WHITHER
WOMANKIND?

Whither Womankind?

The Humanity of Women

by Robert Kress

ABBEY PRESS • St. Meinrad, Indiana 47577 • 1975

Contents

Already in 1673 Poulain de la Barre anticipated many of the contemporary Women's Liberation's objections to books about women insofar as they are written by men. "Everything written about women by men ought to be suspect, for these men are at the same time judge and litigant." I do think things have changed, at least a little. But what about a book about women by a male who is also a professional priest and professional celibate? I can only reply with the request that the book written be the subject of discussion, not the writer of the book.

I can add, in my favor, that my status as a professional celibate does give me at least a certain immunity to the male chauvinist sexist pig's need to prove his virility and manhood, by whatever means deemed apt. My "preening male ego," as Gloria Steinem would have it, has already been somewhat

Introduction

pruned. Since I am institutionally removed from this combat arena, I may also be able to approach the so-called (and badly) "battle of the sexes" more serenely and objectively.

In general we can say that what a man thinks and says about women comes from the context of the women in his life. John Stuart Mill says simply that if you want to know what a man thinks about women, look at his wife. Of both the joys and sorrows of such a wife I have been deprived, but my existence has been deprived especially of that bane I hear so many male friends bemoan, the nagging shrew. Furthermore, my mother decidedly insists that I am not tied to her apron strings. I have, then, perhaps escaped that other bane so roundly denounced by all, momism. Finally, since I have no designs to conquer any one woman in particular or all women in general (the envious suspicions of some of my confreres to the contrary notwithstanding), I consider myself to be in a reasonably liberated state. Freed from the oppression of the fact of possession and the desire of and for possession, I think that I can write objectively about this question: Are women really human? This concept had its origin in an experience I suspect I share with many others who have engaged in marriage counseling. A frequent complaint from husbands is put in this form: "Women! I'll never understand them! Why do they act like that?" Implicit in this question is at least a slight suspicion that women might not be quite as (equally) human as men. Against this background I have used as a title for lectures I give on the subject of this book, "Are Women Really Human?" The shock value of this title is obvious. However, there was a further, and objective, reason.

The question could also have been phrased, "Are men really human?" Historically, however, the question has in fact been asked in regard to women—at least in print and officially.

To a great extent, of course, this can be explained easily—most of the officials and writers were men. In any case, I was heartened in my selection of this title by a remark Gloria Steinem made on NBC's "Today" show (December 14, 1971). She was being interviewed about the need for a woman's magazine completely staffed by women. Wasn't this sexism in reverse? She replied that it wasn't, remarking about the male editors of women's magazines, "One month they say women are human, and the next month, in order to be objective, they say they aren't."

The question I want to concentrate on in this book is precisely the attitude of mankind toward the humanity of women. I shall try to point out the inconsistency between theory and practice. Hardly ever (if at all) can one find an explicit statement that would deny equally humanity for men and women. However, hardly has this statement of equal humanity left lips or pen before the whole practice of society, and especially the males therein, calls that theoretical equality into doubt.

In this book we shall concentrate on that discrepancy with special reference to religion, theology and philosophy. It is from these three that the most important and decisive statements about reality come. Frequently, of course, their abstract statements can become reality in everyday life only when the economic conditions are right. So, we shall not neglect the economic. In the long run all the dimensions of human life are closely interwined. But we can sort them out to describe them and how they are interrelated. Sometimes we can even show how the abstract theories have caused definite social conditions and facts.

The fact is and has been that women generally have been second-class members of society (often their status was such that they could not even be called "citizens"). In this book we are not primarily interested in describing this factual situation—heaven knows that such descriptions abound. Rather, we want to examine the roots, the causes, of this situation. We shall concentrate on the religious traditions of the Jews and Christians, the philosophy of the Greeks. Those two approaches to reality are the fundamental sources of the formation of the so-called "modern mind," especially, but not only in the West. Hence they are also basically the source of the status of women in the Western world today, and of the way we think and act about men and women, male and female.

In sum, in this broader context of the philosophical and theological question, "What is it all about?" we want to examine the more particular and practical question, "Are women really human?"

This question with regard to the human equality of female with male has a wider import than merely redressing the wrongs of an oppressed group or part of the population, even if that group is the greater part of the population. The whole women's liberation movement could run the risk of trivializing itself if it loses contact with this larger context. That narrowed vision is illustrated by such exotic activities as bra burning and such titles and aims as Up From Under. In this brief chapter I would like to describe that larger context in which the relationship between male and female is located.

First of all, the problem of the relationship between men and women is really a particular (and, no doubt, a crucial) instance of the perennial problem of the one and the many, of unity and diversity. From the very beginning the philosophers of ancient Greece were vexed by the relationship of

1/ Is Woman Equally Human?

the one and the many. If there was unity or oneness, how could there be diversity, many? If there was diversity, how could there be unity? It has not been unusual for the philosophers, in mild despair, to deny either one altogether. That resolves the tension. But it leads to the dictatorship of either the totalitarian One or the anarchical Many. It is not difficult to see how this type of solution has been urged in regard to the relationship of men and women.

Clearly this problem of the one and the many is strikingly manifest in the question about the humanity of women. Practically, of course, it means that we must be able to explain why, if the two sexes are really equal (that is, if there is really a unity of male and female in humanity), there are in fact two. Either, if they are really different, how can they be equal?; or, if they are really equal, how can they be different?

I think that this general consideration is especially important because it can help keep us from getting bogged down in the practical difficulties the two sexes experience in trying to live together. It is possible that concentration on the problems men and women encounter in married life can obscure for us the fact that the relationship itself of man and woman is greater than these practical difficulties. In the same vein, women's liberation and equality with men mean more than equal job opportunity and pay. It's another example of the forest and the trees. Keeping the practical difficulties in a wider perspective can in the long run make even their solution more likely.

This wider perspective also includes awareness that if woman and man are indeed equal, and if, at the same time, women are still widely discriminated against, then the development of all mankind is hindered. Again, without wishing to make little of the oppression of one group of people, it is perhaps more effective to keep emphasizing the detriment such oppression causes to the whole society. One need not reduce mankind to the status of Archie Bunker to realize that harping on the oppression of one group is not immediately appealing to other groups.

It is also good, in this context, to recall that in the kingship of Jesus Christ, Christians proclaim a universal kingdom of justice and peace, that is, equality for all. Jesus himself was a liberator of women and of other oppressed groups in his society. To discern the humanity of women and to work for the practical implementation of this discernment is to follow and imitate Christ.

Furthermore, in oppressed societies not only the oppressed but also the oppressors suffer. Of course, the oppressing class usually lives much more comfortably, and that is not to be ignored. But there is always that aching anxiety: When will the next uprising come? How long can the status quo be maintained? The threat is not always as dramatic as that personified by Spartacus, George Washington, Mahatma Gandhi, Malcolm X or even *Ms*. But no group can remain a victim forever. As Abraham Lincoln observed, no nation can long endure slave and free. It is obvious that the oppression of women has been accompanied by an oppression for men too.

For those in the Judeo-Christian tradition it is also important to keep in mind that all creation is the reflection of the being and beauty of the Creator-God of love and majesty. According to the book of Genesis, this reflection is especially present in the sexual society of men and women (1:27; 2:18-24). From the very beginning they were created as male and female in the image and likeness of God, who saw that this created reflection of his goodness was very good. It would hardly do, then, for mankind, which was liberated from nothingness, to oppress one part of itself; to try to deny to it the being which only both sexes together have received.

It is incumbent upon those who claim to be the children of the Creator-God to allow this diversity of his one creation, his one family, to flourish. So, we again meet the problem of the one and the many, of unity and diversity. The diversity of the human family must not be wasted and obscured in either division or totalitarianism, both of which are always oppressive. It is only the unity and diversity of the human family taken together which can be a "very good" reflection of the being of Christianity's Triune God, in whom the paradox of the one and the many has been resolved.

The question of the humanity of women is, then, neither only practical nor only philosophical. It is not even only a matter of justice and peace. In its deepest dimension it is a question of being itself. It is a particular way of asking, "What is it all about?" Therefore the theologian must consider the question.

Our society has been very ambiguous in its understanding of women and the dignity or value it attributes to them. In general woman alternates between being conceived as a weak incompetent and as an irresistible temptation; as the highest and purest revelation of God and as the basest and vilest snare of the material underworld. Angel or devil—which is she? Is it only our contemporary world that is confused? The answer to that last question is easy—it's a loud *no!* In fact, the entire history of the Western world is a history of the ambiguous attitude of society as a whole toward women.

Our modern Western civilization is really the result of the two major influences: the Greek world with its emphasis on philosophy and the Judeo-Christian world with its emphasis on religion. If we are going to understand our attitude toward women, we must look at the attitudes of the Greeks, the

2/ Woman
in the Old Testament

Jews and then, most importantly, the Christians.

Since the most important book influencing our ideas and behavior has been the Bible, we shall start with and emphasize that source.[1] Not only is the Bible the most important book, it is also probably the most misunderstood. And among the most misunderstood parts of the Bible is the book of Genesis. So, we shall start there.

For a long time just about the only literary document Western civilization had from biblical times was the Bible. This isolated state of the Scriptures made its interpretation difficult. However, since about 1850, much other literature from the same era and area has been discovered and translated. This new literature shows how the Jewish writers not only explained the truth of their own religion but also refuted the false doctrines of their neighbors in what we call the Near East. For us that means we shall be able to understand Genesis adequately only if we also know something about the Mesopotamian religions. Between and around the famous Tigris and Euphrates rivers a great civilization flourished two thousand years before Christ.

Around 1800 B.C. Abraham left this society in a religious protest, especially against the polytheism of the dominant culture.[2] This was the beginning of those religions we know as the Jewish and the Christian: for St. Paul, Abraham is the Father of all believers.

The Bible is the written tradition of these religions. It tells us how the Jews and Christians answered the question, What is it all about? Consequently it will also tell us what they thought about man and woman and sex. But it will do this in the context of the Mesopotamian and Greek cultures in which the Jews and Christians lived. So, we must first of all look at the position of woman in Mesopotamian society. It was not an exalted position. However, the origin of the whole world, according to the Mesopotamian theory of creation, was not very inspiring, as the following summary indicates:

As in Genesis, the universe first appears in the Mesopotamian myth as a formless chaos; but this chaos is personified in two divine beings, male and female, the father and mother of all the gods. Through countless eons they beget their offspring, the famous deities of Mesopotamia. A quarrel breaks out between the progenitors and their children; the male deity is slain, and there is war between his spouse and the children. Now let us look more closely at this female warrior, the mother of all gods. She is a monster, described as unspeakably and terribly hideous, gigantic in size and awful in strength. She brings to her aid a host of demons as hideous as herself, whom she spawns from her unfailing womb.

The gods, the children of the monster, do not easily find a defender, for she is a dreadful enemy. There is no doubt that various gods played the role of the hero in the various forms of the myth; in the Babylonian form, which we possess almost completely, the hero is Marduk, the god of the great city of Babylon. It was not unfitting that Babylon, the "City of Light" of ancient Mesopotamia, should see her god as the creative deity, who makes order victorious over chaos. The combat is joined, and Marduk slays the monster. Now Marduk is manifested as the creative deity; for earth, sky, sun, moon, stars are fashioned from the gigantic carcass of the monster. Presumably, also, living creatures are fashioned; but this portion of the myth has not been preserved. Man is made of the blood of a god, an ally of the monster, who dies for his crime.[3]

Genesis is written in opposition to this creation theory which involves many gods in a chaotic struggle (the "polytheistic cosmogony" typical of the ancient Near East). For the Hebrew religion there is only one God, supreme and all-powerful. His creation of the world is effortless. Above all, it is a free gift given out of love. Consequently the world in all its parts is good, and in its human completion it is very good. This is emphasized by the sixfold "God saw that it was good" of chapter 1 of Genesis. Against this general background we can better understand Genesis' specific teaching on man and woman. But it is absolutely important to keep in mind the general teaching of Genesis that all being, and especially human being, is a gift from God. It is not an accident, not a punishment, not a mistake. The Hebrew religion will use its understanding of God to criticize not only other gods but also other religions and societies. It can do this because it understands the world in general and mankind in particular to be the image and likeness of God (Genesis 1:26):

> God said, "Let us make man in our own image, in the likeness of ourselves, and let them be masters of the fish of the sea, the birds of heaven, the cattle, all the wild beasts and all the reptiles that crawl upon the earth."

Hence the Hebrews find the Mespotamian religion deficient not only in regard to its creation myth but also in regard to its treatment of women. In general it can be safely said that in Mesopotamian society woman had no rights. She really was a second-class citizen, oppressed and suppressed. In today's language, which reflects our acute sense of failure in social justice to Black people, she would have been purely and simply the "nigger."

Her whole being was explained in terms of sex, both as fertility and pleasure. Her fundamental function was to provide offspring in order to preserve the tribe as nation, and above all the male family lines. In the very process of doing this, and also in addition to it, woman was also to provide the male with his greatest pleasure. Beyond that, she could be divorced for the slightest reason, even at will. She could be mutilated or executed for adultery, although her rights were not thought to be violated by the husband's adultery. Polygamy of some sort was the widespread practice. In general, woman was the property of man, owned by him whether as wife or slave. In fact, these two states were combined. Woman was a drudge.

> The more austere morality of the desert nomads was some protection against the disintegration of sexual morality; for the woman, while still a drudge, was too important for the survival of the family and of the clan to be degraded. In the teeming cities of the rich valley of Mesopotamia, where woman was less a drudge and more generously endowed with legal rights, the highest eminence which woman could attain was that of temple prostitute.[4]

The book of Genesis takes a strong and definite stand against this state of affairs. It is not that the author of Genesis was a promoter of female equality as such, for woman was also a depressed class within his own Hebrew people. He does insist, though, that this is not the way it was "in the beginning." That is, this is not the way God willed his good world to be. This point is made in different ways in the first two chapters of Genesis.

We must keep in mind that these chapters are neither historical nor physical science. They are religious writings, and as such, concerned with the meaning of the existence of the world and mankind. We have already seen this in regard to the creation of the world. Now we shall look more directly at its teaching about man, woman, and sex. First of all, it is helpful to keep in mind that chapters 1 and 2 of Genesis are not two different accounts of the same event, creation. It is much better to approach chapter 1 as the account of the origin of the world (cosmos); chapter 2, the origin of sex (male and female mankind); and chapter 3, of the origin of evil in the world (sin, suffering, death).

For our particular purpose we can focus our considerations of the question that is still asked—frequently and earnestly, much to my surprise. Does Genesis teach that men and women are equal or does it teach that women are inferior to men and that wives are subject to their husbands? I say "to my surprise" because it seems to me that Genesis' teaching is quite clear and obvious. However, I then remember that even in our day and age scholars like Lynn White, Jr., can make statements such as this:

> By gradual stages a loving and all-powerful God had created light and darkness, the heavenly bodies, the earth and all its plants, animals, birds, and fishes. Finally God had created Adam and, as an afterthought, Eve to keep man from being lonely.[5]

In the first place, the six days of chapter 1 do not describe creation in gradual stages. The six-day schema is, rather, a device to help the reader remember the classifications of all the beings in the world. It simply says that everything—namely, these six groups of objects (all that is)—comes from God and is good. The six days have nothing to do with a chronological process.

Further, verse 27 hardly allows for woman's being an afterthought:

> God created man in the image of himself, in the image of God he created him, male and female he created them.

In verse 26 the word "man" does not mean male in distinction from female. It is, rather, a collective noun and means mankind. In the poetic development of this idea in verse 27, the equal originality of woman is clearly stated. From the very beginning human being, which is the image and likeness of God, is sexual. That means that sex itself is not an afterthought or the result of some primordial evil or fall. As is all of created being, so also sex is a gift of God, and therefore good.

Note also the interplay of the noun "man" in the first strophe and the pronouns "him" and "them" in the second and third. Chapter 1 of Genesis clearly and unequivocally states that man and woman are equally human. Human being is present only when both the male and female are present.

Some would object, though, that chapter 2 has a different theory. They would argue that the woman is clearly subordinate and inferior to man because she is constructed later than the man from his rib. Such an approach, however, obviously does not take into account the literary characteristics of the chapter. This chapter is in the so-called Yahwist tradition: it uses the word Yahweh for God. It also has a very dramatic and colorful style, especially in comparison with the priestly tradition of chapter 1. (Maybe that is why so many people seem to forget chapter 1 entirely and remember only the rib scene!) Furthermore, chapter 2 is not a single original literary unit. It has, rather, been composed of various units that had previously existed separately in the oral tradition. In order to keep the basic story-line flowing, you should go from verse 8 to verse 15. Verse 9 is very difficult because it is the combination of several pre-existing traditions which the editor did not completely succeed in reconciling. Verses 10-14 are a later addition to the basic story and have no essential connection with the matter at hand. For our purpose we can also pass over verses 15-17.

> At the time when Yahweh God made earth and heaven there was as yet no wild bush on the earth nor had any wild plant yet sprung up, for Yahweh God had not sent rain on the earth, nor was there any man to till the soil. However, a flood was rising from the earth and watering all the

surface of the soil. Yahweh God fashioned man of dust from the soil. Then he breathed into his nostrils a breath of life, and thus man became a living being.

Yahweh God planted a garden in Eden which is in the east, and there he put the man he had fashioned.

Yahweh God said, "It is not good that the man should be alone. I will make him a helpmate." So from the soil Yahweh God fashioned all the wild beasts and all the birds of heaven. These he brought to man to see what he would call them; each one was to bear the name the man would give it. The man gave names to all the cattle, all the birds of heaven and all the wild beasts. But no helpmate suitable for man was found for him. So Yahweh God made the man fall into a deep sleep. And while he slept, he took one of his ribs and enclosed it in flesh. Yahweh God built the rib he had taken from the man into a woman, and brought her to the man. The man exclaimed:

"This at last is bone from my bones,
and flesh from my flesh!
This is to be called woman,
for this was taken from man."

This is why man leaves his father and mother and joins himself to his wife, and they become one body.

Now both of them were naked, the man and his wife, but they felt no shame in front of each other.

These adjustments to the text make it much easier to see the point that is being made. We must also keep in mind the Hebrew thinker's desire to refute the Mesopotamian idea that sex and fertility are divine. In contrast to the Mesopotamian goddess of sex and fertility as the ideal or model for woman, the Hebrew emphasizes that woman is the "helpmate suitable for man." She is not meant to share only his sexual activity; she is to share his entire existence—that is, human being. This is the importance of Adam's exclamation in verse 23 that woman is bone and flesh of his; the woman, from man, has the same being. Thus she is different from and superior to the wild beasts, the birds and the cattle—just as the man is. Some scholars think that in these verses Genesis might also be arguing against sexual bestiality. This would again be a confirmation of the equal humanity of the man and the woman who are, indeed, sexually differentiated, but also precisely thereby meant for each other: "This is why a man leaves his father and mother and joins himself to his wife, and they become one body" (verse 24).

In the era of Hugh Hefner and *Playboy's* cult of the woman as a playmate, it might be advisable to avoid the term helpmate. As E. A. Speiser points out; "The traditional 'helpmate for him' is adequate, but subject to confusion. . . . The Hebrew complement means literally 'alongside him,' i.e., 'corresponding to him.' "[6] Or, as John L. McKenzie dares to say, "his partner and, in the context of the story, his equal."[7]

The words "deep sleep" and "rib" are also worth at least a brief examination. The Bible sometimes uses terms like sleep and dream to describe the mysterious and highly important activity of God in the world. The emphasis is not on the man and his sleep as some sort of anesthesia, but on the divine nature of the activity—namely, the completion of the creation of the one human being: male and female humanity. The meaning of the word "rib" is not entirely clear. It is possibly connected with the Sumerian word which means both rib and life. This meaning would be most apt. The heart is an important symbol for us. It was even more important for the Hebrews. I think that it is legitimate to think of the rib in terms of both the heart and the lung, the place of breath. It is significant that in this figurative account of the origin of human (note! human, not female) being the woman comes from the area of the heart and breath. For the Hebrew, heart symbolizes the whole human being and breath the whole life. (See verse 7 where Yahweh breathes life into the clay figure which then becomes a living human being.)

The objection can, however, still be urged that chapter 2 does indeed allow for a later creation of the woman. But this objection, again, fails to take into account the literary form of the chapter. It is not a historical chronicle, concerned with what came before and what came after. Nor is it a work of biological or geological science. It is, rather, a religious book. And here it uses a story to make a point. The point is not *when* men and women first began to exist, but that man and woman are both equally human. Again, humanity—human being—is complete and fully present only when both man and woman are present.

In a different manner from chapter 1, but no less clearly and insistently, chapter 2 not only does not teach the subjection of women to men, but teaches just the opposite. Men and women are equally human and equally original. Furthermore, their origin and value are not to be sought in the myths of warring gods and goddesses of fertility. Rather, they are the image and likeness of the one sovereign God who freely chose them out of chaotic nothingness to live in a garden of contentment, as the word Eden probably suggests.

Furthermore, against the then common practices of polygamy (and also one wife and many concubines) and easy divorce for the male, the Hebrew religion emphasizes the exclusiveness and fidelity of the relationship between man and woman. The original Hebrew theology of marriage was clearly a liberation of, and protection of, woman from the sexual caprice of the stronger male. This will be emphasized later in Jewish history by Jesus when he says, "It was because you were so unteachable that Moses allowed you to divorce your wives, but it was not like this from the beginning" (Matthew 19:8).

But is this really how it worked out? As the quotation from Jesus indicates, the answer is negative.

Chapters 1 and 2 of Genesis were written by a realist. The editor of Genesis was aware of this apparent contradiction between his theology of the origins of the world and mankind and the real world in which he lived. He was also aware that the most striking contrast was in regard to the sexual dimension of human being. Chapter 3 is his explanation of the difference between the garden of Eden intended by God and the desert of thistles and wild plants, sweat and pain, which is man's present abode. It was man's desire to be God instead of God's friend that so disturbed the order of the creation. From the original condition of peace has come the disorder of turmoil and oppression.

For the Bible sin is essentially the destruction of the proper order of relationships that are supposed to exist among the various beings of the world and between the entire world and God. This is illustrated in various ways in chapter 3, which is really a brief but classic history of the way men and women have treated each other. Against the tendency of some people to act as if chapter 3 described the way the world is supposed to be (God's will) we must insist upon the opposite. Chapter 3 is the description of what happened when everything went wrong. It is precisely what God does not will.

The lead-in to this account of the origin of evil is the last verse of chapter 2. "Now both of them were naked, the man and his wife, but they felt no shame in front of each other." This refers not only—in fact, not even primarily—to the absence of sexual disorder. It emphasizes the general original innocence of mankind, with special emphasis on the "mutual trust and esteem of the man and woman for each other."[8]

The result of the first sin was precisely the destruction of this innocent order. Immediately the man and the woman became uneasy in regard to each other. They had to shield themselves from one another with clothing. And the clothing is not just in general, but specifically sexual—loin-cloths. Thus is emphasized that the sin has disrupted the most fundamental and most important order within the world, that between man and woman. The rest of this chapter can be seen as the elaboration of the significance of this disorder. This approach has support in the fact that the key figure in both chapters 2 and 3 is the woman.

Again this must be viewed against the general cultural background of Mesopotamia and the Hebrew protest against certain religious beliefs. First of all, the Hebrew objects to the theory that the female principle is divine. Beyond all the forces of nature, God is therefore also beyond the sexual differentiation of male and female. God is one. Sex is indeed his gift to creation, but it is not itself divine. Thus the sexual woman is also to be seen as God's gift, but she is not divine. The woman and the man are both creatures of God and partners in life and being, not merely in sex. Hence, woman's dignity is not established by her necessary role as the sacred prostitute in the fertility cults of the fertility goddesses.

One of the strongest temptations of the Hebrew nation was to participate in these fertility cults. This was the practical equivalent of making sex and fertility divine. It is possible, then, to see chapter 3 as the explanation of what happens when mankind disregards the true God and tries to make anything else God. In this case the "anything else" is sexual mankind which tries to become the master of life and being on its own.[9] Man is no longer content to be the friend, the receiver of the gift of the being.

The man and the woman become aware of their nakedness, which must be covered. Otherwise they will no longer be able to get along at all, since the original mutual trust and confidence have been destroyed. However, it is not only with each other but also with God, the ultimate source of the creation, its being and order, that they are now in conflict. Hence they hide. Their previously easy-going relationship is now destroyed, and God must search for them. Rather than gods in command of the world, they are now refugees, suspicious of others, in hiding. The rest of the Old Testament—indeed the rest of the whole Bible and of the history of the whole world —will be the account of God's searching out this fallen fugitive, not to condemn but to save (John 3:16).

But chapter 3 immediately takes up the consequences of sin for the man and the woman. Its insights into the psychology of fallen man and woman are profound. The fall from naked trust and esteem is immediately illustrated by Adam's claim that although he did indeed eat the fruit, it wasn't his fault. The woman "made" him do it. But he is not satisfied with blaming the woman. He also blames God—"the woman whom *you* put me with." How far have we already come since that happy and exultant shout in chapter 2: "At last, bone of my bone and flesh of my flesh!" So, in a male claim to innocence typical of all subsequent history, it is not Adam's fault but woman's—in fact, God's.

As for the woman, does she play the role of the meek and submissive woman, to say nothing of the contrite and sorrowful sinner? Does she fall to her knees in humble admission of guilt and prayer for forgiveness? Hardly. Her immediate response is to blame the serpent. (The poor serpent is the end of the line; it can't find anyone else to blame.)

Quite clearly the author of this chapter is relating the ageless general experience of humanity: "Who? Me? I'd never do anything like that." And the mutual recrimination of the sexes: "It's her (his) fault. She (he) made me do it." Of course these observations are not meant as the proclamation of eternal verities. They are simply the religious recordings of the experience of mankind after, and because of, the sinful disarrangement of God's Eden gift. Things are not *supposed* to be this way, but this is the way they are. The disorder is not merely in the world at large, it is in the very heart of the human relationship. It is between the man and the woman.

Consequently not even the family, so highly esteemed by the Hebrews, offers a sure and secure harbor from the storms of strife, abuse, and oppression. This is illustrated especially in the punishment prescribed for the woman. Again, it must be emphasized that this verse does not describe the ideal or what God wills; it describes the world that in fact has come from sin.

To the woman he said:

> "I will multiply your pains in childbearing, you shall give birth to your children in pain. Your yearning shall be for your husband, yet he will lord it over you" (Genesis 3:16).

The punishments respect the division of labor found among the Hebrews. The man is cursed in precisely his capacity as breadwinner, the woman in precisely her capacity as child-bearer. The punishments are directed precisely to what each does to continue the family and the nation. The man and woman are, however, hardly like gods, as the serpent had promised. They are much more like drones and drudges—the woman much more so than the man. And in this drudgery even that relationship which originally was to be the peak experience of the goodness of creation has been compromised and obscured.

As verse 16 states, men and women still yearn for each other. However, their yearning leads not only to pleasure, happiness and fullfillment, but to recriminations, pain, and oppression. This verse explicitly relates the "lording it over" only to the man in his relationship with the woman, but it is legitimate to extend it in the other direction. As Ignatius Hunt notes:

> And, though often maltreated by man, she will nonetheless be unfailingly attracted to him, just as it is man's weakness that he is unfailingly drawn to her.[10]

Here the groundwork is laid for that misogyny which comes to the surface elsewhere in the Old Testament, especially in the Wisdom literature. It must always be kept in mind that this skeptical, if not cynical, attitude toward women is the result of the original sin. In the fallen world where man searches for being he is still, now as then, tempted to find God in his own power, in sex and fertility, an attempt forever doomed to failure. Man and woman both experience disillusionment with the other sex because too much is expected of it. In this disillusionment is the source of the sexual combat which verse 16 describes. Since mankind has succumbed to the temptation to make sex-fertility its Lord, mankind is lorded over by this very same sex-fertility.

So much for the Hebrew theory, which was in principle a protest against the dominant religion of Mesopotamia and a reversal of its divinization of sex, its simultaneous exaltation and degradation of woman. Hebrew practice, unhappily, reflects the pains of man's wounded nature and his disordered world. In fact, the rest of Old Testament history can be regarded as a meditation on and a practice of the curse of the woman:

> You shall give birth to your children in pain. Your yearning shall be for your husband, yet he will lord it over you (Genesis 3:16).

In that battle for superiority and survival which has become the mode of man's life with woman, man seems in general to have been the victor. He has been, in reality, the lord and the woman his servant even when she has enjoyed the "dignity" of being his wife. And the history of Israel, God's chosen people, illustrates this no less than does the history of the Gentiles, the heathen. As we now survey the history of the Old Testament, it will be important to keep verse 16 constantly in mind.

In fact, the Old Testament can be read as the record of man's increasing domination over woman, whose condition becomes more and more depressed. This decline is illustrated by the greater freedom and mobility woman enjoyed in the early part of the Old Testament. To some extent, of course, this can be attributed to the looser social organization and life style of a wandering and nomadic people. As a society grows older it will tend to become more tightly organized. It is also likely to reinforce early practices. In our case this means that the restrictive practices affecting women in the early history of Israel will have become decidedly more inflexible by the time of Jesus.

However, let us begin at the beginning, with Sarai, the wife of Abraham, the patriarch of patriarchs and the father of all believers. Sarai is also important because she illustrates the discrepancy between theory and practice in Israel. By this I mean that if the Hebrews had been consistent they would have recognized that Yahweh's treatment of Sarai the woman paralleled his treatment of Abraham the man. Granted that the promise (Genesis 12:3; 15; 17:15; 18:6-17) is more directly given to Abraham, it is also necessary to note that not just any child of Abraham will be the bearer of the promise. Only the son of Sarai. Yahweh says, "But my covenant I will establish with Isaac, whom Sarah will bear you at this time next year" (Genesis 17:21). It is therefore fitting that when Abram's name is changed to Abraham in chapter 17, so is Sarai's name changed to Sarah. A name change like this always indicates a special role and dignity in the history of salvation. This is expressly noted by the prophet Isaiah when he calls upon Israel to be true to the covenant: "Consider Abraham your father and Sarah who gave you birth" (51:2). Furthermore, the Yahwist tradition does not describe Sarah as a passive and submissive servant; she is certainly not the drudge and drone so typical of women in later Judaism. Whether or not this description of Sarah is strict chronicle or not is beside the point. What is important for our considerations here is that this was the image she enjoyed and the influence she exercised in the history of Israel. However, if this history could overlook her special treatment by Yahweh in the birth of the nation, it is not surprising that it could also nullify this exalted "personal" status of hers.

Sarah was by no means the only heroine in the history of Israel. The other wives of the patriarchs—Hagar, Rebekah, Rachel, Leah—are hardly representatives of a totally oppressed class. The influence of Rebekah in salvation history is both obvious and strong. It is also interesting to note that for all the divine and human ado involved in Isaac's birth, he does not seem to have been a very forceful person. His contribution is to some extent less than Rebekah's since it was she who actually arranged for the promise and blessing to be continued in the way it in fact was. This observation is also important, for it illustrates that the segregation of women from public life and office does not mean that they are therefore entirely without influence. Rebekah is certainly a striking example of this. But one can also think of Jezebel and Athaliah during era of the Kings. Of all peoples who are socially restricted, by custom or law, it is characteristic that they find their own way. The immense influence wielded by women in a country like Italy and the survival in the early days and the current cultural influence of the Negro in America are but two examples of this. No history of women may overlook this "other," or hidden, way of being and influencing.

The era of the Judges also witnesses to the importance a woman could have. As a judge and prophetess, Deborah officially dispensed justice. In the name of Yahweh (Judges 4:4-10), she commanded the chosen people, indeed the person of a male judge, Barak. She even marched to battle with the soldiers assembled by her command. It is, furthermore, possible that she is the author of the oldest extant literary composition, namely the so-called "Song of Deborah" (Judges 5). Deborah is especially important since her achievement was accomplished through neither husband nor child, but on her own.

There are other famous women in the Old Testament. They are, in fact, a rather mixed lot. Rahab (whose profession has perhaps given the color red, or scarlet, its enduring special occupational significance) was a Canaanite as well as a prostitute. In spite of these two handicaps she is considered a heroine of both Jews and Christians because she served Yahweh by hiding his spies. Her deed (James 2:25), interpreted as her faith by the Epistle to the Hebrews (11:31), merits her inclusion among the ancestors whose faith is commended by the author of the latter book.

Michal, the daughter of Saul and sometime wife of David, was by no means a weak-willed drone. She was afraid of neither her father nor her husband, as her story (1 Samuel 14 to 2 Samuel 6) shows. During the time of the Kings both Abigail and Rizpah are notable women. Earlier there was the prophetess Miriam (Exodus 12:20), who led the people in public dancing and singing to celebrate the escape from Egypt under Moses. Later on, and more familiar to us, are such heroic women as Ruth, Judith, and Esther.

However, it must be admitted that by and large the history of Israel is male-dominated. Woman was man's property and could even be used by him in his own defense (Genesis 12;

19; 20; Judges 19). This last cited incident (it will be recalled that the Levite in Judges 19 gave his concubine to a crowd of evil men who were threatening the house where he was staying, allowing them to use and abuse her sexually throughout the night) is certainly one of the most gruesome descriptions of male exploitation of woman in history. But whether it need be made as chauvinistic as Sr. Albertus McGrath would make it is another question. It is to be noted that Yahweh threatens to take away David's wives if he will not reform his ways (2 Samuel 2:11). This would have been a light threat to David if his wives had not been more valuable than just any property in general. Likewise the Levite in Judges 19, who called for massive vengeance for the crime against his concubine, would not have done so had he considered her just one possession among others. The trouble with making things worse than they are by the interpretation one imposes on them in the interests of a thesis is that it sometimes damages the very cause one is trying to defend. This is perhaps the capital error of the more strident vocal advocates of the women's liberation movement. If women had been unremittingly treated as savagely as they claim, one would almost be forced to conclude that female being was so frail that it deserved its fate. What the history of women in the Bible does show, on the contrary, is that woman's being is so strong that in the face of immense obstacles she cannot be reduced to nothing.

A further lowering of the status of women in the Old Testament is noticeable in the Exodus version of the Ten Commandments, which includes woman among the man's property, and not even in first place: "You shall not covet your neighbor's house. You shall not covet your neighbor's wife, or his servant, man or woman, or his ox, or his donkey, or anything that is his" (Exodus 20:17). Perhaps in anticipation of the traditional dining ritual of Catholic rectories, it seems that women did not usually eat with the men (Genesis 18:9; Ruth 2:14).

According to some experts, the legal status of women among the Hebrews was possibly poorer than among the other citizens of Mesopotamia. Although there are laws which afford women special protection (see, for example, Deuteronomy 21, 22), they are most notable for their scarcity. This is counterbalanced, however, by women's greater social status and mobility. At least a partial basis for this is the extremely high esteem which the family enjoyed in the Hebrew religion and society. It must also be remembered that God's covenant promise to Abraham was that "you shall become the father of a multitude of nations. . . . I will make you most fruitful. I will make you into nations, and your issue shall be kings" (Genesis 17:7). Even the most hardheaded male chauvinist could not avoid drawing certain conclusions about the dignity of women from this promise. Nor could the inadequate biological understanding of procreation (which we shall examine later) completely nullify the important, indeed inescapable, role of woman in the fulfillment of this promise. A practical expression of this recognition is contained in the Ten Commandments and other precepts which explicitly include the mother as well as the father in the reverence to be paid by the children (Exodus 20:12; Leviticus 19:3; Deuteronomy 5:16; 21:18).

Although women did not generally enjoy full access to temple worship and knowledge of the Torah, they were not simply and totally excluded. In fact, their singing and dancing were a major contribution to the religious celebration (Exodus 15:20; 1 Samuel 18:6; Psalm 68:25). They also were able to take part in the great cultic festivals. "There you shall rejoice in the presence of Yahweh your God, you and your sons and daughters, your serving men and women" is the command of the Law (Deuteronomy 12:12). Indeed, sometimes it is the woman who must give to the male the adequate theological explanation of a ritual sacrifice, as Samson's mother, Monoah, did (Judges 13:23). Women are also capable of going on pilgrimage to holy places, as did Hannah—nor does Hannah seem to be overwhelmed by timidity in her conversation with either Yahweh or her other lord, Elkanah her husband (1 Samuel 1).

It is also important to note that women are present at both weddings and funerals (Judges 11:40; Jeremiah 16:7; Psalm 45:15; Tobit 8:21). This is especially significant since the worship of ancient Semites was basically in terms of life (and death). If women enjoy access to these festivals of birth and death, then they are at least implicitly accorded the same human dignity as the males. For it is the life of the whole people which was given to the whole people by God that is being celebrated.

Very important is the fact that women had at least some access to the sanctuary, even if it was restricted to festivals. In the sabbatical year women were also allowed to be present at the reading of the Torah during the feast of Tabernacles (Deuteronomy 31:12).

Most important, however, is that women are to participate in the sacred meals of the priest (Leviticus 10:14) and especially the Passover celebration (Exodus 12). The Passover is the most intense celebration of the covenant between God and his chosen people. If women participate in this sacred and cultic meal, then they must be regarded fundamentally as members of the covenant people. The chief temptation, constant and increasingly severe, of the people of Abraham, in whose descendents all nations were to be blessed, was to restrict the benefits of that essentially expansive covenant. From this point of view it was not only women but many other groupings of people who had to battle against segregation from full participation in the covenant blessings. In fact, the book of Jonah is a stinging satire on the narrow-mindedness of the Jews. Even Yahweh is not exempt from the attempts of his people to restrict his blessings.

Precisely the covenant of the chosen people gives us the occasion to examine one of the great obstacles in the way of women's full participation in the life of that people. Yahweh speaks to Abraham: The "sign of the covenant between myself and you" will be the circumcision of the male foreskin (Genesis 17:11). Although the practice of circumcision actually involves no implications with regard to the inferiority of the female sex, it is not hard to see how it might be used as an argument against the equality of the woman. Thus what was supposed to be a sign of the covenant—that is, of salvation from the fallen state of sin and exploitation (recall Genesis 3:16)—in fact opens the way for further sexist exploitation. The question necessarily arose whether women, who could not be circumcised, could nevertheless enjoy full membership in the covenant people. Admittedly circumcision is only the *sign* of the covenant, but as the language of Genesis 17 shows, it was easy to exaggerate the sign and eventually equate it with the covenant itself. Given the already existing male pretensions to supremacy, it is not surprising to see how this "sign" of the covenant did in fact work to the disadvantage of women.

In the same context we can consider the prescriptions regarding ritual purity. Cleanness and uncleanness in the ritual sense means that certain things—including foods and sexual events or acts—which are in themselves morally indifferent become "unclean" in relation to worship. It may be that the unclean thing or act is considered incompatible with worship, but it is also true that its "uncleanness" may consist in its being regarded as holy, and thus reserved for God. The theory and practice of "unclean-clean" had an extremely long history, and doubtless hygienic considerations had entered in. It is possible that neither theory nor practice was any longer fully understood in biblical times. For example, unlawful sexual activity would be considered to render one no more unclean than would lawful sexual activity which had entered the category, temporarily, of "unclean"—nor, indeed, than the eating of "unclean" food. But despite this lack of clarity, the prescriptions for ritual purity were retained, most likely because they had belonged to the people in the past and were part of the traditions handed on by and from the fathers.

The concept of ritual uncleanness was by no means restricted to the Hebrews or even the Mesopotamians: insofar as it is connected with blood it tends to be worldwide. This universality is rooted in the association of blood with life. Often the two words are simply equated: to shed one's blood for one's neighbor is to die for him. Consequently, when we read the words of Jesus at the Last Supper: "This cup is the new covenant in my blood which will be poured out for you" (Luke 22:20), it is not on a container filled with the red liquid from veins and arteries that we are to concentrate but on the *life* of Jesus. It is his life in which the new covenant consists.

In Old Testament thought, blood is clearly conceived as the life of the living being (Genesis 9:14; Deuteronomy 12:23). Hence, as well as murder, which involves the shedding of blood, the eating of blood is prohibited. Here we must again recall the emphatic conviction of the ancients that life and death belong to the sphere of the divine. Blood also, therefore, would belong to the sphere of the divine which is forbidden to man.

Once again, it is evident that the practices with regard to

ritual purity have no actual antifeminine implications. Nevertheless it is most likely that women will be more affected than men because blood is more apparent in their sexual constitution. The "uncleanness" of blood in this connection derives from its holiness by which it is reserved to God. A widespread theory of the "holy" explains holiness as both attracting and overwhelming man. That is, the experience of the holy by mankind has a double effect: reverence, awe, devotion, on the one hand; and fear, confusion, and "shame," on the other. The holy both attracts and repels.

In the face of woman's association with blood in sex and fertility, especially in childbearing and childbirth, it is not surprising that that she should receive greater attention in regard to the practice of unclean-clean. However, it is difficult to avoid the sense of sexist discrimination in regard to the prescriptions of chapter 12 of Leviticus. A woman is unclean for seven days after giving birth to a boy, fourteen after a girl. This should be kept in mind in regard to the difficulty Mary and Joseph experienced in finding room in an inn (Luke 2:7).[11] The entire building could easily have been rendered "unclean" for at least a week, perhaps two, if Mary had been admitted and had given birth there. Consequently it is perhaps not so much the hardhearted exploitation of the poor by the "capitalist" innkeeper that Jesus experiences, but rather a discrimination based on a false understanding of both sex and the holy. Abstention from sexual intercourse is mandatory for another thirty-three days after the birth of a boy, but sixty-six days after a girl. This, of course, complicates the vulnerable position of woman, who is already "unclean" by virtue of her menstruation.

Although such uncleanness was not basically equated with immorality, it is difficult to see how this practice in such an important sphere of life could completely avoid affecting the moral evaluations of the people. The exclusion from cult and worship would seem inevitably to contribute to the transfer of the unclean status to the sphere of morals.

Once again the connection between life and the holy, between fertility (sex) and God seems to work in favor of the male, although even his sexual life can hardly be considered paradisiac under these conditions. In any case, the history of Israel is certainly a fascinating illustration of that leitmotif we found in Genesis 3:16: "Your yearning shall be for your husband, yet he will lord it over you."

I have tried to present the above considerations in a way that illustrates the ambivalent status of women in the history of Israel. Not only its history, however, but also the Wisdom literature of Israel can be regarded as a "meditation" on this incisive verse. The Wisdom books have been accused of being "classically" and "notoriously" (Tavard), even "venomously" (McGrath) misogynist.[12] Indeed they are hardly love songs from the wise man to his fair lady.

Without attempting to gloss over the acerbity of these writers, we can gain a better perspective of their position by considering it as a prolonged meditation and elaboration on the unfulfilled sexual yearnings of men and women for one another.

But first of all a word about the nature and purpose of wisdom literature is necessary. Israel's Wisdom literature was influenced by the wisdom of the East and Egypt, but especially Edom. This type of literature is "practical." That is, in brief maxims it attempts to teach people how to act, how to conduct themselves so that they can get along well in this world. Wisdom was considered the distilled experience and knowledge of the past. Even today we speak of the wisdom of the ages. After all (if such a statement can be allowed in a book like this), "Father knows best." The wisdom was to be learned by the young from the old, or not at all. To emphasize its "practical" nature is not to deprive it of either morality or profundity. Much like Cardinal Newman's later definition of a gentleman, wisdom's basic code of conduct demanded that offense be given to no one. (Exactly how this aim could be reconciled with the frequent blunt misogynism evident in the Wisdom literature apparently escaped the attention of the Wisdom writers.)

Wisdom is to enable the wise man to cope with the practical problems of life, and not primarily to reach abstract decisions. However, books like Job and Ecclesiastes (Qoheleth) do indicate that wisdom was also concerned with the problems of good and evil, suffering and sin. In other words, at least sometimes wisdom did ask the question, What is it all about?

There is one more dimension to Israel's wisdom, and it must be considered the most important: its relation to Yahweh and the covenant made with Yahweh and Abraham as well as the Law (Torah) of Moses. Only Yahweh is wise, and this wisdom of his is revealed in and shared by his creation (Ecclesiasticus 42:15-43:33). Wisdom is present not only in God's creation but also in the history of this creation (Job 12:13).

After these general remarks it is easier to appreciate the relationship of the Wisdom literature to the earlier writings of the Old Testament. "Already" in Deuteronomy the foundation for this relationship was laid:

> Keep them (the laws and customs), observe them, and they will demonstrate to the peoples your wisdom and understanding... they will exclaim, "No other people is as wise and prudent as this great nation" (4:6).

In Ecclesiasticus the relationship between wisdom and the law is made explicit:

All this is no other than the book of the covenant of the
    Most High God,
    the Law that Moses enjoined on us,
an inheritance for the communities of Jacob
(24:23-25).

Later on, the same author emphasizes that the wise man

will grow upright in purpose and learning, he will ponder
the Lord's hidden mysteries. He will display the instruction
he has received, taking his pride in the Law of the Lord's
covenant (39:7, 8).

In the words of Roland Murphy we can summarize by
saying:

For the most part, it (Wisdom) is essentially a postexilic,
religious, interpretation of human conduct, carried on in the
light of the traditional Israelite moral ideals and motivation
of Deuteronomy, but also continuing the experimental,
humanistic tradition inherited from courtly origins.[13]

After all this I hope it is clear that the Wisdom musings
on woman, as lopsided as they may be, can and must be considered as meditation on that fateful sixteenth verse of the
third chapter of Genesis—the frustrating yearning of men
and woman for each other. The Wisdom authors cannot, then,
be regarded simply as ill-tempered old misogynists, perhaps
frustrated in love by a shrewish wife or rebuffed in passion by
a diffident maiden. Their caution in regard to women is more
than the "fools rush in where angels fear to tread." It is,
rather, the continued meditation of that primal religious experience of the Hebrews, that divinity is to be sought only in
Yahweh—not in sex, not in fertility, not in woman. Of course,
the shoe could also and must fit the other foot. However,
given the experience women had had of men by the Wisdom
era, it is highly unlikely that they would have been tempted

to confuse their uxorial lords with THE LORD. Consequently the Wisdom books are not unreasonable when they concentrate on cautioning the young male.

We can legitimately, then, suggest that the Wisdom literature must be read in the light of the entire biblical salvation history. A fundamental factor in that history had been the evil state of affairs resulting from the Fall. A further fundamental factor in this evil state of affairs was the frustration experienced by the male and female in their sexual relationship. To this can be added the necessary caution a young man must have if he is to have both peace of mind and success in business. It is difficult to imagine a male making more of a fool of himself in regard to anything or anyone than he does with regard to his original helpmate.

We shall now examine some of the Wisdom literature directly. It mighet be good beforehand to note that if woman could in fact have been such a great, indeed irresistible, temptation for the male, that is hardly a recommendation for his presumed superior status. If woman is so inferior, how can she possibly exert such influence on the superior lord and master? I have found the same inconsistency in the classic opposition to miscegenation. If white people are so superior to black people, why the great fear that intermarriage must produce a mongrel race? Perhaps there lurks deep down the fear that white might not be all that much better. From the conduct of Jesus with sinners (He is their friend according to Matthew 11:19), we know that true goodness is more powerful than sin and evil. Flight always indicates feelings of inferiority. Can flight from woman indicate anything else?

Furthermore, in the great caution that must be exercised in regard to women there may be an explicit awareness of that survival ability of the oppressed we noted above. Had women been simply the socially depressed dullards we are led to believe they were by certain biblical texts, they could hardly have been the alluring enticements so vehemently inveighed against by the sages. Here again we have further evidence of the ambivalent status, both biological and social, that is the history of women in Israel.

Wisdom's negative approach to women seems to stem from woman viewed as temptress and seductress, an approach that almost every Catholic priest experienced in the seminary (I almost said "learned," but apparently many did not learn). The classic statement of this constantly recurring theme is in Ecclesiasticus:

> Woman's beauty has led many astray:
> it kindles desire like a flame (9:9).

In the first nine verses of that chapter we find the following words: "entangles," "snares," "dally," "wiles," "charms" to which the male "succumbs." The entire exhortation is climaxed with his "slide down to ruin." The same text appears to equate wife, woman, harlot, singing girl, virgin, whore, handsome woman. The wiles of the harlot and adultress are graphically described—it sounds almost like the script for an R movie—in the book of Proverbs (6:7). Apparently a woman intent on conquering a man is irresistible, at least according to Proverbs:

> She has done so many to death,
> and the strongest have been the victims (7:26).

Again we meet the strange paradox that the superior male is viciously set upon by the lusting female and inevitably devoured by her. The consensus of one's priest friends is that one can wait many years for an encounter with the female against whom one has been briefed in the seminary (and per-

---

haps wait for ever). I can't help thinking that suspicions and cautions like those above are much greater indications of the male's weakness and vulnerability than of the seductive prowess of the (supposedly inferior) woman. In any event, the strong man has only to say no. I should think it exceedingly difficult to be seduced from a distance.

But on the other hand, if a man conscious of his superiority has succumbed to the charms of a faithless woman, it is understandable that he should adopt a misogynist attitude toward the sex in general. After all, wounded pride must always find a way to assuage itself, and how better do it than by blaming the other? Now we can recall the Genesis account of Adam's reaction to Yahweh's inquiry about his nakedness: he blamed Eve.

The reaction against women becomes so bitter that Ecclesiastes can say:

> I find woman more bitter than death; she is a
> snare, her heart a net, her arms are chains;
> He who is pleasing to God eludes her,
> but the sinner is her captive.
> One man in a thousand I may find,
> but never a woman better than the rest
> (7:26-29).

The Wisdom books love to inveigh against women who seduce men by their beauty (Ecclesiasticus 9:3-9; 25:16), and then turn into nagging wives, shrews who are never done with talking (Proverbs 19:13; 21:9; 24:24; 27:15). Of course, given the relative physical strength of men and women and the disparity in legal sanctions available to them, about the only weapon available to women then was the tongue. It is highly unlikely that the Semitic lord-husband would have tolerated nocturnal headaches very long.

Of course not only the Wisdom writers berate women. Already the prophets Amos (4:1) and Isaiah (3:16) had taken them to task for their frivolities and extravagances. For downright indignation and disgust, however, it is hard to beat or even match Ecclesiasticus, especially in chapter 25. We shall include here just a sample:

> Any wound rather than a wound of the heart!
>   Any spite rather than the spite of woman!
> A woman's spite changes her appearance
>   and makes her face as grim as any bear's.
> When her husband goes out to dinner with his neighbors,
>   he cannot help heaving bitter sighs.
> No wickedness comes anywhere near the wickedness of a
>   woman,
>   may a sinner's lot be hers! (25:13, 17-19).

In the same book a theme occurs that will be taken up later by St. Paul and some of the Fathers of the Church:

> Sin began with a woman,
> and thanks to her we all must die (25:24).

Here again we see that ambiguity and paradox which mark woman's status in the Old Testament. Although she is supposed to be inferior and weaker than the male, nevertheless she is also apparently *the* responsible one. However, how can she be so responsible if she be's (if you will pardon the grammar) so little? The same ambivalence is continued in St. Paul, as we shall see later on. I have thought it advisable to spend so much time on the Old Testament because otherwise certain problems and insights of the New Testament do not appear in all their sharpness. We shall conclude the discussion of women and death when we discuss St. Paul's attitude toward women.

It would not be in complete accord with the Old Testament to end so sourly. Even the sinful history of Israel as the broken covenant is not allowed to end on a down note. The account of the Kings of Judah, certainly an uninspiring collection, ends only with the liberation and elevation of King Jehoiachin (2 Kings 25:27). The chronicle of Israel's historical downfall does not end with exile, but with the proclamation of Cyrus King of Persia that the exiled Jews are to return to their homeland and rebuild the Temple (2 Chronicles 36:22). Consequently we can do no better than to end our examination of the Old Testament doctrine of women on the upbeat—and presently shall—by reading the Song of Songs.

But even elsewhere in post-exilic Judaism women were accorded at least some status. They are, for example, present to hear the reading of the Law of Moses. They are included in "the assembly, consisting of men, women and children old enough to understand" (Nehemiah 8:2). This text is important as indicating a significant difference between the Judeo-Christian assembly and the Greek polis, one that will be extended in the Christian Church, which will also include all—men, women, and children. Furthermore, the text indicates that women are regarded as capable of understanding. We read (Nehemiah 8:9) that all the people wept as they heard the words of the Law—men and women alike, we may assume, when they heard its requirements. Implicit here is the statement that first-class citizenship is a matter of demands as well as privileges. For neither men nor women is it an unalloyed joy to belong to the covenant people. We may also assume that the feasting which followed the reading of the Law was equally celebrated by men and woman.

Our misogynist Wisdom writers can also regard woman herself as a cause for feast and celebration. In fact, even that dourest of all, Ecclesiasticus, must confess:

Happy the husband of a really good wife;

the number of his days will be doubled.
A perfect wife is the joy of her husband,
he will live out the years of his life in peace.
A good wife is the best of portions,
reserved for those who fear the Lord;
rich or poor, they will be glad of heart,
cheerful of face, whatever the season (26:1-4).

The same doctrine is also found in Proverbs (12; 18; 19), which lists in detail the virtues of a good wife (31:10-31). With the exaggerated reactions so typical of celibate clergymen intent on being liberated and relevant, G. Tavard comments on this verse, "Interpreted literally, as a description of the ideal wife, this describes a slave, a person who is entirely dominated by another."[14] In that paragraph he omits verse 30, which allows even a woman to have wisdom: "the woman who is wise is the one to praise." Verses 10-31 do indeed describe a very energetic and busy wife. But they also and equally describe an extremely competent and able person.

We can, of course, agree with Tavard when he goes on to relate this text to the Wisdom literature which delights in speaking of the divine wisdom in feminine terms. In the book of Proverbs wisdom is personified, and contrasted to Dame Folly (14:1; 9:13). The same book regards wisdom as present at the first creation and active in the further creation (8:22-31). It is precisely this (feminine) wisdom who is to instruct and gladden Israel, hence both male and female (8:32-36). Chapter 9 describes wisdom as a hostess whose banquet offers the bread and wine of life in contrast and opposition to the kingdom of the dead, Sheol. This chapter will play a great role in the theology of Jesus as Wisdom, whose bread is for everlasting life (John 6) and whose kingdom is one of life against the gates of the netherworld, the kingdom of the dead (Matthew 16:16-19).

The book of Ecclesiasticus, for all its bitter misogyny, attributes even greater being to wisdom. She is now a heavenly being.

> From eternity, in the beginning, he created me,
> and for eternity I shall remain (24:9).

This wisdom is very active in salvation history, from creation (24:3 plays on Genesis 1:2) to the pillar of cloud in the Exodus (24:4), to the sacred worship of Yahweh in the Temple (24:10). Indeed wisdom

> is no other than the book of the covenant
> of the Most High God,
> the Law Moses enjoined on us (24:23).

Wisdom's exemplary status is established at the very beginning, for she is regarded as the source of the four rivers of paradise (24:25-27). Thus the feminine principle is postulated from the very beginning, before the cosmic creation of the world and mankind. This is very important for our later considerations in chapter 12.

The book of Wisdom attributes twenty-one perfections to Wisdom. In the symbolic number system (3 x 7) of the Bible this is incredibly perfect (7:22-8:1). Wisdom, even here, is not god. How could she be for the decisively monotheistic Jew? But Wisdom is the reflection or manifestation of God.

> She is a breath of the power of God,
> pure emanation of the glory of the Almighty...
> She is a reflection of the eternal light...
> image of his goodness.

Wisdom reveals to men the intentions of God, who as divine remains hidden and unknown, so that they can be saved (9:13-18). Wisdom is thus clearly revealed to be that knowledge of good and evil and of life which the serpent promised, but which Eve and Adam did not obtain from him. It is interesting that this wisdom so desired by the first woman should be revealed in feminine terms. It is also interesting that it is feminine wisdom which "delivered him (Adam) from his fault" (10:1). Even more striking is that the feminine principle is active so that "The father of the world, the first being to be fashioned" (10:1) could be fashioned. God had certainly been thought of in male terms, but here the "female" wisdom is active in the very creation of the first male. Certainly, then, at least the foundation has been laid for the equality of women "in God's eyes."

So we come finally to the Song of Songs. Because of its unusual characteristics, namely the absence of reference to God and the presence of sexual passion, this book has been the target of repeated efforts to remove it from the Bible. The same two characteristics have also prompted many and outlandish theories to explain its meaning and how it could be included among the *sacred* books of the *Holy* Bible. Even as late as 1973, Tavard[15] would interpret it in the prophetic tradition which, from Hosea on, has described the relationship of God and his people in terms of husband and wife. This prophetic approach is applied to Christ and the Church from the New Testament on. However, the contrast between the prophets and the Song of Songs is clear and indisputable. That means that such an interpretation has no evident basis within the Song of Songs and must be introduced from outside.

It would be much easier to avoid all the complicated allegorical and historical explanations, and to accept the Song of Songs for what it is—a love poem celebrating the delights of sexual human being. We need not succumb to those Puritan and Jansenist misconceptions which equate the sexually frigid with the religiously fervid. In fact, there is no better way to conclude our considerations on the ambivalent sexual history of Israel than to see the Song of Songs as an intense protest against that fateful verse from Genesis which has been our leitmotif for all these pages:

"Your yearning shall be for your husband,
Yet he will lord it over you (3:16)."

Genesis 1 and 2 maintain that it doesn't have to be this way and indeed wasn't always—not "in the beginning." The Song of Songs makes the same point: it didn't have to be that way; not in the Garden, at least. In fact, it doesn't have to be that way even here and now, outside that Garden. For sex remains the good gift of God to his creation. It may now be obscured and hindered. But it is still God's good gift. And woman and man remain, not alone, but helpmates suitable for one another. She is still bone of his bone, flesh of his flesh. They are still meant, and able, to cling to one another and become one body.

What is the Song of Songs really all about? That's simple. It is the declaration that Genesis 3:16 is not the last word. It is the proclamation that the ambiguity sin introduced into the world and sexual humanity is not absolute. In its own words it reveals itself as the invincible conviction that man can still say to woman as the bridegroom does:

How beautiful you are, how charming,
My love, my delight (7:7).

And the woman to the man, as the bride does:

My Beloved lifts up his voice,
he says to me,
"Come then, my love,

my lovely one, come.
For see, winter is past,
the rains are over and gone.
The flowers appear on the earth.
The season of glad songs has come,
the cooing of the turtledove is heard
in our land.
The fig tree is forming its first figs
and the blossoming vines give out their fragrance.
Come then, my love,
my lovely one, come.
My dove, hiding in the clefts of the rock,
in the coverts of the cliff,
show me your face,
let me hear your voice;
for your voice is sweet
and your face is beautiful."
My Beloved is mine and I am his.
He pastures his flock among the lilies (2:10-14, 16).

As the early Hebrews had to contend with the doctrines of the Mesopotamians, so did the later Jews and the early Christians have to contend with the doctrines of the Greeks and Romans. Jesus himself lived in a world that was geographically Semitic, religiously Hebrew, and politically and culturally Hellenistic. Although the political power was Roman, the cultural influence was largely Greek.

Before we examine the gospels to see Jesus' attitude toward women, we should look at least briefly at the status of women in Greece and Rome.

Both Greece and Rome were intensely patriarchal societies. The families were like miniature states, governed by a rigid code under the authority of the *pater familias* (normally the eldest male in the family). This family head had almost absolute power. He could sell the members of his household

3/ Jesus and Woman

into slavery and even put them to death. His sovereignty was limited only by an unwritten law according to which he had to call a family council in regard to the more serious offenses against the family code. His death gave the adult males their personal freedom. Then they were able to become "fireside despots" of their own. Woman, however, could never escape male tutelage. Unmarried, she was the subject to her father; married, she passed into the power of her husband; widowed, she would belong to her son, or some similar representative or relative.

In the course of history this absolute patriarchal domination was modified, especially by the dispersion of the family members. Trade, travel, and warfare loosened the bonds of the family in general, but especially for the female members. There was also a growth in the understanding of the dignity of men and women, and this brought to both an increase in freedom. However, this development was slow and unequal. For example, in Greece the domination of the young by the old ended long before the equality of the sexes was established (if indeed, it is yet). However, in Rome the dominion of the father was legally intact until Constantine (A.D. 324-337), although its extreme provisions were practiced less and less frequently. In 63 B.C. a Roman nobleman executed an adult son without interference from the law—the last case on record.

Most significant with respect to the status of woman is the practice of infanticide by exposure. In Greece infanticide was widely practiced after 200 B.C. in order to achieve a stable population. Infanticide, of course, applied selectively to girl babies and crippled males. Roman custom prohibited the exposure of sons who were not cripples and of the first-born daughter. Even if its implementation were not widespread, such a distinction hardly indicates equal humanity for both male and female.

In Greece the restriction of women to the home was generally greater than in Rome. For the Greek males, womanly companionship, wit, grace, and charm were provided not by the wives (they were to bear and rear legitimate children), but by the *hetaera*. More than mere prostitutes, these professional women were rather like high-class call girls who could be kept as mistresses affording more than merely sexual companionship. Greek marriage was basically monogamous, but marital fidelity was not enforced for the men. In Greece, as in the whole Mediterranean world (and perhaps at least the whole Western world), woman tends to be regarded as a nymphomaniac—without constant supervision, only sexual errancy is to be expected of her. Therefore she must be kept at home. And if she cannot be kept physically within the walls of the home, then a sort of mobile home must be provided— the ample robes for the body and the veil for the face. This "home away from home" provides for her seclusion even when she ventures out of doors. As we remarked earlier in regard to the Hebrews, though, the question remains whether such male suspicions point to female unreliability or male insecurity and weakness. The increasing incidence of male impotence today points up the physiological inadequacy of the male to satisfy the potentially insatiable female, who does not labor under such physiological difficulty.

Roman wives and mothers generally enjoyed greater freedom and dignity than their counterparts in Greece and the Near East. In fact, as early as 450 B.C. a Roman woman whose father had died or one who had reached the age of twenty-five under a guardian became independent. She could then terminate a marriage as the husband could—that is, by a simple declaration of her intention to divorce. By at least the second century B.C., what could be called "free" marriage had become the practice. That is, the previous restrictions in favor of the parents, prearranged marriages, and the like, had yielded to the free choice of the partners. In regard to property ownership and freedom of movement in society, the Roman woman enjoyed much greater independence than the Greek. In the later Republic and early Empire this Roman woman's liberation was, in fact, a source of consideration difficulty for the early Church, especially St. Paul. The liberation of Roman women, as is the wont of such liberations, was accompanied by a wide-ranging sexual freedom. This led to a license and a deterioration in family life that could only distress someone like St. Paul, who had grown up in a strict Pharisiac Judaism. However, it was not only on the basis of the traditional reverence for the family but also on the basis of the Christian respect for the human body as the temple of the Holy Spirit that this liberation become libertinism was unacceptable to the early Church. We shall discuss this further when we come to St. Paul.

It is possible, however, that the most influential element in a culture's attitude toward women is not the strictly legal. The estimation of women found in the philosophers and poets can be even more indicative of their real position and status. Thus Homer's dictum is extremely valuable testimony: "There is no more vile and devilish creature than a woman whose heart is bent on evil." This sentiment is echoed by Euripides' "There is no evil so terrible as woman" (although Greek drama is certainly replete with strong-willed and noble women). Reminiscent of the Hebrew ambivalence, on the other hand, is Homer's view that life can offer nothing better than a happy marriage. Furthermore his poems, which were very influential in forming Greek opinion, feature women who are both honorable and important. In fact, the ancient world's best-seller, the *Odyssey,* was an epic of matrimonial loyalty and devotion.

Plato was grateful not to have been born a slave or a woman. The fifth book of the *Republic* is hardly a love letter. Near the end of the *Timaeus* (90) Plato speculates on the origin of women:

> Of all the men who come into the world, those who were cowards or led unrighteous lives may with reason be supposed to have changed into the nature of women in the second generation.

What could prompt a man as intelligent as Plato to come up with such an explanation? His statement can provide us with the occasion to see how such ideas originate. Given the culture in which Plato lived, he could certainly be accused of at least some sexism. But that alone is not sufficient explanation. Some people then have recourse to wild speculations or ivory tower, abstract theories. But this explanation also misses a very important point, namely that philosophers generally begin with the real and factual world they experience around them. Philosophy is really the philosopher's attempt to explain this real world of his—the one he experiences. This real world is the starting point and subject of all his explanations and theories.

The *fact* was that in the society of Plato's time women were socially oppressed and depressed; they were second-class citizens. What Plato had to do was to discover why. He was aided in forming his explanation by his general suspicion and distaste for things material. Real being was not material, not sensual, not corporal; it was immaterial, spiritual. For Plato the material human body was basically the prison of the immaterial soul, which was being thus punished for some fault. Ideally the soul would be without the body, and heaven was attained by flight or escape from the body.

Now, join the theory that bodily existence was a punishment with the fact that women were oppressed, and Plato's conclusion is not far-fetched. Women are those who in their previous existence lived very unsatisfactory lives. Hence they are being punished all the more. The difficulty with Plato's approach is that it does not avoid the vicious circle in which the fact and theory mutually reinforce each other. The result: although the theory is originally intended to explain the fact, it eventually can also create the fact.

There is an interesting contrast between Plato's conclusions and those of the Hebrews. Both find the depressed state of women to be the result of "sin." For Plato this oppression is inherent in human nature, itself a "fall," and therefore in feminine human nature. For the Hebrew, however, the oppression is not inherent in human nature. Nor, if our interpretation of the Song of Songs is correct, is this sexual disorientation and oppression inevitable even in this world.

Stronger and longer-lasting than Plato's was the influence of Aristotle's philosophy. Even more than Plato, Aristotle based his thought on the observation and description of the reality he experienced around him, as the following quotation indicates (*History of Animals,* IX, 1;608b):

> Hence woman is more compassionate than man, more easily moved to tears, at the same time is more jealous, more querulous, more apt to scold and to strike. She is, furthermore, more prone to despondency and less hopeful than the man, more void of shame or self-respect, more false of speech, more deceptive, and of more retentive memory. She is also more wakeful, more shrinking, more difficult to rouse to action, and requires a smaller quantity of nutriment.

It is not, however, for such general observations that Aristotle is most famous—or infamous. It is, rather his theory that in the generation of offspring woman is the passive partner. This would not itself have been fateful. But from women's passivity, which he would claim to have observed as a fact, he concluded women were inferior (*On the Generation of Animals,* 729a, 728a, 737a):

> But what does happen is just what one would expect, since what the male contributes to generation is the form and the efficient cause, while the female contributes the material.
>
> That, then, the female does not contribute semen to generation, but does contribute something, is clear from what has been said, and also from a general and abstract survey of the question. For there must needs be that which generates and that from which it generates; and in those animals that have these powers separate in two sexes the body and nature of the active and the passive sex must also differ. If, then, the male stands for the effective and active, and the female, considered as female, for the passive, it follows that what the female would contribute to the semen of the male would not be semen but material for the semen to work upon.

From Aristotle's thesis that action is more perfect than passion (receptivity) is derived the logic whereby the passive partner is regarded as imperfect and defective. He describes woman as a multilated or incapacitated male:

> Now a boy is like a woman in form, and the woman is as it were an impotent male, for it is through a certain incapacity that the female is female, being incapable of concocting the nutriment in its last stage into semen.
>
> For the female's contribution also is a secretion, and has all the parts in it potentially though none of them actually; it has in it potentially even those parts which differentiate the female from the male, for just as the young of multilated parents are sometimes born mutilated and sometimes not, so also the young born of a female are sometimes female and sometimes male instead. For the female is, as it were, a mutilated male, and the catamenia are semen, only not pure; for there is only one thing they have not in them, the principle of soul.

These lengthy quotations are important because the concepts they express will enter into the biological and philosophical foundations of Christian theology, which will by and large consign women to an inferior position sexually, socially, and even religiously in the sense of depriving them of the participation in the life of the Church of which they are capable. We shall discuss this further in connection with the question of women's ordination to the priesthood later on.

We need not prolong our examination of the culture of Greeks and Romans. Even this short summary has adequately revealed an attitude toward women much like the ambivalence we saw in the Hebrews. There are, however, major theological differences, since neither Platonic nor Aristotelian philosophy is capable of providing a basis for the establishment of human equality between male and female. The influence of this Greek thought in the development of later Christian philosophy and theology will impede the understanding of Genesis 3:16 and indeed contribute to its misunderstanding: the lordship of the male over the female will tend to be interpreted as the way things should be instead of the way they are because of sin. Once again we have encountered a reduced dignity and status of women in the context of sexuality and procreation. It is against this background of Mesopotamian, Hebrew, and Hellenistic thought, sketchy but we hope adequate, that we can now proceed to Jesus.

In considering the impact of the man Jesus on the society of his time, some commentators insist upon calling him a revolutionary. However, the word "revolutionary" has certain overtones which don't really fit. In view of this, others have said that he should be described not in terms of revolution but of liberation. Jesus did speak of himself in terms of freedom. For example, "You will learn the truth and the truth will make you free" is his promise to those who become his "disciples" and "make my word your home" (John 8:31, 32). Nevertheless liberation is such a wide-ranging term that its application to Jesus is by no means without serious difficulties. The word as such specifies neither "from what" nor "for what" man is freed. Still another suggestion comes from German scripture scholar F. J. Schierse, who would prefer to call Jesus "oppositional": that is, Jesus opposes himself to various kinds of evil and to the groups which represent or encourage these evils.

None of these suggestions, however, takes fully into account the most important dimension of Jesus' life, with respect both to attitude and action. Although Jesus is certainly not tolerant in face of evil, he makes it evident that his mission is not one of condemnation but one of love. As we read in the gospel of John:

> Yes, God loved the world so much
> that he gave his only Son,
> so that everyone who believes in him may not be lost
> but may have eternal life.
> For God sent his Son into the world
> not to condemn the world,
> but that through him the world might be saved (John 3:16f.).

Likewise, he rejected the intolerance and hypocrisy so often involved in the judgment of one man by another:

> "Do not judge, and you will not be judged; because the judgments you give are the judgments you will get, and the amount you measure out is the amount you will be given" (Matthew 7:1).

In his encounters with persons, he generally stresses the positive factors in their personalities and lives. More of his time, during his public life, is spent proclaiming the will of his Father than in condemning the wicked. In this sense Jesus can be said to be a liberator. As we have seen from Genesis 1-3, God's being and will are liberating, not oppressing. God's relationship to the world and mankind is a liberation from both original nothingness and sin's later desire to return to nothing. Insofar as Jesus is this being of God in the world (John 1:14 and Hebrews 1:1-4), his very presence is a continued liberation or new manifestation of that original liberation described in Genesis. We shall examine the gospels to see how this freedom of Jesus is manifested in his words and deeds.

First of all, and perhaps most striking, is the complete absence of that misogyny we have seen in the Hebrews, Mesopotamians, Greeks, and Romans. Nowhere in the record of Jesus' life is there any trace of a male superiority to which women are subordinate. That women should be subject or submissive to the male as to their lord is nowhere even hinted. Nor can one find in Jesus the suspicion that deep down women are secretly nymphomaniacs and seductresses. As we shall see, this is especially evident in his association with women. In fact, even fallen and "professional" women do not disturb Jesus. Nor do they lead him to blame them for the male's legendary weakness, from Adam on.

This attitude toward women is illustrated not only negatively but positively. Jesus seems to regard women as capable of the same virtues and good acts as men. It is not as if he started from men and then extended both the expectation and ability from the original male to the female. This distinction apparently never entered his mind.

Some people make much of Jesus' familiarity with the daily duties and life of women. For example, he knows about baking (Matthew 13:33), the bridal party (25:1), the woman's lost coin (Luke 15:8), and the widow's lawsuit (18:1). However, it is hard to imagine that anyone, even a Hebrew male, would not *know* about these things. What is surprising is that such a Hebrew male, Jesus, would not be ashamed or reluctant to use such examples in his public teaching.

Even more revealing is the presence of parallels from both the male and the female "world" in his parables. Even Matthew's gospel, which is supposed to have a greater Hebrew orientation than the others, shows this concern, which must be a deliberate effort. In chapter 13, the kingdom of heaven is like a mustard seed in a field (male) and the yeast in the flour (female); in 24, there are men in the fields and women at the grindstone; in 25, the kingdom of heaven is like both the man and his servants and the bridesmaids. Luke parallels the cures of a male leper and a widow (ch. 4), the condemnations by the men of Nineveh and the Queen of the South (ch. 11), the shepherd's search for the lost sheep and the woman's search for the lost coin (ch. 15). Sometimes such parallels are not contained in the same chapter. So, for example, the persistent neighbor at midnight (Luke 11:5) has his female counterpart in the widow who won't give up "pestering" the evil judge (18:1).

Not only men but also women are present at the miracles of the loaves and fishes (Matthew 14:21; 15:38). In John 6 the only designation is a "large crowd" and the "people." Since a small boy is mentioned, we can conclude to the explicit presence of women. Their presence at this "eucharistic" event is most important. Just as women were present at the liberating Exodus meal of the Old Testament, so do they also participate in the liberating Eucharist of the New. Jesus also cures women, starting with Simon's mother-in-law (Mark 1:29). Given the precarious position of widows at the time, we could also say that when he raised the wdow's son to life at Nain, he also simultaneously restored her life (Luke 7:11-17).

It is also very noteworthy that Jesus performs miracles at the request of women, especially since women were not supposed to be forward in regard to their lord-husbands and other males.

Similar to the parallels we noted above, immediately after honoring the official's (male) request, Jesus honors the request of the woman with a hemorrhage (Matthew 9:18-26). Here we can also recall our considerations about clean and unclean from the Old Testament. Although the woman's ailment is the discharge of blood, Jesus does not object when she touches him. In fact, he praises her faith. Even more striking is the cure of the Syrophoenician woman's possessed daughter (Mark 7:24-30). It is quite possible that this is another male-female parallel with the Gentile centurion whose servant was cured (Matthew 8:5-13; Luke 7:2-10). Perhaps even more important for our considerations here is the fact that Jesus does not discriminate against this doubly disadvantaged person. Not only was she a woman, she was also an alien—a non-Jew. (Such women were traditionally accorded little respect in society, being very subject to what is known as "couch" politics: in return for her favors she could receive a favor from the male.)

The Bible of Jerusalem obscures another possible interesting interpretation. In this translation she says "Sir" to Jesus. However, if we translate the Greek "Kyrie" by "Lord," then we have a profession of faith which far outstrips that of the disciples. Is it also impossible that she anticipates the proclamation of faith made by the Gentile centurion at the foot of the cross: "In truth this man was a Son of God" (Mark 15:39)? In contrast to the "favored" but slow to understand male disciples, women both before and after the resurrection believe first. Thus women from Eve and Sarah on illustrate that God is no respecter of persons, as St. Paul will insist. Hence the "superiority" of both male and Jew is revealed to be a misunderstanding. The only true "above" is God's Spirit, which blows where it will (John 3:8). As a consequence, Jesus is even willing to cure a woman on the sabbath and thus face the indignation of the officials for having violated the sabbath (Luke 13:10-17). It is not without interest for us that the following chapter of Luke begins with the cure of a man on the sabbath (14:1-6). It is difficult to avoid the conclusion that Jesus' dealings with men and women were so fair and so equal that the gospels could not be written without clearly manifesting this trait.

Thus it is important for Luke to note that women also accompanied Jesus on his missionary journeys (8:1-3). It is most interesting that these women are not included only in general among the disciples. They are, rather, placed in a certain parallel to the Twelve, whose chief purpose was symbolic and not practical or missionary. As the symbol of the new Israel, the fulfillment of the original twelve tribes of Jacob, they must almost necessarily be men. Hence it must have been quite clear to the early Church that the presence of women among the foundational disciples and missionaries had to be explicit and emphatic. Thus the women are not only there, but active participants. They "provided for them out of their own resources" (8:3) is a clear statement that women as well as men shared in the mission of Jesus. (Unfortunately the Churches have not yet been able to draw the inevitable conclusions from this fact in regard to the arrangement of their ministry and priesthood.)

Jesus was willing to risk his good name and reputation for the sake of "fallen women." Only Luke's gospel has preserved the incident of the sinful woman who washed Jesus' feet in the house of Simon the Pharisee (7:36-50). In contrast to Simon, who would have rejected the sinful woman,

Jesus accepted her company, even allowing her to touch him. He did this even though her basic unacceptableness was increased by her act of letting her hair down. In the male chauvinist society in which she lived, this would have been regarded as the brazen affront of a hussy. Her action must have been doubly disconcerting to the Jews of the strict observance, for she was not only a woman but a sinner. Often their concept of holiness did not allow for a relationship of love between God and the sinner; and, as we have seen, they could also be reluctant to admit that the divine holiness could communicate itself to women.

Again, when the woman caught in the very act of adultery is dragged before Jesus, his conduct is in bold contrast to that of her accusers and would-be judges (John 8:1-11). Even more here than in the previous incident, Jesus dares to risk his personal safety. It is quite possible that the woman's accusers were trying to trap him (v. 6). If he should decide in favor of the woman and free her, he would violate the Law of Moses, which is quite clear on this point. However, if he agreed that she should be stoned, he could be in trouble with the Roman occupation authorities, since it seems that at this time the Jews no longer had the right to inflict capital punishment. It is significant, then, that Jesus did not abdicate his role as liberator at the expense of the woman. He continued to insist on the mercifulness of God to the sinner. And he expends himself to find a way to effect this, even, we might say, in regard to a lowly female sinner.

How different Jesus' attitude was from that of other men is highlighted by the theory of at least some scholars that the woman's husband set a trap for her. Of course, her apprehension in such a sin and crime would have allowed him to divorce her even in the stricter interpretation of the Mosaic Law. This is, perhaps, the ultimate in the double standard of morality for men and women. We shall see later how Jesus' rejection of divorce clearly rejects this double standard.

St. John's gospel also contains two more instances of Jesus' liberating attitude toward women. The first again involves a fallen woman, the Samaritan woman at Jacob's well (John 4:4-42). Since Jews were allowed to have at most three marriages, five husbands plus her present companion would indicate that this woman was really, in today's idiom, a "swinger." Whether the same standards existed among the Samaritans or not, the moral code of the Near East could never have approved of so many marriages. In any case, verse 29 presumes that she is aware of her guilt. Still, Jesus not only speaks to her but does so respectfully: the word translated as "woman" was a courteous title for someone who was past the stage of being "Miss." When the disciples return and see Jesus speaking with a stranger, they are apparently more shocked that it is a woman than that it is a Samaritan. Given the very low esteem in which the Jews held the Samaritans, their shock must indicate how really differently Jesus treated women. This is supported by the verb: "were shocked" is in the imperfect tense and indicates not a moment's surprise, but a prolonged amazement. Certainly Jesus here liberates woman from that suspicion we have seen in Ecclesiasticus 9:1-13 and which prompted later rabbis to warn men against even speaking to women in public.

However, even more to the point for us is that Jesus discusses religion and theology with this sinful and Samaritan woman. (While I was writing this chapter I had to attend a convention of university theology professors. During one of the discussions a religious sister from St. Mary's of the Lake reminded us that she was not allowed to be granted a degree in "theology"—it had to be in "sacred doctrine." For the same reasons the present College Theology Society was originally named in terms of "sacred doctrine." The difficulties women experience in obtaining theological degrees within Protestantism is also a fascinating story, as Elsie Gibson has shown in her book *When the Minister Is a Woman.*)

Although the dialogue between Jesus and the Samaritan woman seems to presume almost too much knowledge on her part, scholars still think that an historical occurrence in the life of Jesus is the basis of this chapter. It is also noteworthy that the woman becomes a "missionary" for Jesus. Although her townsfolk eventually believe in Jesus because they have heard him themselves (v. 42), they were led to belief in him by this woman and her testimony.

In both Luke (10:38) and John (11:1-44) two sisters are mentioned, Martha and Mary. With these two women we leave the company of the "sinful women," since it is not likely that the Mary "who anointed the Lord" here is the sinful Galilean woman mentioned in St. Luke's gospel (7:38). Mary and Martha have certainly been overinterpreted in the history of theology. There has been a tendency to value Mary more highly. But, as Raymond Brown points out, it is quite possible that the original character in this account is Martha, and that Mary's role is an afterthought. In both Luke and John the characterization of the two women is consistent. They have been described as active (Martha) and sedentary—or prostrate— at the feet of Jesus (Mary). Luke's statement (10:42) that Jesus told the listening Mary that she had chosen the better part has become a standard argument for the contemplative life being preferable to the active life. The "one thing necessary" has also been invested with great theological and mystical significance. However, I really think this is all basically an exaggeration of a much more practical attitude on the part of Jesus. Nowhere does he show great concern for what we call "material" things or comforts. Consequently he might just be telling Martha, "Relax, woman. All this running around is not necessary. Not every meal has to be a banquet, not every visit a royal reception. Why don't we all just sit down and talk!" Furthermore, it is fully possible that Mary, far from being a contemplative in the religious sense, is simply the more passive type. It is Martha, after all, who first goes out to meet Jesus, who "believes" that whatever Jesus asks God will be granted, who believes that Jesus is "the Christ, the Son of God." This confession of faith is certainly the climax of the entire scene. Mary really seems only to echo Martha.

For our purpose, though, most important is the contrast between the faith of the women and the absence of such faith on the part of the Jews in general (v. 31; 37). Again, exactly how much understanding Martha and Mary may have had is not the point. Rather, in the gospel narratives concerning Jesus, it is clearly women as well, and perhaps better than, men who recognize and believe in him. Hence it is clearly revealed that God's gifts are equally intended for women and men.

Martha and Mary also show once again the free-and-easy access women had to Jesus. There relationships are immediate and even intimate. Martha can complain to him, Mary can try to be his favorite. Is it "typical" feminine attentiveness to a pleasing male guest that brings her to the feet of Jesus—rather than fussing around the house? And Jesus finds this very acceptable.

The anointing scene in the next chapter is quite confused. However, for our purpose the point is quite clear that women can believe in and love Jesus directly. An auxiliary point would easily be that women are also courageous enough to do this publicly, in the face of scornful opposition. Whether planned or not, contrast between the believing female Mary and the betraying male Judas could hardly be overlooked.

Finally, according to Mark (14:9), by virtue of this "faithful act" Mary has entered permanently into the proclamation of the gospel "in the whole world."

From Mary's anticipatory anointing of Jesus for his death it is only a short and logical step to the presence of women at the crucifixion. According to the gospels, probably four women were present. Although the disciples had fled, at least "the disciple he (Jesus) loved" (John 19:26) was there. And Luke mentions both "his friends (male acquaintances) . . . (and) also the women" being present, so that "they saw all this happen" (23:49). It would be dramatic to emphasize the complete dereliction of the males in deserting Jesus and the complete devotion of the women in staying with him. However, this would be an oversimplification and exaggeration. Neither would it be true to that apparently deliberate effort of the gospels to provide an equal, parallel and balanced presentation of men and women in the life of Jesus. According to this, theoretically both men and women should have been at the foot of the cross. And both were.

The precise role of Mary in the life and ministry of Jesus is only briefly presented by the gospels. This sometimes alarms people, who are then tempted to overinterpret what is there. Although Jesus establishes a certain distance between himself and his mother, he always remains filial. For example, even at Cana he grants her request while at the same time he asserts his basic independence. It is also important to realize that not only Mary but everyone, male and female, is "excluded" from planning the life and mission of Jesus. He does only the will of God in heaven! But, in doing this divine will, Jesus invites all, without any discrimination, to be associated with him.

A comparison between Mary and other people in the gospels is interesting. She is in obvious contrast to Zechariah, whose lack of belief leaves him unable to sing the praises of God (Luke 1:20). Mary is "blessed" because "she believed" and is thereby able to "proclaim the greatness of the Lord" (1:45f.). Likewise, Mary is the mother of "the Son of the Most High" while Zechariah is the father only of the preparer. The gentleness of the angel's dealing with Mary could have been a revelation to subsequent Christians about how God treats women. But it obviously has not been. In the so-called Infancy Gospel there is also an indication of the male-female parallelism we noted above: both Simeon and Anna prophesy about Jesus (Luke 2:25-38). Furthermore, when the boy Jesus is found in the Temple, it is Mary's words which are recalled. Of course, it is not all and only Mary. In Matthew's gospel, Joseph is the one who receives communications from God (1:20; 2:13, 19). This is important because it is one more example of how God favors neither male nor female, nor does "he" discriminate against either. Rather, both are fully able to participate in God's gifts, both receptively and actively.

Mary also provides another occasion for Jesus to clarify the status of woman. Along with some other relatives, she has come to speak with Jesus. They approach Jesus on the basis of their blood or family relationship. To this Jesus replies that the *true* relationship to him is established not by flesh and blood, but by the ability to hear the word of God and to do his will (Luke 8:19; Mark 12:46). This has prompted one Catholic women's libber to exult that women are not just wombs! That, in any case, was obvious even for ancient sexists. For them women were, however, restricted to the pleasures of sex and to the bearing and rearing of children. To restrict the liberation afforded by Jesus' explanation above to the bearing of children is to have missed the point. It is rely the physiological sexual capacity for procreation ἰ relativized here; it is rather the whole idea that "salva-᾽ or "meaning" can be found in the family or in the sexual and/or procreative nature and activity of humanity. What this indicates is that sexual differentiation does not provide the fundamental dignity of men and women, but only the modality in which they enjoy their humanity. It is a restatement of that "original" Genesis teaching that man's fundamental dignity is his being related to God. This relationship-being is God's gift, not man's own accomplishment or achievement. Hence even the Mother of Jesus does not find the ultimate basis of her "perfection" in her maternity, but in her "I am the handmaid of the Lord . . . let what you have said be done to me" (Luke 1:38).

There is confirmation of this in another scene, and also an admonition to those who tend to belittle maternity, as if mothers were nothing but "baby machines." In chapter 2 Luke tells of the woman who praised Jesus and Mary in terms of procreation: "Happy the womb that bore you and the breasts you sucked" (v. 27). Jesus does not deny this. Indeed his reply must be understood as an emphatic restatement of the original goodness of sex and procreation—as long as they remain the gifts of God and are not made divine themselves. He says, "Still happier are those who hear the word of God and keep it" (v. 28). The comparative form of happy is not without its significance. It means that sex and parenthood are indeed important. They are ways of sharing in God's gifts, but they are not the sum total of his gifts. Most importantly, they do not provide men and women with that "immortality" which is the completion of the original gift of being. How this final triumph over nonbeing would have happened in a sinless world, in Eden, is not known. What is known, however, is that it would not have been through man's

---

own sexual and procreative achievement. Hence, not even Mary's human motherhood is the source of her final blessedness. That source is the will and grace of God, which Mary experienced and lived as mother. Certainly the Mother of God would know and bear witness that motherhood itself is not divine.

A final—and perhaps the most important—incident in our examination of Jesus' liberating approach to women is supplied by his debate with some Pharisees about divorce, and some subsequent conclusions about the unmarried state:

> Some Pharisees approached him, and to test him they said, "Is it against the Law for a man to divorce his wife on any pretext whatever?" He answered, "Have you not read that the creator from the beginning made them male and female and that he said: This is why a man must leave father and mother, and cling to his wife, and the two become one body. So then, what God has united, man must not divide."
>
> They said to him, "Then why did Moses command that a writ of dismissal should be given in cases of divorce?" "It was because you were so unteachable," he said, "that Moses allowed you to divorce your wives, but it was not like this from the beginning. Now I say this to you: the man who divorces his wife—I am not speaking of fornication—and marries another, is guilty of adultery."
>
> The disciples said to him, "If that is how things are between husband and wife, it is not advisable to marry." But he replied, "It is not everyone who can accept what I have said, but only those to whom it is granted. There are eunuchs born that way from their mother's womb, there are eunuchs made so by men and there are eunuchs who have made themselves that way for the sake of the kingdom of heaven. Let anyone accept this who can" (Matthew 19:1-12).
>
> So then, what God has united, man must not divide. Back in the house the disciples questioned him again about this, and he said to them, "The man who divorces his wife and marries another is guilty of adultery against her. And if a woman divorces her husband and marries another she is guilty of adultery too" (Mark 10:10-12).

The text from Matthew reflects a dispute then current between two rabbinical schools, based on Deuteronomy 24:1. The dispute concerned the obscure phrase "some impropriety of which to accuse her." It can also be translated "something shameful." Rabbi Hillel tended to permit divorce for any reason—for example, the love of another woman or even poor performance in the kitchen. That would correspond to the "on any pretext whatever" of our translation. Rabbi Shammai's school allowed divorce only for adultery. Apparently Jesus is being asked to decide which of these two interpretations is correct. His decision rejects both by going beyond the Law of Moses to the original order of creation by God. Here again is confirmation that woman's yearning for man who will lord it over her (Genesis 3:16) is not the will of God, but the result of sin. In the older translation Jesus calls this their hardness of heart; in our translation it is because they "were unteachable."

This is really a liberation of women from male domination. Among the Jews, of course, it was only the male who could divorce the female. Hence, when Jesus simply forbids divorce, with no qualifications or exceptions, he certainly liberates women from this subjection to the whims of the male. However rare or frequent divorces may have been in fact, they were always theoretically and legally available. St. Mark's gospel was written for a Gentile audience. Consequently it does not apply Jesus' saying to the rabbinical dispute, but to the problem of divorce purely and simply. This is significant because, as we have seen above, by this time Roman women as well as men could initiate divorce proceedings. It would be the view of Jesus that the original divine plan "freed" men and women by allowing them to be faithful to each other. They could thus avoid the sexual Olympics which some of our our contemporaries propose as liberation. This view of Jesus is entirely his own. It is found neither in the Old Testament nor in the later rabbinical and Qumran literature. In this context the statement of Jesus in Mark that a man can commit adultery *against his wife* is no less astonishing. It would have been especially unsettling for the Jews. For them adultery was always intercourse between a married woman and a man other than her husband. A woman could commit adultery against her husband, but a husband could commit adultery only against another husband, not against his own wife.

However, Jesus does not stop here. The newness of his teaching is clearly shown in the startled reaction of his disciples. As Matthew indicates, the Jewish male had no intention of remaining married to a wife who did not give due respect to her lord husband. They said, "If this is how things are between husband and wife, it is not advisable to marry" (19:10). Apparently the disciples understood that Jesus had just closed their privileged playground. It is important to note that Jesus does not require anyone to be celibate, but he does allow it—freely, for the sake of God's kingdom.

This is a liberation not only of women but of humanity. It is clear that if one does not have to get married, then salvation does not come from sex, whether for pleasure or procreation or both. In a sense we have now returned to the teaching of Genesis that neither sexual pleasure nor sexual fertility is divine. Hence, although men and women are God's greatest gifts to each other, they do not thereby become the all-sufficient sources of being and happiness. That remains the gift-giving God. Consequently, however great the abuse of women may have been in the past, from the time of Jesus on she certainly could never have been regarded as inferior to the male, certainly never as a baby- or pleasure-machine. Or could she? Indeed, the liberating teaching of Jesus was not always readily understood; hence its application was not always immediate. As we shall see in the next chapter, the early Church did enjoy a great emancipation of women, but it was not completely without its restrictions.

But if we look only at the gospels' record of Jesus' words and deeds, then we are brought face to face with a fascinating record of amazingly liberated and liberating behavior. For Jesus woman is clearly the "helpmate for man" of Genesis, clearly his partner and equal in humanity. She is not elevated to the status of sex or fertility goddess and consequently not subject to the male as sexual drudge and drone. She is clearly in the image and likeness of God, able to hear his word and keep it.

It would be difficult to find a better way to end this chapter than the one chosen by the evangelists to end their Gospels. And that is with the appearances of the risen Jesus. The Gospels are really only being consistent when they all report that the angels announced the resurrection first of all to women (Matthew 28:5; Mark 16:5; Luke 24:5; John 20:12). Likewise, Jesus shows his risen self (that is, he completes his revelation of God and His relationship to the world) first of all to women. They then became the first missionaries of the risen Christ and the new creation. However, in keeping with the old and fallen world, their message "seemed to be pure nonsense" to the male apostles, "and they did not believe them" (Luke 24:11). Once again the male shows himself to be reluctant in regard to the reliability and truthfulness of woman. But equally once again the Gospels indicate that Jesus does not share this male reluctance. The risen Jesus again emphasizes his lack of sexism. For him women are not secondary, inferior and cursed. They are, rather, chosen, privileged and blessed. Truly the curse has been undone by the resurrection.

The beginning of the Church's history bears eloquent witness to this new concept of woman. After the Ascension the apostles returned to Jerusalem "to the upper room where they were staying. ... All these joined in continuous prayer, together with several women, including Mary the mother of Jesus" (Acts 1:14). This would also have been the group which received the Holy Spirit on Pentecost. It is important to keep in mind that the Church can be defined and described in various ways. A classic description has been to emphasize the praying Church as the liturgy of the world. If we keep this definition in mind, then women are obviously full members of the Church from the very beginning, for it is this praying community which receives the Holy Spirit and thus becomes the Church. Another classical description of the Church is Temple of God (Holy Spirit). In this case women

4/ The Church in New Testament Times

would also be full members from the very beginning.

This is confirmed by Peter's action upon being freed from prison. "He went straight to the house of Mary . . . where a number of people had assembled and were praying" (Acts 12:12). Here we should also recall that in the New Testament the word "church" has three fundamental applications. There is the universal Church, the local church, and the domestic or house church. The domestic church is considered the Church in the full sense. That does not mean that this house church is all there is to the Church. But it does mean that in the house church the event of the "Church" is really happening! It is not merely a private devotional meeting. Hence, for women's status in the Church it is of immense importance that such a domestic church should be woman's.

Furthermore this history of the early Church in New Testament times shows no reluctance to be explicit about the number and identity of women converts (Acts 5:14). Not only is Lydia converted, but her entire household too (Acts 16:13). Even more striking is Lydia's success in overcoming St. Paul's extreme reluctance to accept help from anyone. Recall how he boasts that he has always paid his own way (Acts 20:33; 1 Corinthians 9). But Lydia is able to persuade him to "come and stay with us; and she would take no refusal" (Acts 16:15). So Paul, whom certain women's libbers so sharply castigate for his supposed male chauvinism, is not able to resist the persuasion of a woman. It is also to Lydia's house that Paul and Silas return after they are freed from prison (v. 40). It is difficult to believe that Paul could have been so much of a misogynist and still have associated so closely with women like Lydia.

In chapter 17 there are three explicit references to women converts. There are some who think that Damaris (17:34), otherwise unknown in biblical literature, must have been a *hetaera* (as will be recalled, a high-class concubine or para-mour, a courtesan). Otherwise she would not have had the freedom to come to hear Paul preach publicly in the Areo-pagus. Jesus himself, as we have observed, had also been able to "convert" morally marginal women.

Women are not only recipients of the good works of the Church, like the widows in Acts 6:1; they are also the active agents of these good works, like Dorcas in chapter 9. In turn, she receives the Church's greatest temporal gift; her life is restored to her by Peter. Clearly, in the earliest history of the Church women were active in the whole life of the Church. They were by no means restricted to menial tasks.

This is illustrated especially by St. Paul's friends, Aquila (male) and Priscilla (female; also spelled Prisca). They were active not only in general support activities but also in cate-chesis. Thus they give Apollos, who was already a powerful preacher, further instructions in the Christian religion (Acts 19:26). Luke seems to indicate that this additional theological instruction enabled Apollos to be included officially in the teaching body of the primitive Church. Although there is no univocal record that women actually engaged in the official proclamation of the word, they were certainly active in the ministry of the Church. Priscilla and Aquila even accompany St. Paul on missionary trips (Acts 18:18). They are men-tioned six times in the Acts and St. Paul's epistles. Quite con-trary to normal Jewish usage, Priscilla's name is mentioned first in all but one of these references. It is extremely difficult to imagine that she is not the more important of the two. St. Paul's affection and esteem for her is obvious in the greeting in the last chapter of the Epistle to the Romans (16:3). It is interesting to note the number and ranking of women in this chapter. The first person mentioned is a woman, Phoebe. She is, indeed, the carrier of the epistle, certainly a missionary activity. More interesting, she is called a "deaconess of the church at Cenchreae" (16:1).

Whether this term designates a special religious structure in the local church is not clear. It could also be merely a generic description of assistance or helpfulness. The term deacon is used in this general sense in 2 Corinthians 3:6; 11:23; 1 Thessalonians 3:2. However, other texts point in the direction of a specific title, which could quite possibly indicate the existence of an "order" of deaconesses in the primitive Church (Philippians 1:1; 1 Timothy 3:8, 12; Titus 1:9). We do know that there was an office of widow for the fulfillment of various functions in the Church (1 Timothy 5:9). Some kind of teaching office for women in the Church is also recorded in documents outside the New Testament (see *Hermas the Shepherd,* written in stages between 96 and 150 A.D.).

There is another interesting pair of names in the last chapter of Romans. In verse 7 two "outstanding apostles" are listed, Andronicus and Junias. Junias is a masculine name, but in the original language could also be translated "Junia," female. Indeed some versions read "Julia." Some ancient commentators understood the female "Junia" to be the correct name and identified her as the wife of Andronicus. It is interesting to speculate about the significance of this in connection with the discussion of the ordination of women to the priesthood, to which we shall turn in a later chapter. Although most modern commentators understand it to be a masculine name, their conclusion could also be, at least in part, the end result of the generally restrictive tendency which had already set in for women in the apostolic Church.

A similar situation exists in regard to verse 3 in the last chapter of the Epistle to the Philippians. St. Paul is asking someone (Syzygus can be a proper name, but can also mean comrade or companion) to mediate a dispute between Evodia and Syntyche, two women in the Philippian church. In the Bible of Jerusalem translation (the one we are generally using) St. Paul says of them, "These women were a help to me when I was fighting to defend the Good News. . . ." This is really a very general designation—"a help." It could mean almost anything from cooking and laundering to debating or preaching—or fisticuffs! The original Greek verb is general, but it does convey much more than merely "help." It means to struggle along with, to be the associate in hard work. Other translations do better in conveying this more direct cooperation in St. Paul's evangelizing mission. The Revised Standard Version says: "they have labored side by side with me in the gospel. . . ." The Goodspeed translation has "they toiled at my side in spreading the good news. . . ." If the translation of any text is always difficult, how much more so the Bible. Consequently, I don't want to labor the point. However, it is possible to understand some of this "minimalism" in translations of the Bible and in regard to women in the Church if we keep in mind that the primitive Church itself underwent a restriction of women's freedom to participate in the evangelical and apostolic mission.

Before we examine this, we can conclude with a summary of the expanded activity women clearly exercised in the early days. Although the possibility of women apostles and office in the Church for women is important, it is probably not decisive—not even for the question of women's ordination to the priesthood. What is decisive, however, is their active and open participation in the work of the official preachers and teachers of the Church. Of this there can be no doubt, as we have just seen. This fact has been obscured in later times, but it cannot be simply nullified or eradicated. Nevertheless there was tension and ambivalence. Nowhere is this better illustrated than in the life and writings of St. Paul.

St. Paul himself certainly experienced in his own body the liberation effected by Jesus Christ. In all religious literature there is hardly a more eloquent testimony to this than chapters 7 and 8 of the Epistle to the Romans. The Epistle to the Galatians, which preceded but covered much the same ground as Romans, reaches a climax in chapter 3, verse 28:

> All baptized in Christ, you have all clothed yourselves in Christ, and there are no more distinctions between Jew and Greek, slave and free, male and female, but all of you are one in Christ Jesus.

Later, in Colossians, we have a similar insistence that in Christ "there is no room for distinction between Greek and Jew, between circumcised or the uncircumcised, or between barbarian and Scythian, slave and free man" (3:11). It is important to note that these are not merely random couplings or contrasts for a literary effect. St. Paul is here claiming that the most fundamental oppositions and hostilities known to the ancient world are no longer operative. How strange and overwhelming this must have been to even St. Paul himself is readily apparent if we recall his own background and education. As he himself says, "I was ... a Hebrew, born of Hebrew parents. ... As for the Law, I was a Pharisee ... as far as the Law can make you perfect, I was faultless" (Philippians 3:6). And to King Agrippa he described himself: "I followed the strictest party in our religion and lived as a Pharisee" (Acts 26:5). Without doubt this Pharisiac background would have provided St. Paul with a tendency to regard the female as inferior to the male. And this tendency would certainly have been reinforced by the Greek culture of Paul's home, Tarsus. (As we have already seen, the Greek woman was probably even more socially depressed than the Hebrew.) To these two "negative" influences must be added a third, that of the Essene Jews. How great this third influence on Paul may have been is not absolutely clear, but that it was present is beyond doubt. Certainly the Essene understanding of woman would have been denigrating. Only males could belong to the elite and be fully initiated; celibacy was required of them (although there were also married members of the Essene community at Qumran). Although Paul was a fully authorized rabbi and rabbis were required to marry, it does not seem that he himself had married (1 Corinthians 7:8).

Against this background it is not so puzzling that Paul may have insisted on some restrictions for women. What is amazing is that he could have been so liberated in his own behavior and writings, as we saw earlier. But the question reasserts itself: after such a glorious beginning in which St. Paul clearly and fully celebrated the freedom Christ gave mankind, why did he begin to levy restrictions on women? We shall see that the church at Corinth was the occasion for many of these restrictions. Later on, the Pastoral Epistles will reinforce some of them. However, before we look at the Corinthian file we must consider some other factors in St. Paul's life and mission.

First of all, it is important to keep in mind that as the Christian converts become more and more aware of their new and special identity, they had to devise ways of behavior consonant with this identity. It is only those whose minds are unstructured who think that freedom is unstructured. Hence, even some one like St. Paul who revelled in the freedom Christ had effected would not think that the Christian individuals and communities were meant to be anarchical. In practical terms this would mean patterns, rules or norms of conduct and behavior. Furthermore, it is obvious (see, for example, Romans 12-15) that St. Paul emphasized the importance of not scandalizing the weak members of the community. It was also of great urgency to him that believers should give no scandal to those outside the Christian community, so that these latter might be converted. "We who are strong have a duty to put up with the qualms of the weak without thinking of ourselves" (Romans 15:1). "I personally am free. . . . So though I am not a slave of any man, I have made myself the slave of everyone so as to win as many as I could. . . . I made myself all things to all men . . . for the sake of the gospel" (1 Corinthians 9:1, 19, 22). Perhaps the best summary of this whole approach to right behavior is: "For me there are no forbidden things; maybe, but not everything does good" (1 Corinthians 6:12), or "helps the building to grow" (10:23). This principle governed the entire life and work of St. Paul. If we are going to understand his restrictions on women in the Church, we must never forget it.

St. Paul was certainly aware that women had received the Holy Spirit and shared in his various gifts just as men had (Acts 2:17). That they were also prophets was clear (Acts 21:9; 1 Corinthians 11:5). As we have seen in Galatians, for St. Paul Christ's freedom has nullified all separatist and oppressive distinctions. There is no more male and female. Why, then, does he draw back from his first impulse to grant unrestricted freedom?

First of all, it is noteworthy that the restrictions are concentrated in the Epistle to the Corinthians. This busy seaport was a large cosmopolitan city and an important commercial and religious center. It was also a city notorious for sexual license—indeed, sin city. Its fame was such that terms like "Corinthian girl" became a synonym for a prostitute and "Corinthian businessman" for a whoremonger; "to play the Corinthian" meant to visit a house of ill fame. The greatest of Corinth's many temples was dedicated to Aphrodite. It housed 1,000 *hierodules*—that is, sacred prostitutes.[1] It is hardly surprising that the Corinthian church had problems and even scandals; what is surprising that there was a church at all. Certainly Paul's own background would seem to make him an unlikely missionary to such a populace. But, just as Jesus had been the friend of sinners (Matthew 11:19), so does St. Paul go to these lowly, weak, and insignificant people (the Greek text summarizes by calling them *ta me onta,* which can best be translated as "the nonentities").

He was successful in preaching the Good News of Christ's freedom to these "nothings," and they took to heart their liberation. But they also took it awry. It was to these Corinthians that St. Paul wrote the following admonitions:

> You have done well in remembering me so constantly and in maintaining the traditions just as I passed them on to you. However, what I want you to understand is that Christ is the head of every man, man is the head of woman, and God is the head of Christ. For man to pray or prophesy with his head covered is a sign of disrespect to his head. For a woman, however, it is a sign of disrespect to her head if she prays or prophesies unveiled; she might as well have her hair shaved off. In fact, a woman who will not wear a veil ought to have her hair cut off. If a woman is ashamed to have her hair cut off or shaved, she ought to wear a veil.
>
> A man should certainly not cover his head, since he is the image of God and reflects God's glory; but woman is the reflection of man's glory. For man did not come from woman; no, woman came from man; and man was not created for the sake of woman, but woman was created for the sake of man. That is the argument for women's covering their heads with a symbol of the authority over them, out of respect for the angels. However, though woman cannot do without man, neither can man do without woman, in the Lord; woman may come from man, but man is born of woman—both come from God.
>
> Ask yourself if it is fitting for a woman to pray to God without a veil; and whether nature itself does not tell you that long hair on a man is nothing to be admired, while a

woman, who was given her hair as a covering, thinks long hair her glory?

To anyone who might still want to argue: it is not the custom with us, nor in the churches of God (1 Corinthians 11:2-16).

As in all the churches of the saints, women are to remain quiet at meetings since they have no permission to speak; they must keep in the background as the Law itself lays it down. If they have any questions to ask, they should ask their husbands at home: it does not seem right for a woman to raise her voice at meetings (1 Corinthians 14:34-35).

The specific situation at Corinth which led St. Paul to institute such restrictive measures with regard to women was this. Traditionally, as we have noted, a city famed for its sexual activity, it was currently undergoing a further "moral expansion" in terms of the growing emancipation of women in at least certain sections of society. It seems that precisely those sectors of society were attracted to Christianity. This feminine emancipation, as is its wont, was accompanied by an increase in sexual libertinism.

But there was more than that. In this society St. Paul's converts comprised what can only be called an exuberant and enthusiastic church. Having found release through Christianity from the oppression of the ancient Hellenistic culture with its emphasis on necessity and fate, these former "nonentities" (recall 1 Corinthians 1:28) really celebrated their freedom. Apparently they also experienced an abundance of the extraordinary gifts of the Holy Spirit. In the midst of this exuberance certain practices arose which disturbed a least some of the community. A letter of complaints was forwarded to Paul. Whereas it was once thought that he replied in four letters, a growing number of scholars today think the two "lost" letters have really been incorporated into the two epistles to the Corinthians as we have them today.

Be that as it may, we do know that Paul had to address himself to the following problems in the church at Corinth: the eating of meat which had been sacrificed to idols; factionalism and cliques within the community; a case of public incest; disbelief, on the part of some members of the community, in the resurrection of the body; disorderly—apparently raucous in some cases—celebrations of the Eucharist; the role of extraordinary charisms; marriage, celibacy, and divorce; and the conduct of women in the public worship assemblies.

Paul's proposed solutions are generally moderate and temperate, even when, as in the case of the incestuous man, he is adamant. We shall examine only those problems relating directly to men and women.

In regard to the relationship of the sexes in chapter 7, St. Paul exhibits an almost perfect parallelism in his directions to men and women. This is certainly reminiscent of the gospel record of Jesus' own conduct. Both husbands and wives have rights over each other (v. 3); sexual abstinence is legitimate only by mutual consent (v. 5). Divorce is legitimate for neither husband nor wife (v. 10). Is this an explicit reference to the words of Jesus preserved in Matthew 5:32 and 19:9? In any case, Paul's statement clearly and certainly implies equality of the sexes. Both believing husbands and wives are to remain with their unbelieving spouses, and for the same missionary reason: the salvation of the partner (vv. 12-16). Likewise, both men and women are free to marry if they so choose (vv. 25-28).

In this chapter occurs a statement of great importance for understanding St. Paul and the entire primitive Christian community: "Our time is growing short . . . the world as we know it is passing away" (vv. 29, 31). These verses explain "these present times of stress" in v. 26. Consequently St. Paul can urge: "those who have wives should live as though they have none" (v. 29). That is, given the imminent fulfillment of the reign and kingdom of God preached by Jesus and happening in the churches, things which would otherwise be most important become less important.

Will it not be possible to apply this same principle to Paul's restrictions on certain activities of women in the Christian community and especially in the liturgical assemblies? After all, he himself says that he does not want "to put a halter round your necks, but simply to make sure that everything is as it should be, and that you give your undivided attention to the Lord" (v. 35). We shall return to this later.

It is also important to note that when St. Paul allows celibacy he is already freeing both men and women, since it was generally held that men and women had to be married. St. Paul, of course, realizes that celibacy, especially if the celibate is in close contact with the other sex, is not easy. Hence, the celibate may change his mind and legitimately marry.

Verses 36-38 can be interpreted two ways. The traditional exegesis, the one adopted by the Bible of Jerusalem, understands the problem of celibacy in regard to the father-daughter situation. Here we can recall from the Wisdom literature that an unmarried daughter was a major source of concern for her family (Ecclesiasticus 42:9-14). In both this and the following interpretation, favored by many moderns, St. Paul clearly and essentially limits the traditional *patria potestas* and ensures the girl's freedom in regard to marriage. Many modern exegetes prefer to interpret the man ("anyone" in the Bible of Jerusalem translation) and "his virgin" ("daughter" in the same translation) as an engaged couple who have become or already were Christians.[2] What should they do in the light of St. Paul's teaching on celibacy and the passing away of this world? The answer would be that they may stay together in a "spiritual" relationship, an anticipation of the heavenly existence "in the other world and in the resurrection from the dead (when they) do not marry" (Luke 20:35), if they are able to do so. If, however (like the widows mentioned earlier), "they cannot control the sexual urges, they should get married, since it is better to be married than to be tortured" (v. 9).

In all of this, St. Paul displays none of that misogyny so typical of his Jewish religious and Hellenistic cultural compatriots. He is not unaware of the strength of human sexual attraction, but he in no way regards woman as the sly and serpentine seductress so popular in all literature. In sum, St. Paul is again very temperate and balanced. Whether one marries or not—one may do either—the overriding concern must be "undivided attention to the Lord" (v. 35), and, as we have seen earlier, avoidance of scandal to the weak and those outside the Christian community. In passing, we can note that St. Paul clearly does not share the modern rigidity of the Roman Catholic Church in regard to celibacy. For St. Paul celibacy was desirable only insofar as it corresponded to the needs of the Christian community and would further its goals.

We would have to say, then, that in this part of St. Paul's directives to the Corinthians he is just the opposite of being oppressive to women. How, then, did he come to those restrictions in the texts cited earlier? First of all, it can be pointed out that there is some textual difficulty with 14:34, 35. Some scholars think that they are a later addition inspired by 1 Timothy 2:11-14, which forbids women to teach or hold authority, and even to speak. Verses 34 and 35 do seem to interrupt the natural flow of the text. They are clearly not in harmony with chapter 11:5 which assumes that women do and may speak in the liturgical assemblies. There St. Paul seems only to require that she not "pray or prophesy" unveiled. This is a far cry from the injunctions in chapter 14 and 1 Timothy. The purpose of the insertion would have been to reinforce with Pauline authority the prescriptions of the latter kind in the Church "ordered" by Timothy. Generally, contemporary biblical scholars do not attribute authorship of the pastoral epistles (1 and 2 Timothy and Titus) to St. Paul in the same sense as the other Pauline epistles. They consider them to have been composed by disciples of St. Paul. An author could, they say, have collected the correspondence that remained between Paul and his former associates, collated it, and applied it to the needs of the Church in his time. This process could have been completed as early as the end of the first century. The document known as *1 Clement* was written about 95 A.D. and has a more sophisticated hierarchical structure than that of the pastoral epistles. Hence, in these later epistles we are probably provided with a partial picture of the life and concerns of the Church in the last third of the first century. It is clear testimony that the original freedom experienced by Christian women has eroded. From even later sources we know that women were still active in the Church. However, the pastoral epistles do show a restriction of the emancipation of women; in fact, almost a retrogression to the prevalent Old Testament view of women as exclusively wife and mother (see 1 Timothy 2:15, which we shall examine later).

Let us now return to the topics of silence and the veil in chapter 11. Some people have tried to explain the contrast between these directives and St. Paul's Galatian (3:28) statement that there is neither male nor female in the Lord by referring that statement to a later heavenly state. Thus St. Paul would not have meant that these divisions and hostilities were already overcome, but that they would be in the final fulfillment of the eschatological reign and kingdom proclaimed by Christ. However, this explanation collapses because St. Paul certainly regarded the other divisions mentioned in Galatians 3:28 as no longer valid in *this* world. True, he concentrated his efforts on the Jew-Gentile problem in preference to those of the male-female and the slave-free. But, if the one is real now, so must the others be. We cannot say St. Paul ignored the latter two. His collaboration with women would certainly void such a contention.

However, he clearly did not give the same attention to all. He was willing to compromise on the male-female question, as the texts here show. But he was not willing to compromise on the Jew-Gentile question, as his conduct at the Jerusalem Council and in regard to Simon Peter's equivocation on this question shows (see Acts 15 and Galatians 3:11).

Why should St. Paul so concern himself with unveiled women speaking in the assemblies? Obviously because they were upsetting or giving scandal to some of the other members. Perhaps also because they were alienating unbelievers who were permitted to come to the assemblies (1 Corinithians 14:23). In St. Paul's estimation, such conduct on the part of these women was not sufficiently important as an experience or an expression of Christian freedom to outweigh its possibly more destructive influence on the weak members of the community and on prospective converts. In making this decision, Paul would have tried to strike a balance between what could be termed the right and left wings of the Christian community. Since he himself had not exercised his freedom fully and indiscriminately, he could feel justified in asking the women for the same restraint. This attitude is a far cry from preening male egoism and chauvinism, no matter how much—from a later vantage point, at least—one might wish that he had refused to compromise the principle of sexual equality and thus solved this female discrimination problem once and for all.

St. Paul's attitude apart, all history amply testifies that it is usually those who have been discriminated against, however the discrimination is justified, who come up short when the principles of accommodation and adaptation (read frequently: give in) are invoked. And so here: the males, who would have generally been threatened by this new feminine freedom, benefited from the compromise, along with the conservative females.

To be realistic: could St. Paul have been expected to resist those who urged "not too fast" or "with all due deliberate speed" (which we know means as slow as possible, if at all)? His own personal background, as we have already seen, would not favor such resistance, although he seems to have overcome that factor in regard to other problems. There is this additional element to consider: St. Paul could very possibly have been protecting the women themselves. Reliable evidence indicates that in Corinth such open and forward speech on the part of a woman was sufficient grounds for divorce by her husband, without return of her dowry. Among Jews and Greeks the veil was required of wives, but not allowed to slaves and whores. If a Jewish wife was accused of adultery, the priest was enjoined to "unbind her hair" (Numbers 5:18). Upon proof of her innocence, her veil was restored to her. A Jewish wife who removed the veil of her own volition could/should be divorced by her husband without her dowry being returned, and a pagan wife could be locked out of her house. We can also recall the indignation of Simon the Pharisee when the sinful woman undid her hair to dry the feet of Jesus (Luke 7:38), and the commentators' difficulty in trying to find an adequate explanation for the same conduct on the part of the demure Mary (John 12:3). We can also recall here that Jewish women did not speak in the synagogue and that in Greece only ladies of easy virtue spoke in public.

It is quite possible, then, that in insisting on the veil and silence (if 14:34, 35 are originally from Paul) he was protecting not only (patriarchal) marriage but also those spirited women whose celebration of their freedom could have cost them dearly. Some scholars think that the prohibition of speaking applied only to married women. It is difficult to overestimate the importance of the family for someone like Paul with his background—Jew, Pharisee, rabbi. Consequently his stategy to avoid the scandal to weak and prospective Christians is understandable, again, even if one wishes he had chosen another course.

Far less acceptable is the baneful use to which these *ad hoc* solutions were put in the subsequent nineteen centuries. Other equally firm prohibitions from the Pauline writings have certainly not enjoyed such rigorous enforcement. For example: against 1 Corinthians 6:1, Church members do take one another to court; against 1 Timothy 2:9, Christian women do braid their hair and wear expensive gems and clothes. I already know the response to this: "But that's different." But that's precisely the question, not the answer! Why is it different?

We cannot complete this consideration without examining St. Paul's reasoning, especially in 1 Corinthians 11 and 1 Timothy 2:13, 14:

> A woman ought not to speak, because Adam was formed first and Eve afterward, and it was not Adam who was led astray but the woman who was led astray and fell into sin.

In fact, his reasoning might be more important than the actual directives he thereby justifies. We can call this reasoning typically Pharisaic and rabbinic. It is based on the Yahwist account in Genesis 2, ignoring completely the teaching of Genesis 1 in which the equal and simultaneous humanity of men and women is clearly asserted. It also interprets Genesis 2 in a manner not true to its literary form. As we have seen, the rib story does not imply a subordinate status for women, as created after man. Rather, in dramatic story form, it asserts that humanity is essentially bisexual, that both male and female are necessary before human being is present. The text from Timothy simply violates the text of Genesis 3 when it claims that Adam was not led astray. According to Genesis, both Yahweh and Adam knew that he had gone astray, and although Adam blamed Eve, Yahweh didn't. This also clearly contradicts what Paul had taught in Romans, especially 5:12-21. Inconsistencies like this are one reason the Scripture scholars tend to think that the pastoral epistles do not come directly from Paul's hand or mouth. Furthermore, it must be recalled that the word Adam really refers to mankind, not to a single male man. In these respects the letter to Timothy resembles what one expects from a Jewish rabbi, not a Pauline Christian.

St. Paul's reasoning in the fully authentic 1 Corinthians 11 is not nearly as hardheaded. In fact, I do not think it fanciful to detect in verses 2 to 16 that impatience which a busy man displays when he must divert his time and energy from the really important things to the trivial. Picture yourself in Paul's sandals—a proclaimer of the reign and kingdom of God brought near in the crucified and risen Jesus Christ, missionary par excellence—and then you have to talk about women's hair and veils because some obviously cramped and inflexible souls can't cope with the Christian's newfound freedom—or perhaps more to the point, simply with change! Rather than expend the energy necessary to show how even these minor liberations are but the manifestations of that fundamental freedom Christ has brought all mankind, Paul remains true to his missionary strategy. But then he has to find some way to justify the customary veil. So he invokes the traditional rabbinic and Pharisaic piety, although he has at other times rejected it.

It could also be that St. Paul himself had difficulty in applying the principle of Christian freedom thoroughly and to every situation. His reasoning does seem to reflect a struggle about the nature of man and woman. In his tradition he can find reason for a priority of the male; but he can also and immediately find reasons which counterbalance this priority, as verses 12, 13 indicate. It is indeed true that according to Genesis 2 (not 1; note again the prevalence of chapter 1 over 2!), woman came from man, but even the defective biology of Paul's time could not obscure the obvious origin of every male from the female. So, what to do in the face of the old chicken and egg conundrum? Paul finds the only feasible solution: both come from God, and therein lies their ultimate dignity. He does not, however, make the rigorous application of this insight, which we can only regret. Instead, he returns to the familiar customs, "Ask yourselves if it is fitting. . . ." The argument from nature about the relative length of men's and women's hair is conclusive only if you already know the right conclusion. Paul's abrupt termination of the whole discussion reinforces the unavoidable impression that he himself is neither impressed nor convinced by the arguments he has just presented. And he need not have been. After all, he was trying to solve a practical problem with practical measures.

Finally St. Paul cuts off any and all further argument. He will simply not discuss it anymore. His clinching reason is simply: 'It is not the custom with us, nor in the churches of God" (11:16). These "churches of God" were the primitive communities of Judea to which even the great Apostle of the

Gentiles continually recurred as to the mother and model Church of all Christianity.

A very important text, and one which has often been used to urge the subjection of women to men, is in the Epistle to the Ephesians. There is considerable debate whether this epistle comes directly frim St. Paul himself or from a Pauline disciple or school of disciples. Even so cautious a scholar as R. Schnackenburg thinks that it was not written directly by St. Paul, and also not before 90 A.D.[3] Hence, although it is incontestably a mature development of Pauline thought, it will also reveal a later stage of development in the life and practice of the Church.

The text which is of interest to us is 5:22-32:

> Wives should regard their husbands as they regard the Lord, since as Christ is head of the Church and saves the whole body, so is a husband the head of his wife; and as the Church submits to Christ, so should wives to their husbands, in everything. Husbands should love their wives just as Christ loved the Church and sacrificed himself for her to make her holy. He made her clean by washing her in water with a form of words, so that when he took her to himself she would be glorious, with no speck or wrinkle or anything like that, but holy and faultless. In the same way, husbands must love their wives as they love their own bodies; for a man to love his wife is for him to love himself. A man never hates his own body, but he feeds it and looks after it; and that is the way Christ treats the Church, because it is his body—and we are its living parts. For this reason, a man must leave his father and mother and be joined to his wife, and the two will become one body. This mystery has many implications; but I am saying it applies to Christ and the Church.

The proper context of these verses is indicated by Heinrich Schlier, who divides the entire epistle into two parts: (1) the mystery of the Call of the Pagans into the (mystical) Body of Christ (1:3-3:21); and (2) the conduct of Life corresponding to this call (4:1-6:22).[4] The second part concentrates on the unity of the Church in view of the many and diverse gifts (charisms) of Christ. Steeped in the Spirit of God, the new Christians are not to turn back to their former pagan ways. Rather, they are to presevere in the light and love of Christ, in which they participate primarily through the celebration of the Eucharist. St. Paul moves from the orderly life of the Church to the orderly celebration of the Eucharist to the orderly life of the Christian home, and that is the context of Ephesians 5:21-32.

From 5:21 to 6:9 we have what the Germans call a *Haustafel*—that is, a list or table of directives which enable the household to function well and peacefully. The general principle enunciated in v. 21 will be applied to husband and wife, parents and children, master and slave. The motive for all this conduct is fundamentally Christ.

The Bible of Jerusalem translation is somewhat misleading when it adds the verb "should regard" to verse 22. In the original Greek text this sentence has no verb. I think that this is important. In fact, St. Paul makes the transition from the Christians' liturgy to their home so smoothly that it is not entirely clear whether v. 21 goes with the liturgical section or, as is more likely, with the section on the family. But this fact plus the absence of a verb in the following sentence indicate clearly that v. 21 is more of a general principle of Christian behavior. It is not to be applied immediately and exclusively to the wives so that they would be "subordinate" to their husbands, although the husbands would not be "subordinate" to their wives. A better translation would read: "Establish a reverent relationship among yourselves out of reverence for Christ: wives to their husbands. . . ." One would expect a later parallel applying this principle of reverent relationships to men (husbands). There is one, of course, but the parallel is obscured because the author switches verbs between verse 24, where wives are to submit, and verse 25, where husbands are to *love*.

I realize that my suggested translation "establish reverent relationships" can be accused of undertranslating. The Greek word does mean to subordinate, subject, submit. However, we must also note that this is to be done "in Christ." Various translations render the term as obedience, reverence, fear of Christ. Schlier chooses fear, on the basis that it is a submission dictated by the conscience "fearing" Christ as the judge.[5] I also find support for my translation in that the Bible of Jerusalem translates the Greek word *phobos* (normally "fear") as "respect" in verse 33. Be that as it may, the admonition to be subject to one another applies to all Christians. The mode differs, depending on the particular Christian's state in life.

In older pious literature we were urged to "anticipate" one another. This would fit Ephesians 5:21 beautifully. All Christians are to be alert to the needs and conditions of others. The model for Christian behavior is not the single-minded and single-directed bulldozer or tank. The Christian looks about himself constantly so that he can "anticipate" how he will be able to relate, and need to relate, to the "brethren" (if that word be allowed in this book). It is, of course, clear that the author has the ancient family in mind when he writes these admonitions. It is also clear that the Greek word *hypotassomai* as such calls for more than reverent relationship. But since this verb forms a superinscription for the whole following section, and since, in the ancient family, husbands, parents and masters could never be subject to their wives, children or slaves, it is not illegitimate to seek a new translation. It is not at all clear why the Bible of Jerusalem should translate the same verb as "give way" in the universal admonition of verse 21 and as "submit" in verse 24 when it is a matter of wives and husbands. Surely the Church could as well "give way" to Christ as to "submit." Given the unsavory overtones of "submit" today, we would be well advised to avoid it and search for a better expression.

In any case, this passage cannot be used to urge the inferiority of women in general or of wives in particular. That is clear from the whole context, which demands at least as much if not more from the men. In particular, it is extremely difficult to imagine what love would be if there were no "submission" or "subordination" to the beloved. Unfortunately it seems that by "submissive" wives nowadays is meant mousey little creatures who are dominated by their husbands, or sado-masochistic sex objects. And a submissive husband— who can even *hear* it! Since husbands are admonished to love their wives, we may legitimately conclude that they are also to be "submissive" (not enslaved) to their wives.

It is also worth noting that in the Pauline literature this Greek verb of submission can also be applied to Jesus Christ: "the Son himself will be subject in his turn to the One (God)" (1 Corinthians 15:28). Obviously there is a difference in being subject to God and to one's husband. However, it is still interesting to note that there can be a submission in the New Testament that is neither exploitative nor demeaning. Furthermore, if the husband is to imitate Christ, he can be reminded immediately of Philippians 2:7: Jesus "emptied himself to assume the condition of a slave . . . he was humbler yet." This is certainly submitting, if that is what one is interested in. And in the Ephesians passage itself husbands are reminded that Christ's relationship (whether it is called anticipation, submission, or love) to the Church was such that he freely died for it. Such a sacrifice is certainly "submitting."

Furthermore, St. Paul takes the "become one flesh" of

Genesis and shows that it was only a foreshadowing of that awesome mystery which has now been fully revealed in the Christic union of God and man in the Church, the Body of Christ. In this union, in whose grace Christians participate, all divisive distinction has truly been overcome. Hence, when a husband loves his wife it is truly himself that he loves (28, 29), for we are all one in Christ—there is no more male and female (Galatians 3:28). As far as "submit" and "subordinate" go, they have *gone*. How could one submit to oneself? What we have here is another example of the inability of the traditional customs and language to describe the new creation in Christ. The reality (customs and language) of the old and fallen world keeps intruding in both the living and thinking of this new Christic creation.

If we keep the new creation in mind, then we shall never confuse the unique and universal headship of Christ with a lesser. This headship is both the goal of the Christian life and mission (Ephesians 1:10) and its source (Colossians 1:15, 18)—a truth to which we always advert when descriptions like the husband as head of the wife are encountered. It is very easy, especially given the history of male dominance, to slide from metaphor to fact in such usage. We must constantly remind ourselves that the author of Ephesians was using the de facto social conditions of his time as the frame work[6] of his explanation that Jesus is the Savior of the Church, which is his body, which is mankind freed from all oppression for the glory of God.

This fundamental truth is always the point that really matters: all else is only to help explain and illustrate it. As a fitting conclusion to these remarks on the term submission in Ephesians, we need only recall how Jesus subjugated no one except the evil powers and principalities, the demons. People, on the other hand, he healed and freed and raised up. If this Jesus is the model proposed by the author of Ephesians for the conduct of Christians, then there will be no fear of subjection. For Jesus promised that the truth he revealed would not enslave but free us (John 8:32).

There is one more text we should examine before we conclude our investigation of the New Testament. As we have already noted above, the pastoral epistles present a later picture of the Church, one in which the first free-wheeling enthusiasm has settled into more institutionalized patterns. It had become clear that the Church would be around for a long time. The world had not been converted, nor had the divine cosmic judgment happened. Against this background the status of Christian women begins to decline from its earlier liberation. All the factors we have already seen—Jewish and Hellenistic traditions, the threat of secular emancipation, the male's own sense of insecurity—combine to restore Jewish patterns of life for women.

A major object of the pastoral and of other, later epistles is the legitimation of this status quo. Thus the First Epistle of St. Peter urges women to obey their husbands, since this submission might be conducive to the husband's conversion if he is not already a Christian (3:1). This is much like the admonition of St. Paul in 1 Corinthians 7:12, although unlike Paul, Peter does not seem to allow for the separation of the partners and dissolution of the marriage which the Church has called the Pauline Privilege. Likewise, and for the same reason, women are not to be ostentatious in their dress and self-adornment (1 Peter 3:4-6):

> the ornament of a sweet and gentle disposition—this is what is precious in the sight of God. This was how the holy women of the past dressed themselves attractively—they hoped in God and were tender and obedient to their husbands; like Sarah, who was obedient to Abraham, and called

him her *lord.* You are now her children, as long as you live good lives and do not give way to fear or worry.

It is interesting that Peter speaks of the women of his day as being thus the children of Sarah. Is this an explicit inclusion of women in the covenant "seed of Abraham"—receptively but also actively—in Sarah? And although the real revival of the Semitic male superiority is indicated in the admonition that women should imitate Sarah who called her husband "lord," Peter does not explicitly draw the obvious conclusion: that the women to whom he is writing should call *their* husbands lords. In this perhaps a sign that the original freedom Paul celebrated with his "neither male nor female in Christ" will not give way entirely to the established custom of male superiority?

As for the husband (v. 7):

> In the same way, husbands must always treat their wives with consideration in their life together, respecting a woman as one who, though she may be the weaker partner, is equally an heir to the life of grace. This will stop anything from coming in the way of your prayers.

Note that the traditional Semitic male chauvinism reasserts itself here, at least momentarily: woman is "the weaker partner" (also translatable as the more familiar "weaker sex"), a statement not found elsewhere in the gospels or in the Pauline epistles. But this feeble female is nonetheless the male's co-heir to grace. There is an at least remote resemblance here to St. Paul's conclusion of the veil discussion in 1 Corinthians 7:11. After making various distinctions between men and women, and not always favorable to the latter, the whole discussion is resolved by a declaration of equal relatedness to God as the source of being, life, and grace. So, I would repeat that we must regard much of the man-woman discussion of the epistles as the struggle of believers to understand the saving freedom of Christ in the real context of their cultural and historical world.

A less than successful instance of this is found in 1 Timothy 2:13-15:

> A woman ought not to speak, because Adam was formed first and Eve afterward, and it was not Adam who was led astray but the woman who was led astray and fell into sin. Nevertheless, she will be saved by childbearing, provided she lives a modest life and is constant in faith and love and holiness.

We have already examined the first verse. It bears repeating here because it is another illustration of the gradually diminishing freedom, and hence equality, of Christian women. However, even this epistle recognizes women deacons (3:11) and an "order" of widows (5:9). Experience has taught that the eschatological sign of celibacy so vividly urged earlier in the Corinthian church (7:8, 40) is not without problems of its own. So, in this later epistle, young widows are counselled "to marry again and have children and a home" (5:14). Indeed, the Church is settling down and making a home for itself in this world.

Nevertheless, has it so settled down as to lose sight of the eschatological import of celibacy that belonged to the vision of earlier days—to the extent of holding that women are to be "saved by childbearing"? This is the rather precipitate interpretation given by Tavard and McGrath to verse 15, which they render sterile by excising the last clause: "provided she lives a modest life and is constant in faith and love and holiness"—a provision which is hardly unimportant. It is worthwhile to quote their remarks directly, since the note of righteous indignation sounded is not untypical of many of today's reformers and liberators:

> Are there to be no virgins? What if, as is true now in

the United States, there are more women than men? Is the answer a return to polygamy? Or will the unmarried and the sterile be eternally damned?[7]

The meaning is plain: she will be saved by the fulfillment of her curse, by which she was condemned to multiple pregnancies and to her husband's domination. Yet, if this is the true way of life and salvation for the Christian woman, then in no sense can she be said to have been saved by baptism in Christ Jesus; again, this is not Pauline. Furthermore, if this is the correct teaching, then there should be no room, in the Ecclesia, for unmarried women. Clearly, this runs counter to the position of Paul.[8]

It is difficult to imagine that a theologian like Tavard could attribute childbearing to the curse in the Garden, unless his Gallicism contained a latent Jansenism. "Long before" the curse, man and woman were commissioned to "be fruitful, multiply, fill the earth" (Genesis 1:28). One assumes that this was not to be accomplished vicariously through the stork! It is ironic that Tavard, who complains of the neglect of chapter 1 of Genesis, should himself neglect it.

It is also remarkable that neither of these writers places the text within its historical context of gnosticism, relating it to the false teachers "who will desert the faith and choose to listen to deceitful spirits and doctrines that come from the devils . . . they will say marriage is forbidden" (1 Timothy 4:1-3).

The Gnostics tended to stress the doctrine that the material and the bodily are evils to be shunned. Hence marriage and procreation are evil because they involve and produce the material body. Later on there were sects which urged fornication instead of marriage since fornicators would be more diligent in avoiding conception and hence bodily children. Obviously such a doctrine would appeal to restless women, since it was precisely marriage and children that did most to confine them and restrict their freedom.

In passing we can note here what is perhaps the first case of the Church's failure to promote unequivocally a Christian value; later it would exert its attention in the secular order. Had the Church really and uncompromisingly asserted the freedom of Christian men and women, perhaps this pseudo-freedom of the Gnostics would never have enjoyed the success it in fact did. It is not beside the point to note that gnosticism had its own ardent women missionaries. It is the general understanding of scripture scholars that the statement of 1 Timothy 2:15 is in opposition to this gnostic doctrine that marriage is evil and to be avoided in principle. Obviously McGrath and Tavard are overreacting. Nothing in the statement itself or in its context indicates that childbearing, alone or primarily, is the source or means of salvation. In fact, the second half of the sentence "provides" the possibility that childbearing may not even be all that important. It apparently occurred to the author of 1 Timothy, unlike our two celibate critics, that women do bear children, that nobody else can, and that it is a way or mode of being a Christian, and hence of salvation. This should not be all that difficult to understand, unless one is perhaps a cryptic Gnostic.

In conclusion we can, unfortunately, note a parallel between the Old and New Testaments. Both were faced with following and living a truly liberating beginning. In the Old Testament the beginning was the liberation from nothing and the many false gods (especially of sex and fertility) of paganism. This included the human and precisely sexual liberation from exploitation and enslavement. As we have seen, though, the people of the Old Testament preferred a dubious interpretation of the Yahwist account of creation and experienced so acutely the unfulfilled and oppressive longing of the sexes for one another.

In the New Testament the beginning was the liberation from

the Law and sin, and from lording it over one another in the new creation, Christ. But the Christians also chose the same dubious interpretation of Genesis 2. Consequently we have all shared and witnessed less of the Song of Songs and more of the battle of the sexes (Genesis 3:16).

Without being unduly pessimistic, we can sum up our biblical considerations and anticipate our post-biblical history with St. Paul's remark: "We too (still) groan inwardly as we wait for our *bodies to be set free*" (Romans 8:23).

The history of the Church after the New Testament era will reflect the same ambiguity with regard to sexual equality that we have already found in biblical history. Perhaps it would be well to recall, at this point, that the People of God, whether under the old covenant or the new, are subject to the working out of cultural processes. The Church is in the world and also of necessity partly of it; it is historically conditioned. And so in any period, cultural factors will have a bearing on the elements of Scripture which are stressed in the Church's practice. We shall continue to find that of the two options available to the Church in developing the sense of Genesis, chapter 1 or chapter 2, the latter will be selected—and, indeed, in that misleading interpretation which would make woman both a later creation than man and an inferior one. Consequently there will be a twofold tendency: to make

5/ The Church in the Post-Apostolic Age

the "curse" of Genesis 3:16 almost normative and to regard it as the way things should be instead of the way they unhappily are.

Among the cultural factors bearing on the early Church, there was initially a strong influence of Jewish Christianity— that is, of those converts from Judaism whose churches were in the Holy Land. From them Christianity received a strong infusion of misogyny, based both on the Wisdom literature, which we have already examined, and on certain apocalyptic writings marked by extreme moral and ascetical rigor. (Some authors do not hesitate to state that this literature regarded women not only as inferior in the sense of being prepetual minors but also as dangerous, if not evil.) Fortunately, this influence was not long-lived. By the middle of the second century, after the Romans had almost annihilated the Jewish population, these communities ceased to exist. Many Christians had already fled the Holy Land before that.

While the flight from the Holy Land freed Christians from some of the excessively rigorous Jewish ideas, it also brought them into contact with Hellenism, and with the gnosticism so pervasive in the general culture at that time. The Church had to battle the Gnostics throughout its early history. Even when the Gnostics as such were no longer formally a challenge, their ideas were—especially their denigration of the material world and their doctrine of salvation through knowledge and asceticism.

Almost from the beginning, too, the Church had to do battle with a theory and heresy known as encratism, which taught that sex was evil in principle and to be avoided. In the actual conditions of a male-dominated society this position is equivalent to saying that woman, already regarded as weak and as a source of temptation to man, is evil.

At the risk of becoming repetitive, I think that the anomaly of this position should again be pointed out. If woman is so weak and inferior, how can her power of seduction be so irresistible to the stronger male, and hence so dangerous? If we are to try to understand the ambivalence toward woman out of which the later European understanding of womanhood developed, we must take into account the pagan mythology which associated sex with the divine. Thus woman will come to be regarded as a temptation, but as a temptation to a fulfillment which neither she nor any other creature can provide. And since she falls short of what her beauty seems to promise, she is regarded as a deception and a disappointment. Shades of the ancient Mesopotamians, who demanded of woman that as a sex goddess she be both virgin and mother—and then subjugated her as a drudge or whore because she was unable to fulfill these demands! This simultaneous exaltation and degradation will be a hallmark of the modern European attitude toward women. However, it is first of all in view of the encratic devaluation of sex—marriage, procreation, the family and, in particular, woman—that we must approach the Church's teachings in the earliest period after the New Testament writings had been completed.

The Church was armed with one very potent weapon—apart from the direct statements, especially of Jesus and Paul —in favor of the dignity and statue of woman. This weapon was the flourishing theology in whose figurative language the Church is symbolized by a woman. Before we proceed into this discussion, which will lead us into the center of the present-day controversy regarding the Judeo-Christian concept of woman and have a bearing on the question of woman's full ordination to the priesthood, a clarification is in order. It must be understood that God, as conceived by the inspired writers of Scripture, is neither male nor female but infinite Spirit. That Scripture speaks of God in terms of Fatherhood and Sonship plainly derives from the necessity man has of expressing the divine in human terms, which are the only terms within his competence. The question of the modern critic, then, is whether the element of masculinity has so predominated in Scripture and in religious writing and practice as to constitute discrimination against the female sex. Now, to return to the symbol of woman in early Christian theology.

Its basis, of course, was in the Old Testament practice, from the prophet Hosea on, of describing the relationship between Yahweh-God and Israel in terms of the husband-wife relationship. As we have seen, this approach was strong in the prophets. It was not well represented elsewhere, although many scholars try to read it into the Song of Songs. And it is also tacitly assumed by basically the same people that this theme is also present in the gospels. However, as Joachim Jeremias has clearly shown, this is not the case:

> The bride is never mentioned [in Matthew 25:1] the words [bride] are an addition. Just as the comparison of the redeemed community to the bride is frequent in early literature ...so the same comparison is unknown in the whole of Jesus' teaching. It is rather Jesus' custom to compare the messianic community with the wedding guest.
> ...for the allegorical representation of the Messiah as a bridegroom is completely foreign to the whole of the Old Testament and to the literature of late Judaism, and first makes its appearance in the Pauline writings (2 Corinthians 11:2).... Since the allegory in question is also not found in the rest of the preaching of Jesus, we must conclude that Matthew 25:1-13 is not an allegory of Christ the heavenly bridegroom.[1]

The absence of this metaphor from the gospels does not, of course, mean that it is not scriptural. From its early appearance (in 2 Corinthians, probably written in 57), the theme enjoyed a rapid development in both Pauline and

Johannine writings, especially Ephesians 5 and the Apocalypse. Although some will be able to use the figure of woman in the Apocalypse against women, it does nevertheless bring the element of feminine being into the very heart of theology and the Christian understanding of salvation. The concept of the Church in the image of woman makes it impossible to categorize Christianity as a "masculine" religion. How well the theologians and overseers of the Church will actually make use of the possibilities it contains is another matter entirely.

Outside Scripture, the theological metaphor of the Church as woman is stressed in *Hermas the Shepherd,* a book which, we will recall, was written in stages between the years 96 and 150. It is primarily a sermon on penance designed to combat an increasing rigorism. Hence Hermas insists that there is forgiveness of sins committed after baptism, and upon this as the "traditional" doctrine of the Church. In the course of his book he gives a vivid picture of the life of the Church at that time; thus its value for us, since it provides at least some indications of the status of women in the practice and theology of the Church during the first generations after the apostles.

In the second of a series of visions, the identity of an elderly woman is revealed. Earlier she had given Hermas a book of revelation or instruction to report to God's elect (II vision, IV):

> "Who, do you think, is the elderly lady from whom you took the book?" "The Sibyl," I said. "No," he said, "you are mistaken." "Who is she then?" I said. "The Church," he said. "Why is she elderly?" I asked. "Because she was created before all things," he said, "For this reason she is elderly and for Her sake the world was erected."[2]

It is already interesting that a woman should be the agent of Hermas' vision. But even more so that the Church, as "elderly lady," should have been created before all things.

This is clearly in line with the Wisdom literature, which, as we have seen, also allowed for a feminine dimension to the divine creativity. In Vision III the lady explains that "the tower which you see being built, that is I, the Church." Furthermore, the elderly lady is able to explain to the "persistently enquiring" Hermas "whatever can possibly be revealed."

Also in Vision III there is a catalogue of seven virtues personified as seven women: Faith, Continence, Simplicity, Knowledge, Innocence, Reverence, Love. Their function is to support the tower (the Church) in accordance with the Lord's command. It is not without interest that continence should be symbolized by a woman, in view of the tendency we have seen to regard female virtue with so much dubiety.

But although Hermas was able to use feminine symbolism so intensively and extensively in his book, he personally appears to have had an inclination toward encratism. At the very beginning of the book he speaks of a woman (to whom he had been sold as a slave) he loves as a sister. A little further on, he is able to decipher the book given to him by the elderly lady, and among other things it admonishes him to "make this message known ... to your wife who is to be as your sister." Later, he is encouraged with words which include "your great continence is saving you."[3]

There is a sense in which we can already see, in Hermas, what will become a standard theme in later theological and spiritual writing: woman enjoys considerable status and activity as a "symbol," but only insofar as she is de-sexed. As a real, living, sexual human being she tends to be too strong a temptation for the male: on that plane she must be avoided and accorded minimal participation in the things of God and man (which easily becomes male man). We must note, to be quite clear, that Hermas is called upon to give up not adultery or fornication, but an apparently perfectly legitimate sexual relationship and activity, namely marriage. From this we can conclude to that gnostic mentality which thinks that the victory over the "curse" of Genesis 3:16 coincides with, if it does not equal, "victory" over sex itself. This attitude will influence some Christians like Tatian to found his own sect and the great theologian Origen to castrate himself. Their distaste for sexuality readily lends itself to special distaste for female sexuality.

On the other hand, we must recall that during Hermas' time women still enjoyed a very active role in the Church. Hermas is told to write "two small booklets, one for Clement and one for Grapte (a woman) . . . and Grapte will instruct the widows and orphans."[4] In this activity Grapte enjoys a role similar to the roles of Clement (certainly Pope Clement, who wrote his Epistle to the Corinthians about 96) and Hermas and the presbyters. Her sphere of activity is perhaps more restricted, but nonetheless of basically the same kind as that of individuals who, we may assume, enjoy what is now called the sacrament of holy orders. Furthermore, Hermas was considered an inspired prophet by late Church writers (for example, Irenaeus and Origen). The close cooperation of women in this prophetic activity is also worthy of note.

Apparently the church at Corinth did not settle down to a calm tranquil life after St. Paul's admonitions. The apostles, and even the presbyters whom they had appointed as their successors, had already died or become inactive owing to their age when Pope Clement had to direct his attention "especially to the abominable and unholy schism among you." In the course of his exhortation to right and orderly living, Clement invokes the example of "those who have perfectly served His magnificent glory." Among them he includes

Rahab the harlot, of whom he says: "you see, beloved, that not only faith but also prophecy is found in this woman."[5] Given the history of the Corinthian church and its problems with prophets and in particular women prophets, the insistence that prophecy was already present in Rahab is interesting.

A second epistle has been attributed to Clement,[6] although it certainly did not come from his hand. It was probably written about 150 and possibly at Corinth. This writing is sometimes called the oldest extant Christian homily—after those of the New Testament, of course. It is an exhortation to live in such a way that God's majesty is glorified and eternal life gained. It is valuable for us because it is the first document to refer to the Church as Mother: "By saying 'Rejoice, O thou barren, that bearest not' He meant us, for our Church was barren before giving children." The New Testament idea of the Church as the bride of Christ is obviously being developed, its implications being drawn out.

The Pesudo-Clement also conceives of the Church as having existed before creation. Furthermore, the Church is feminine: "The male is Christ, the female is the Church." The influence of St. Paul, especially of Ephesians, is obvious. But it is also interesting to note the similarity between this pre-existent female Church and the pre-existent female Wisdom of the Old Testament. All this female symbolism— Hermas' elderly lady, the pre-existent Church and pre-existent Wisdom—could have prevented the "masculinization" of the concept of God in Christian theology. But here, once again we can see the tendency in favor of the male. Nevertheless these earliest of Christian writings do provide a basis for the full liberation of women and their full incorporation into the life and theology of the Church.

Pope Clement's defense of prophecy in women is also important in connection with the later religious movement known as Montanism which originated in Phrygia, Asia Minor, about 160. It was intended to be a spiritual renewal, and in its be-beginning, at least, it emphasized a rigorous asceticism in view of what was thought to be the impending end of the world. It likewise advocated a renewal of the prophetic activity we saw in the Corinthian church. Such prophecy had declined, perhaps almost to the point of extinction.

Among the Montanist prophets, two of the most famous were women, Priscilla and Maximilla. The latter of these, according to Epiphanius, claimed that she, Maximilla, would be the last of the prophets: after her the end would come! The Montanists called forth a rather antagonistic reaction from many contemporary writers, and even more from later authors, owing to the form which prophecy took among them. Whatever the facts of the matter, the Montanists were accused of valuing the prophetic character above all others. This is important for our study because of the extent to which the controversy centered on women. It was said that Priscilla and Maximilla were held in greater esteem among the Montanists than the apostles—perhaps even more than Christ himself. It was also charged that in Montanist groups there were women bishops and priests.

Of course, all this would take its toll of the esteem in which prophecy in general was held. But more importantly for us, this reaction to Montanism marks the definite and continuing decline of women's right to teach in the Church. And not only women: from this point on, the Church will begin to adopt a very cautious attitude toward the laity in general.[7] Let us note in passing, however, that here is a striking instance of that double morality which has reigned for so long. Women must always pay more dearly for their "crimes."

The great theologian Tertullian, in North Africa, came under the influence of Montanism. Always austere, he became

---

even more rigorous in his moral and ascetical demands—including, for example, the rejection of remarriage and the strict insistence that women's hair should be veiled. In such matters he claimed he was only being faithful to the Bible and to the tradition of the Catholic Church. He did not want to be either innovator or sectarian.

Among historians of women he is most famous (infamous may be a better word) for the following paragraph:

> You give birth, O woman, in pain and anxiety, and your desire is for your husband, who will lord it over you. And every one of you should be clothed in mourning and tatters ... God's judgment on your sex continues to live in the present. Thus it cannot be otherwise than that your guilt is still alive. You are the door that gave entrance to the devil. . . . You too are the one who persuaded him whom the devil was not able to attack. . . . As a result of your guilt the Son of God had to die.[8]

In this passage Tertullian has clearly sided with that dubious misogynist interpretation of Genesis which puts all the blame on Eve. However, there is another side to him. He can also write lyrically about the beauty and holiness of a marriage blessed by Christ. To this marriage Tertullian applies the words of Jesus, "For where two or three meet in my name, I shall be there with them" (Matthew 18:20).

However, Tertullian will meet the same fate as his like-minded predecessors—his disparagement of vain, primping women will be remembered, but his praise of marriage and affection for his wife, "my beloved companion in the Lord's service," will go unnoticed.

During this period of the Church's history the great persecutions of the Church began. For our theme it is of interest that women as well as men enjoy the honor of martyrdom. Of these, two of the most famous were Felicitas, a slave, and

Perpetua, a noblewoman. Their fame was such that they were included in the canon of the Mass in the Roman liturgy. It is also in connection with such martyrs that the Roman liturgy developed the prayers which praise God's power that was able to work the miracle of martyrdom even (or also) in the weak(-er) sex.

Although Clement of Alexandria was much more cosmopolitan and humanistic than many of his contemporaries, he could still comment that a woman should be covered with shame at the very thought that she is a woman. In defense of woman, however, he did oppose compulsory marriage. The woman must be free in regard to marriage. She is her husband's helpmate; that role adequately describes her being, and she is to conduct herself accordingly. This does not mean, however, that she is to be deprived of an education equal to that of men.

The Gnostics depreciated woman by insisting that her salvation could be accomplished only through her transformation into a male. The "pagans" depreciated woman by transforming her into a sex- or pleasure-object. Against both of these Clement defends woman. Heaven will involve not the masculinization of the woman, but the cessation of all divisiveness such as that described in the curse of Genesis 3:16. Since the human being, hence woman, is more than merely sexual, Clement insists that "we (can) praise virginity and those to whom God has given this" (*Stromata,* 3, 1, 4). In one of his major works, *Tutor (Paedagogus)*, Clement defends marriage against the Gnostics, who maintained that it was evil. In the process he also gives an eloquent description of the equality of men and women:

> The virtue of man and woman is the same. For if the God of both is one, the master of both is also one; one Church, one temperance, one modesty; their food is common, marriage

an equal yoke; respiration, sight, hearing, knowledge, hope, obedience, love all alike. And those whose life is common, have common graces and a common salvation; common to them are love and training.[9]

Clement also applies the words of Jesus about two or three gathered in his name (Matthew 18:20) to marriage and the family. Since he held that even death does not fully dissolve this union, he was basically opposed to remarriage.

Clement's successor, and perhaps Alexandria's most famous theologian, was not nearly as favorably disposed toward marriage and women. Origen displayed much more of that suspicion of, and disdain for, matter which we have seen in both Plato and the Gnostics. He was true to that tradition in that he also had a low opinion of women, who were considered to be more closely involved with the material universe and in that legendary exegesis of Genesis 3 according to which they are the weaker sex and prone to temptation and sin. In many ways Origen was a classical misogynist. He used misogyny as a literary device. However, it is clear, and unfortunate, that his misogyny was not only allegorical but also substantial. It became part of his doctrine—what he taught, not merely how.

Origen was intensely mystical and ascetical. For him all material being is secondary; it is all passing away in the face of God's eternal kingdom. Unfortunately this led Origen not merely to relativize sex, marriage, family but also to demean woman.

In Origen we can see a definite twofold trend which will steadily increase in scope and in intensity. For Christians in general there will be a movement from the "sacramental" to the ascetical: that is, what at one time had been regarded as the gracious gift of Christ's saving action came to be regarded as the goal of man's own striving and achievement.

For example, the transcendence of the separation of male and female in Christ as St. Paul described it in Galatians 3:28 is attributed less to the grace of baptism and more to the preservation or attainment of a virginal soul.

For women there is a further modification of the practical Christian life. From their role as educators and co-workers in the apostolate, from their offices as deaconesses, widows, and virgins they are directed even more into the way of asceticism and virginity. This will be their mode of achieving equality with men in the life of the Church. This is the second trend to the ascetical, this time away from what is called the "diaconal." It will eventually lead to the nearly total exclusion of women from the Church's official public life. Consequently, although women are promised freedom and equality in the ascetical endeavor, they are more and more restrictd in the Church. The increasing emphasis on virginity as a "replacement" for the eschatological fulfillment promised by Christ and begun in baptism is applied much more vigorously to women than to men. The monastic movement, with its emphasis on contemplation, conspired with the virginal ideal to further heighten the danger women posed to the (male) Christian. Henceforth she will be a distraction to his prayer (contemplation) and a threat to his chastity. Thus the desirability of virginity for women increased twofold. Here we have another instance where woman as symbol—the virgin— enjoys great prestige; but the sexual being in the real-life world suffers considerable attrition.

In the metaphor Eve-Mary which had begun to become so popular from Justin the Martyr on, there is a definite tendency to dwell on the concept of Eve as weak and tempting. Mary will become more and more idealized until she is no longer a real model, in fact, hardly even an inspiration.[10]

Christ became man by the virgin in order that the disobedience which proceeded from the serpent's might receive its destruction in the same manner in which it derived its origin. For Eve, who was a virgin and undefiled, having conceived the word of the serpent, brought forth disobedience and death. But the Virgin Mary received faith and joy when the Angel Gabriel announced the good tidings to her, that the spirit of the Lord would come upon her, and the power of the highest would overshadow her; wherefore the Holy Thing begotten of her is the Son of God; and she replied, "Be it done unto me according to thy word."[11]

The title of this chapter gives a hint of things to come: the Fathers! The process we observed in the preceding chapter continues and intensifies; the Church becomes more and more settled down into this world, which has not passed away. The Lord has not returned to receive his consummated kingdom and hand it over to the Father; the *parousia* is still outstanding. With the conversion of Constantine the hitherto persecuted Church is not only free to exist publicly but becomes the state religion; the factual real world, which was the Greek and Roman civilization we examined earlier, becomes firmly ensconced in the Church as the Church's fuller participation in it becomes compulsory.

The whole situation is complicated by the advent of the barbarians from the North. Rome is so far from forgetting this invasion that the idea of it has never entirely vanished

6/ The Fathers of the Church

from Roman mentality.

As for this newer element in society, the condition of woman in the Germanic tribes bore certain resemblances to that among the Greeks and Romans. She had no political rights and could not participate in the assemblies which decided the policies of the tribe or community. Marriages were made by the agreement of the families involved: among the Germans, social organization was on the basis of kinship groups. The society was, of course, patriarchal. This accounted for the disparity of divorce rights between husband and wife and the legitimacy of polygamy, at least in theory— its practice was probably infrequent, limited to the higher social classes. There were also Germanic fertility goddesses. However, it does not seem that this particular approach to religion enjoyed the same influence among the Germans as it had among the Mesopotamians.

Woman was basically viewed as the property of the tribe. In marriage the exercise of the ownership was transferred from the father (or in his absence, the senior male) to the husband. However, even when wives were still purchased, they were not defenseless in regard to their owner-husbands. Violence on the part of the husband could evoke vengeance on the part of the wife's relatives. The literature of these peoples is filled with sagas describing the savage feuds which did in fact arise on this basis. Theoretically the father could sell both his wife and children. However, the available evidence does not indicate that this took place with any frequency. Likewise, it also seems that the wishes of the daughter were taken into account in the arrangement of her marriage, although this was not absolutely required. Even though divorce was readily available to the male, it was not very desirable in view of the property arrangements designed to protect the woman in case of divorce or widowhood.

Apparently the wife enjoyed major control over the household and its affairs. (It will be recalled that in the epic *Beowulf* the Queen of Hrothgar enjoyed considerable social status and influence.) Widows were quite unlikely to be immolated with the corpses of their husbands. Such devotion would be the noble warrior's dream (hardly only then and not today!), but the practice can be documented from only a very few exceptional cases.

Familial relationships would seem to have been stronger among the Northerners and to have provided more protection for the wife (though when one thinks of the family feuds of the Mediterranean world one wonders how much difference need be allowed for).

In general, the cultures which came to make up the Christian world emphasized the procreation of offspring as a primary desideratum. This was obviously important for the continuation of the tribe, the nation and, on the familial level, the family line. In point of fact, this meant the continuation of the male family name.

Among the early Greeks and Romans an explicitly and directly religious dimension was operative in the continuation of the family. The hearth of the family was the symbol of the deceased ancestor and consequently a religious symbol. The fire was "divine," everlasting. Each family had its own liturgy in regard to the fire and hearth. One could even say that each family had its own religion. This domestic hearth was always attended and never allowed to die out. On this basis it is obvious that procreation was a religious act, the family a religious order. Such an understanding of religion and the family could obviously provide great positive support for fidelity and perseverance in marriage. It could also support monogamy and even further the dignity of the woman. However, by the Christian era this understanding of marriage was no longer operative. One of the consequences was a much looser and more pleasure-oriented approach to sex and marriage. It is the latter social condition with which the writers of the New Testament and the Fathers of the Church had to deal.

Here we should again recall that Christ and the early Christians were not revolutionary However much they might criticize a given social or religious institution, they did not advocate its overthrow and replacement with a new one. The most often cited example of this mode of action is slavery. Neither Jesus nor St. Paul, for example, led an uprising, although their "principles" could hardly have found slavery congenial or even acceptable. Later Christianity will follow basically the same path. Like Jesus and the primitive Church it will tend to give a new meaning to or interpretation of the older tradition (condition). Hence St. Paul was willing to use the customary patriarchal family to explain the relationship between Christ and the Church. The husband remains head of the family. But his role or situation hardly remains unchanged. Henceforth, if the image is not to be a lie or mere literary device, the husband's role as head in imitation of Christ will require of him that his love likewise be unbounded; he must even be willing to die for his wife. One can legitimately question whether such a "translation" of the husband's headship really leaves him "head" of the wife. However, to call this new interpretation a revolution would be to stretch the latter term out of all recognizable shape.

Like St. Paul, the Fathers of the Church had to wrestle with the fact and truth of Christ in the facts and customs of their social and cultural world. If St. Paul was not able to sustain the purity of Christian origins as he perceived them in the everyday reality of his churches, should we be surprised if the later Fathers of the Church at times succumbed to the weight of their society's unchristian customs? And not only the Fathers, of course, but the Church itself too.

By the fourth century virginity had come to be the ideal form of Christian living. The process noted in the preceding chapter had matured. The "total" freedom of the Christian, promised by Christ and begun in baptism, is achieved and enjoyed in the virginal state. There, whether male or female, one is freed from the solicitude of pleasing one's wife or husband. For St. Paul this state of life was a logical consequence of the imminent end of this world, which was already passing away in any case (1 Corinthians 7). For the Fathers of the fourth century this lively eschatological expectation was no longer strong, if it still existed at all. In their approach there is discernible the lack of enthusiasm for the body characteristic of the Neoplatonist.

The third century had witnessed a great achievement in Greek philosophy in the synthesis of Platonism and Aristotelianism by the greatest of the Neoplatonists, Plotinus. But it was a synthesis in which the Platonic elements predominated, and hence the strongest influence on the thought of the Church Fathers came from Platonism.

It will be recalled that for Platonism the corporal world is not important; in fact, it is often called *me on*—that is, not being. The physical cosmos is a shadowy and only semi-real world in comparison with the world of ideas. The human being is really an invisible soul from this world of ideas, temporarily exiled in the world as a punishment. This soul is a prisoner of the material body; and "redemption" or "salvation" consists in its escape. In view of this, the discipline of the body was greatly advocated, to bring it into subjection to the soul. The body was to be mortified—literally, "made dead"—so that the soul could be free to live. As the concepts of redemption through the imminent end of the world

and through martyrdom passed away, each in its turn, with
the flow of history, the patristic age developed the theology
of virginity as the mode of salvation for the Christian.

For the Fathers, Christians marry as true philosophers do,
not in the heat of greedy passion like the pagans. The Christians are the true philosophers, the true seekers of wisdom.
However, since wisdom can be sought without and apart from
marriage, marriage is not necessary. In fact, sometimes the
cares of marriage can even be a hindrance to the pursuit of
wisdom. Their philosophical background is also evident in
the close connections they find between wisdom, contemplation, and virginity. Catholics are familiar with this approach
in the still surviving assertion that virginity—the virginity of
the religious—is a higher state in life than marriage.

Although the Fathers of the Church did not necessarily
disparage marriage when they extolled virginity, they did not
always succeed in avoiding invidious and demeaning com-
parisons. And these usually came to bear oppressively on
women. The fact that the theologians of the Church tended
to be almost exclusively male was compounded by the increasing incidence among them of celibacy. Celibate males
do not have to be chauvinist males; but the absence of active
women theologians means that no system of checks and bal-
ances is provided in case such male chauvinism should begin
to assert itself.

There is an ironic example of this in the case of the Desert
Fathers, who have received, quite justly, great acclaim in
history for their efforts to live without reserve, without solicitude for worldly concerns, in the freedom and the spirit of
Christ. According to the monk Palladius, writing his *Paradise
of the Holy Fathers* in the year 420, there were 20,000 women
in the desert and only 10,000 men. The sexist mentality does
not see women in the history of the Church because it al-

ready "knows" they cannot be there. That this is not a willful blindness is perhaps even more tragic and saddening.

From our own day comes the unfortunate incident of the unintentional affront to women given by Pope Paul VI, reported by Sister McGrath.[1] Celebrating Mass in the Yankee Stadium during his visit to the American church, he repeatedly greeted the thousands in live attendance and the millions in the television audience with the salutation "Brothers and sons!" Unless all the sociological research on Mass attendance and church participation in general is awry, "Brothers and sisters" would have been a far more accurate description of the audience!

As we have said, in extolling virginity the Fathers did not necessarily disparage marriage. In fact, many of them included beautiful defenses of marriage in their writings in general and even in their works on virginity. But, following Origen's views, there is also a tendency to place the origin of sex and sexual procreation after the Fall, conceiving the life of Eden as closer to the angelic. Once more the general influence of Plato and the Gnostics is clear.

In the viewpoint of the Fathers, marriage has two purposes: first, the alleviation of concupiscence by means other than licentiousness (it is better to marry than engage in debauchery); and second, the propagation of the species to fill the earth. However, since the propagation of the species would seem to have been achieved, the first purpose becomes the chief justification of marriage. But self-denial and self-discipline can accomplish the same end, and better. So, why marry? The married (man) has to put up with endless bickering and nagging, from both spouse and children. Furthermore, there are the worries about money, health, and even fidelity. (It is interesting to note that among the ancients a recurring justification of marriage is the ability of the wife to care for the health of her husband. The hypochondriacal male is of legendary proportions.)

St. John Chrysostom is most famous for arguing this negative view of marriage and woman: "Woman," he says, "is a foe to friendship, an inescapable punishment, a necessary evil. Among all the wild beasts there is not one that is more harmful than woman."[2] He was severe in his opposition to remarriage, emphasizing in his argument against it the stupidity of such people: obviously they had not learned their lesson the first time. In his later years, however, he mellowed and could write beautifully about the love and community of married life. It must also be noted that he took a quite negative view of virginity that was merely physical or virginity for the wrong reasons (e.g., gnostic). What is essential is the virgin's inner disposition. In fact, even married people can be considered virgins if they direct themselves totally to God.

I think it worth noting that here again, of two aspects which it would be possible to record for posterity, history has elected to record the one less favorable to women. Although John Chrysostom may have written as much or more that is favorable to women, history has highlighted his misogyny.

The Fathers of the Church also had to deal with the traditional problems of theology and the interpretation of Scripture, especially the first three chapters of Genesis. Like the teachers of the Old Testament, those of the New stressed chapter 2, understood in the interpretation we have already seen as unfavorable to woman. Their arguments took several lines.

For example, the image and likeness of the omnipotent God must have the aspect of power. Consequently some Fathers are unwilling to grant that woman is in the image of God, for she is powerless. I think that here we have a theory produced to explain a fact. We recall Plato's theory of the origin of woman: she is the reincarnation of a soul that failed in a former creation and thus bears the onus of a heavier punishment which is seen in her inferior status in society. But here, too, the theory tends to perpetuate the fact, and a vicious circle comes into play: because women are powerless they are not (in) God's image. And since they are not (in) God's image, they may not have power—so on and so forth.

The influence of Plato and the Gnostics can also be seen in Gregory of Nyssa's theory that the image of God was in the soul itself as God originally created it. It thus transcends the male-female distinction, which is due to a second creation. Marriage and sexual creation became necessary in view of the Fall wherein sin introduced death into human being.

The generally strong influence of this view, which removes sexuality from humanity considered as the image of God, makes readily understandable the great appeal of virginity. Especially for the female, it was the way to overcome or escape the "curse" of Genesis 3:16. The virgin was clearly no longer subject to the lordship and dominion of the male. She was likewise free of the pangs of childbirth. And finally, a genuinely spiritual virgin would also be free from that longing for the male which had made her so vulnerable to both subjection and pregnancy. Truly, virginity was a return to paradise, an escape from the painful thorns and thistles into which the Fall had transformed the original garden of Eden.

As far as woman the helpmate is concerned, the Fathers would not escape accusations of sexism. Using the same second chapter of Genesis, they were able to assign to the male dominion over not only the earth and animals but also Eve. Here again we can see clearly the neglect of Genesis chapter 1 and preference for 2.

St. John Chrysostom already provides an example of that division of labor into men's and women's work. Man is charged with the really important things: government, war, making money, philosophy. In general man is destined to take care of public matters, woman of the private and practical concerns. Specifically this means that woman is in charge of the home and the children. She may not acquire new property or wealth, but must preserve and pass on to her children the family's *patrimony* (note even the word!) if she is widowed. Here we can again see how the fact of the world's customs weighs so heavily upon the Christian (theologian) who is trying to figure out how he (she) must live the Christian fact and do the Christian truth in his everyday world. Unfortunately, it seems that not infrequently the secular fact wins. So St. John Chrysostom ends up, to a great extent, exhorting women to live according to the customs of the Greek society in which they find themselves.

Again, virginity is a way to escape from this subordination and subjection. However, woman finds herself in a bind, since she is man's helpmate primarily in regard to sex and procreation. Thus she is for his consolation. This could be taken as the anticipation of that later moral and ascetical "theology" which regarded woman as man's night-time "reward" after a hard day at the office, the mine, the factory, or wherever.

The difficulty with virginity as woman's escape or salvation from the fallen world of the curse was that it was not available to great numbers. Apart from familial and social pressure to marry, the urgency of sexual fulfillment itself would have tended to limit the number of women who could have chosen this avenue of redemption. Virtue, especially virginity, enables the women to overcome their weakness and submission and become equal to men. Thus not only martyrs but also very "holy" women are graced by the spiritual writers with the adjective "virile." Is this a forerunner of that "compliment" sometimes given to courageous women, namely that they act like men, not like (typical) women?

It would be easy to stoke up a pseudo-rage and roast the Fathers for their inability to see more clearly that the fact of fallen mankind is not the eternal truth of mankind. It would have been well had they been more perceptive and creative in their theological insights and ecclesial prescripts. However, given the generally unfavorable conditions of woman's status in society, perhaps they did better than we tend to credit them with. And the one thing we must not overlook in the Church's history is those valiant women who not only survived in the increasingly male-dominated Church, but who flourished in spite of all. Not only the famous like Melany and Etheria, not only the elite like the Desert Sisters and Mothers, but also the ordinary and common wives and mothers who lived in the Lord, in the worship of God and the service of the members of Christ's body. And all this in spite of the Church's inability to accord them the full practical participation in the community of freedom and grace which is the Church as the place where the many and diverse gifts of the one divine Spirit of Christ are celebrated.

Much of what the Church Fathers of the Latin West wrote about women coincides with the doctrine of the Fathers of the Greek East. There was much travel back and forth and a lively exchange of ideas. Furthermore, there was the similar effort to understand the same Christian fact and revelation in the context of the culture of that time. There, of course, is a clue to those differences we do in fact find between the Greeks and Latins. As we have seen, among the Romans during the Christian era woman had become immensely emancipated, especially socially and morally. By and large, she was allowed to do whatever she wanted—if she could. Unfortunately this emancipation of women coincided with a general emancipation from morals. Some would claim that the Roman culture had reached its lowest ebb during the first few Christian centuries. In any case, in the West women did undeniably have a much greater degree of freedom than in the East.

Otherwise, however, many of the cultural influences were identical in East and West. This is especially important in regard to philosophy. The influence of Plato lived on in various ways in various philosophical schools. Furthermore, the gnostic approach to reality was still very strong, as the Manichean influence on St. Augustine manifests. These latter two ways of thinking coincide in their generally negative attitude toward matter and the body. As we have seen, this generally tends to become specific in a negative attitude toward women. She becomes the focus of all man's (male) disillusionment and disappointment with the material universe.

This whole tendency will be reinforced by the rigorism and misogyny of Tertullian. There is a special reason for this influence. Tertullian is the Father (Mother?) of Latin theology. He it is who first forged the vocabulary of theology in Latin. It is also important to realize that whoever chooses the vocabulary will also have great influence in choosing the problems and the state of the questions to be theologized.

One other element peculiar to the Latin West was the ancient Roman institution of the Vestal Virgins, dedicated to the mythological goddess Vesta. It is difficult to determine precisely what influence this institution had on the general theory and practice of womanhood in the society at large, but it is certain that these Vestal Virgins posed a problem for Christian theologians extolling virginity as *the* Christian vocation. St. Ambrose felt compelled to attack them, but not (oddly enough) for sexual dereliction from their official virginity. The object of his strictures was the pomp and luxury of their life style. (One wonders what he might have to say about those monsignorial celibates of our day who argue that since they have no better halves to enjoy, they therefore deserve better quarters!)

Already Cyprian had argued for a recognizable life style for virgins. The virgin (apparently female sex is taken for granted, an assumption certainly not without interest) should avoid all occasions where she would give scandal by luxurious and glamorous living, especially with respect to the arts of beauty. She should also avoid all occasions where she could be a temptation to men. Apparently the "stronger and superior" male still lives constantly on the precipice, where his virtue is in perpetual peril. Cyprian is by no stretch of the imagination a classical misogynist, and he can write movingly, as one says, of marital love and affection. On the other hand, his extolling of virginity tends toward that "denaturing" of woman we have already pointed out in the earlier Christian and the Greek writers. Only by ceasing to be a "normal" woman can woman achieve liberation from the "curse" and thereby "equality" with men.

St. Ambrose is a welcome relief to the sexist interpretation of Genesis 2. He points out that God himself noticed that it was not good for the man to be alone.[3] This bisexual nature of man does allow for the possibility of sin. However, if Eve could be considered sin's point of entrance (as we have seen, this is a favorite theme of the Fathers), she must also be seen as the mother of the Redeemer.

The tendency to conect woman and sin does not completely obscure her nature as the "source (mother) of all the living," but especially of the Redeemer. St. Ambrose does not concentrate on Eve (woman) as the first sinner or perpetual temptress. He develops the idea of the Church as woman because for him the female symbolizes fruitfulness. But she is not merely a baby machine, she is an essential and natural part of mankind. Her origin from the rib of Adam clearly establishes that there is only one human nature in both man and woman. In itself the human soul is not sexual; but in relation to the subhuman, it can be thought of as male; in relation to the divine, it can be viewed as female. Even here there are visible traces of that equating of the male gender with power and dominion, of the female with receptivity and passivity. Although such pairing does not have to work to the disadvantage of the woman, it always does.

For St. Ambrose, Eden's human being as such does not appear to be sexual, at least not sexual in any recognizable sense. This does not lead him to reject or demean marriage. He sees it as an honorable and holy way of being a Christian, intended not only for procreation but also as a graced society of reciprocal love and help.

Chastity is not restricted to virgins but is also available to spouses and widows in their own proper ways. In this sense, even married people can participate in that freedom which Christ has given his Church. St. Ambrose can write about the trials and tribulations of marriage, of the subjection which women (can) experience from their husbands. But he can also write beautifully of the marriage of free Christians, whose freedom is not destroyed by or in their marriage:

> Woman must respect her husband, not be a slave to him; she consents to be ruled, not to be forced. The one whom a yoke would fit is not fit for the yoke of marriage. As to man, he should guide his wife like a pilot, honor her as his partner in life, share with her as a co-heir of grace.[4]

Thus marriage is different for Christians and pagans. For the latter it is the experience of the curse in lust. For the believers, however, it can be the experience of that freedom and grace of Christ which makes them able to live in the praise of God and the service of one another. However, virginity remains by far the preferred and "more perfect" state of life. It is the clear anticipation of heaven, the univocal overcoming of the curse, the royal return to the pre-sinful, innocent garden.

As we have seen already, this emphasis on virginity, with the human ascetical effort it demands, will have undesirable effects. The theological understanding that woman enjoys freedom and equality with man through this effort will lead to an increasing de-emphasis of baptism as the source of Christian freedom. This will create an elitist concept of freedom and "perfection," which will be restricted to those few able to achieve so special a way of life. Against the heretical sects, the Church will remain the "great Church," but its theology will not provide a liberation available to all. As we have seen so often, such restriction always works to the detriment of the already restricted. In our case this means that women's already restricted and inferior status will become even more so.

St. Jerome is, among all the Fathers of the Church, most notorious for his misogyny. His ire was enkindled by three contemporary writers, Helvidius, Jovinian, and Vigilantius. They were not major theologians by any means. What the three had in common was a lack of enthusiasm for the ascetic striving which had become so dear to people like Jerome. This tepidity with regard to asceticism also embraced the concept of virginity. Helvidius denied both Mary's perpetual virginity and the superiority of the virginal to the matrimonial state of life. For Jovinian all ascetical strivings were of secondary value since baptism established the freedom and equality of Christians. Vigilantius denounced both celibacy and asceticism. Just by the by, it is interesting to speculate what Christianity would be like today if these three mavericks had carried the day.

In any case, their writings stirred up Jerome's considerable ire. In his calmer moments he acknowledged the goodness of marriage, although he clearly preferred virginity as the better and higher state of life; higher because it is the anticipation of the kingdom of heaven. This would only be a logical conclusion for Jerome, who like many of his contemporaries, supposed human existence in paradise to have been "asexual," or at least virginal, and marriage to have come only after the Fall. Thus it is not merely ill temper, but a certain theological approach that leads him to conclude that "women are the gate of hell." His enthusiasm for virginity and his uncurbed capacity for indignation conspired to produce some of the most misogynist rhetoric the world has ever known. However repetitious it may be, it is not out of place to remark once again that posterity could have chosen to record the utterances of the moderate Jerome, but it preferred the Jerome who regarded marriage as a catastrophe and woman as a shrew.

St. Augustine's writings on marriage were at least partly occasioned by the extremist rhetoric and ideas of Jerome and Tertullian. He also disagrees, of course, with Jovinian. However, for St. Augustine the superiority of virginity is not to be preserved at the expense of marriage. Nor is virginity to be embraced as a flight from the trials and tribulations of marriage.

St. Augustine's doctrine about women is not, however, purely flattering to the fair sex. Indeed, for the vocal ideologues of the women's liberation movement he occupies a deep dark pit next to Sigmund Freud. Rosemary Ruether's penchant for bombast has prompted her to entitle one of her presentations "St. Augustine's Penis: Roots of Misogynism in Christian Theology."[5] Apart from being an exquisite, if unintentional, substantiation of Freud's theory of penis envy, this title also clearly manifests the tendency to single out St. Augustine as *the* culprit in the sexist history of the Christian Church. Such critics delight in emphasizing St. Augustine's early life of lascivious libertinism. To compensate for the wild oats he sowed as a youth, he is now compelled to play the "mature" moralist. Or perhaps better, having eaten his cake, he now wants to have it too. Whether Augustine was all that profligate is a question we can leave to the historians. One cannot, however, always avoid the impression that some of his highly caustic feminine critics operate on a basis of envy—they themselves having passed the sweet years of their youth as academic drones and drudges in the pursuit of equality with their male professors.

Others delight in pointing out the Manichean dimensions of Augustine's personality and doctrine. They apparently are unable to see that his writings against St. Jerome are at least partly intended to defend sex and marriage against such tendencies and interpretations. In contrast to many Church Fathers, St. Augustine clearly teaches that sex does not originate only after or because of the Fall. The first creation of "Adam-man" is already bisexual. Man and woman are equal to one another insofar as they come from God and are related to him. However, insofar as they are mutually intended for procreation, they are unequal. In the spirit of Aristotle the male is described as active, and therefore superior. The female is passive and therefore subordinate.

Augustine's Neoplatonic background is manifest in his understanding that as souls men and women are equally in the image and likeness of God. However, bodily man is superior to woman because he is more powerful. Consequently, insofar as human nature is corporeal, the male alone is the image of God. Hence St. Augustine will conclude that insofar as woman is human she is pleasing to the Christian; but that insofar as she is precisely woman, she is not pleasing. Thus, even though he would have nothing to do with the approach to virginity which debases marriage, he ends up in a position which is really similar. Woman is man's equal as a human being only insofar as her specifically feminine being is nullified —whether by ascetical discipline or theological anthropology is not important.

Augustine holds that in paradise mankind was already male and female but that their mutual attraction and subsequent cooperation in procreation would not have been in and through sexual passion had it not been for the Fall. In the true spirit of intellectualist philosophy, their decision to procreate would have been the fully free choice of a sovereign reason. In fact, sexual intercourse itself would not have deprived the man and woman of their virginity, if indeed they would have engaged in it at all. (His position is not clear on this question of intercourse, although his final conclusion seems to be in the negative.) It is possible to see here the reformed and celibate Augustine, now a theologian, trying to reconcile the insistent urging of sexual passion with the idyllic tranquillity of peaceful paradise.

In all this we must not overlook St. Augustine's generally pessimistic attitude toward human nature and the salvation of humankind. This could readily combine with his own former sexual errancy to produce a basically suspicious attitude toward sex and women. A practical solution to the problem of sexual desire and discipline could be found, he thought, in the direction of limiting one's association with women to the basically procreative activity—that is, if one cannot avoid them completely through virginity. Woman is to be likened to the field in which the farmer—man—sows his seed. Apart from this tie with the female, the male would be better off associating with other males. In all matters except the generation of other human beings, the male is a more adequate companion and "helpmate" than the female. Do we here have overtones of that debased idea of women we saw among the Mesopotamians, for whom woman's only purpose was procreation and pleasure? St. Augustine's position is not identical to theirs because he urges that the pleasure of sex be as minimal as possible. In fact, if procreation could happen without sexual desire and pleasure, that would be preferable by far. (And that would certainly have influenced the world's current population problem.)

St. Augustine was not narrowly or exclusively concerned with the unruliness of sexual desire in particular. In keeping with his Platonic preference, all that distracts the mind or spirit is reprehensible and to be done away with. Whatever the state of affairs in paradise might have been, since the Fall mankind is tossed to and fro on the waves of desire. Of all the human bodily desires, the strongest is the sexual. It must, therefore, be the recipient of greater attention and discipline. In the pattern of other great thinkers, however, St. Augustine also succumbs to the temptation to equate the object of his temptability with the temptation itself. Since sexual temptability is the greatest, this confusion will undoubtedly mean that woman will be the greatest temptation—and hence the greatest evil. At least in this fallen and sinful world, that was the conclusion later generations would draw from the writings of St. Augustine. But they could have concluded differently, for St. Augustine also knew that not only virgins but all the faithful, even the married, are able to be brother and sister and mother of Christ (Matthew 12:50). All they must do is hear the word of God and practice it (Luke 8:21), that is, do the will of Jesus' heavenly Father.

It is difficult to offer a concise summary of patristic doctrine concerning women. This is partly because the Fathers did not write specific tracts on "The Theology of Woman."

Their considerations on women are scattered throughout their writings, especially their commentaries on the Bible. However, there is another and more serious reason, namely that the Fathers themselves did not know simply and clearly what they thought about women. And there is an even more important reason behind this, namely that they did not know simply and clearly what they thought about mankind in general. And the same must also be said about their understanding of Christ. Now, when I say all this I do not want to sound like a minimalist and skeptic. However, we should recall the difficulty St. Paul himself had in understanding and applying the fact and truth of Christ. Consequently it is not surprising that the Fathers didn't achieve a totally consistent and liberating doctrine about the status of woman in the world and the Church. We can be disappointed at the misogyny which is so grossly present in some of their writings. On the other hand, to maintain that they are solely and consistently misogynist would certainly be erroneous. A text from Ambrosiaster's commentary on 1 Corinthians 2 illustrates the ambivalence of the Fathers very well.

> Although man and woman are of the same essence, the man should neverthless be superior since he is the head of the woman. On the basis of his being the cause and virtue of his intellect he is the greater; not, however, by reason of a greater essence or nature is he superior. Therefore the woman is subordinate to the man. She is indeed a part of him because the man is the origin of the woman. That is the source of woman's being subject to the man and to his command.... The man, not the woman, was created in the image of God.... She must wear this sign (the veil) because sin had its origin in and through her. In the Church reverence compels the woman not to appear before the Bishop with her head uncovered; she must be veiled. Likewise she is not to enjoy the power to speak, for the Bishop takes the place of *(represents)* Christ.[6]

Not all the Fathers are so restrictive, but this passage does provide a nice summary of the themes and problems that run through all their writings: who is in the image of God and who are able to be "officials" in the Church. It is time to recall what we said at the beginning of this book, namely that the problem of the relationship of men and women is a philosophical problem. Beyond all the more practical and perhaps more urgent psychological and sociological problems is that fundamental philosophical problem of the one and the many, diversity and unity. How can men and women be different and still equal? This problem receives a practical intensity from the de facto social conditions of woman's subordination. Hence the philosophers and theologians do not start their thinking from a pure state of nature where men and women would indeed be different, but equal. They must start from their real world where men and women are indeed different, but also unequal. The influence of this *fact* on the *reasoning* of the philosophers and even of Christian theologians cannot be overemphasized. As we have seen, the search for an *explanation* of the fact can easily turn into a *justification* of the fact. Thus the fact of woman's subordination in society provided the occasion for the theologians to interpret Genesis in a way which was not demanded by the text itself; in fact, not even allowed by the text. It also provided the occasion for them to pick those New Testament texts less favorable to women and to omit others more favorable, and with a point of view which would prompt them to prefer the minimalist and negative in regard to women.

Nevertheless certain theological metaphors (Mary-Eve, the Church as woman or mother, the individual soul and whole world as feminine) stood in the way of a simple suppression of woman in the Church. The increasing devotion to Mary in the Church also served to promote the dignity and status of woman. A disadvantage for women was in the emphasis on virginity as the means to escape the primal curse and to achieve freedom and equality with men. Although this doctrine entailed a positive and affirmative view of feminine human nature formally, its material content—namely, virginity—automatically and severely restricted the number of women who could benefit from it. It also supported and furthered the increasing elimination of women from the "public" and "official" life of the Church. More and more women were removed from the public *diakonia,* or service of the Church, to the monastery. They were no longer to be deacons, but to become ascetics. Their churchly lives would not be in terms of their "natural'" womanly (sexual) nature, but in terms of their ability to "overcome" this world. Their freedom in Christ is seen to originate less from the sacrament of baptism and more from the achievement of their ascetic love of God. With typical linguistic aplomb, the Germans will describe this as "metaphysical erotic." There has been, indeed, a certain "denaturing" of woman as a condition for her participation in the Church and freedom of Christ. The ambivalence which haunted women throughout the Old Testament has not simply disappeared in the New. The Church will have to continue to struggle against those demonic powers and principalities which still harass the world although their power has been broken in principle by Christ.

Before we turn our attention to the status of women in the Middle Ages, it might be well to pause here on a topic which spans the centuries in the life of the Church, namely that of woman as the source of scandal. A variety of factors have been involved, including, as we have seen, certain biological and philosophical understandings.

First, the idea of ritual cleanness and uncleanness, which we examined in its Old Testament context, has continued to be influential in the exclusion of women not only from the cultic priesthood but even from the place where this office is exercised. Some theologians have urged the total exclusion of women from the sanctuary, and as late as our own century Pope Pius X wanted them excluded even from the choir. It is also not too many years since an Oklahoma priest produced a furor when he allowed girls to be altar "boys." A striking

---

7/ Woman as Scandal

expression of the sense of woman's "uncleanness" is found in Origen:

> What is seen by the eyes of the Creator is masculine, not feminine; for God does not deign to look at that which is feminine and fleshly.[1]

Long after such radical views have been lost in history, their influence persists.

We have seen, too, how the reported presence of woman priests among the Montanists strengthened the already negative attitude of the Church Fathers toward the participation of women in the Church's ministry. The rejection of woman priests easily leads to a more widespread exclusion of women from public and official ministry in the Church. Hence the diaconal office exercised earlier by women will come under more and more pressure of rejection. It will survive in the East until the twelfth century, although in a greatly reduced form. In the West it cannot be considered to have survived much beyond the fourth century. Opposition to the participation of women in the public life of the Great Church intensified and spread. The synods of Orange (441), Epaon (517), and Orleans (533) mark the definite exclusion of women from the hierarchy in the West. Henceforth only the monastic or the lay way of being active in the Church will be open to them.

There was still another factor contributing to the image of woman as a scandal in the patristic era: the practice designated by the terms *virgines subintroductae* or *agapetai*. These are Latin and Greek terms for women virgins who were the companions of males also dedicated or consecrated to virginity either as Church officials or as "simple" faithful. The companionship consisted in various kinds and degrees of living together. The origin of the practice can be traced back to St. Paul's First Epistle to the Corinthians, from which the question arose: Can the Christian virgin remain in the general company of society? Or must she (he) retire to the desert as a solitary or, at most, in the company of the same sex? If men and women have really been freed from sexual differentiation and discrimination by baptism and the ascetical achievement of virginity, can they not live together in various degrees of community and intimacy? In the early years of the Church there seems to have been a widespread affirmative answer. And this affirmation was not restricted to only the enthusiastic Corinthians.

Unmarried priests, deacons, and monks shared their living quarters with women dedicated to the virginal state. Apparently even some bishops adopted this life style. The general ideological background providing for this practice is indicated by the Second Epistle of Clement.

> For the Lord Himself, when asked by someone when His kingdom would come, said: "When the two shall be one, and the outside as the inside, and the male with the female neither male nor female." And "the male with the female neither male nor female" means that a brother seeing a sister has no thought of her as female, nor she of him as male.[2]

The phenomenon evoked a considerable and negative reaction within the Church at large. There was, of course, no opposition to the communion and equality of souls. The same cannot be said about the equality and communion of bodies. The anti-*agapetai* literature does not seem to emphasize woman as a temptation, as other religious and philosophical literature had, but it does urge the danger and impracticability of virginal cohabitation. Cyprian, for example, urges the deacon who was sharing even his bed with his virginal companion to change life styles while there is still time. But the emphasis and tone of this and similar warnings are free of that demeaning and misogynist attitude which regards every woman as essentially temptress and seductress. Although the anti-*agapetai* writings are very insistent that such relationships be dissolved, they do not tend to blame the woman. They urge, rather, the difficulty of preserving virginity in such a close relationship and in such close quarters and call into question the prudence of those involved in such relationships.

However, it was perhaps the fear of scandal more than anything else that led to the attacks on this way of life. Certainly its advocates had the whole tradition of both sacramental and ascetical (virginal) liberation on their side. If St. Paul was right about baptism, and if the Church Fathers were right about virginity, then there was certainly no *theological* reason to oppose the practice of virgins living together heterosexually. The opposition could only be on "practical" grounds. But if theology is not practicable, then what good is it? And if pagans or cynical and skeptical Christians do not believe that this eschatological sign is being lived, should that not be their problem and not that of those Christians who choose to live this sign? However, common sense and prudence won out, as they are wont to do. And as, perhaps, they should. But win they did. And this sign of the freedom Christ had brought for both men and women ceased.

As in so many other things, of course, the cessation of this practice had more serious negative consequences for women than for men. It reinforced the increasingly male dominance in the Church. Henceforth the male officials of the Church will have less and less contact with women—not only because they are temptations, but also because one must avoid scandal. (In passing, one might wonder whether such great weight is also placed on the avoidance of other scandals.) Intentionally or not, another Church practice has clearly contributed to promoting a lesser status of women in the Church.

A final factor in this whole process was the increasing demand for and practice of celibacy by the officials of the Church. Already around 300 the Synod of Elvira in Spain called for celibacy on the part of bishops, priests, and deacons. Likewise, clerics were enjoined to have only very restricted contact with women. In 325 the council of Nicaea made the first attempt to legislate celibacy for the universal Church. Canon 3 of this council forbids any bishop, priest, or other cleric to have a *mulierem subintroductam* unless it be his "mother or sister or aunt or at least those persons who are beyond suspicion."[3] The practice of the Church varied at this time. Those who advocated complete celibacy for the clergy, for those already married and ordained as well as for those not yet ordained, were not able to carry the day. By the end of the fourth century the practice of the East was well established. It basically allows those married before ordination to remain so, but after ordination the unmarried may not enter marriage. In the West there were many and various attempts to require universal clerical celibacy. Candidates for the priesthood and their wives were often required to promise continence. From the sixth century on, the separation of husband and wife was required. However, only after the council of Trent in the sixteenth century can one really speak of a universally effective law and practice of celibacy by the clergy in the West.

Celibacy is not, of course, our main concern. It is of value for our present consideration, however, because it does reveal an attitude toward sex, and consequently toward women. The huge expenditure of the Church's time and energy in urging clerical celibacy cannot have been without major, if unintended, side-effects on women. It certainly had the effect of removing women even further from the councils and counsels of the Church. If only men may be priests and bishops, and if these men are forbidden the company of women, then the latter will surely and increasingly be devoid of influence in the Church at large. Furthermore, if the macho-male ego delights in regarding women as temptation and seduction, how much more the celibate male ego. Is it any wonder that often these ministers of Christ's gospel of freedom sound like Ecclesiasticus meditating on Genesis 3:16?

This exclusion of women not only from the priesthood itself but increasingly from all public Church office and even from contact with the hierarchy will continue throughout the Middle Ages. In fact, it will intensify, for there will be a further theological elaboration of women's "incapacity" to be ordained to the priesthood. A noticeable exception on this incapacity, namely "The Hidden History of Women with Clerical Ordination and the Jurisdiction of Bishops," will be just that —a hidden history.[4] But these developments belong to our next chapter.

It has been necessary to spend so much time on both the Bible and the Church Fathers because the subsequent history of the West has been but a commentary, pro or con, on their insights. We can summarize the theory of women at the start of the Middle Ages in terms of the thought of Augustine and Tertullian: although woman has also been created in and is God's image, she is not to be regarded and revered equally with the man because she bears the stain of Eve. Of course, there was great ambivalence and inconsistency among the Fathers; but as a not entirely inadequate summary, the above sentence can stand.

In the Middle Ages the grounds for woman's inequality will be expanded, or at least intensified, by Aristotle's biological philosophy, on which we touched earlier. This will lead to the description of woman's nature as defective. That is, if

8/ The Medieval World

the process of procreation had been totally and simply successful, the outcome would have been a male; the female outcome indicates that the process was in fact somehow defective. Once more, I think, we have a case of the search for an explanation becoming the justification of that which was to be explained. Of course, by the time the medieval writers got around to doing this, they had a whole army of examples to follow, from the Greeks, the Hebrews, and the earlier Christians. The one exception to this type of antifeminism seems to have been Peter Abelard. His influence, however, if there was any at all, was minimal. It is not without value to wonder whether his generally unacceptable philosophy and theology also contributed to the final unacceptability of his ideas about woman. We have already seen how the general unacceptability of Montanism influenced the seclusion of women from public Church life. And in regard to the *virgines subintroductae,* we know that the influence in woman's favor of even a bishop, Paul of Samosota, was negative because other elements of his life and some of his doctrinal position were suspect. It is another instance of that "law" which seems to require perfect purity on the part of the advocates of practices not considered to be in the mainstream of any given society.

In general we can say that three factors describe the status of women in the Middle Ages. There is an undeniable antifeminism in the Church, although, as in the patristic era, this was neither consistent nor absolute. We shall see the theologians trying to understand the realities of the social, economic, political, and biological worlds in which they live as well as the Christian fact and revelation. By this time, of course, the original Christian experience or "fact" will have developed into a whole tradition. The task of discerning the true tradition from the false will complicate the work of the theologian even further.

A second factor was the development of the erotic culture of the Minnesinger era. The interpretation of love and human being on the part of these "love singers"' will not only influence the practice of sex in society in general, it will also provide a foil for the activities of the theologians who will have to deal especially with the morality of the lyrics. Although we tend to think of the Middle Ages as the Christian era, we must not forget the strong pagan influences still present at this time. As J. Huizinga has pointed out:

> To find paganism, there was no need for the spirit of the waning Middle Ages to revert to classic literature. The pagan spirit displayed itself, as amply as possible, in the *Roman de la Rose*. From the early Middle Ages onward Venus and Cupid had found a refuge in this domain. But the great pagan who called them to vigorous life and enthroned them was Jean de Meun. By blending with Christian conceptions of eternal bliss the boldest praise of voluptuousness, he had taught numerous generations a very ambiguous attitude toward Faith.[1]

Obviously, then, the Church had not yet been able to "Christianize" the sexual passion of humankind. Although virginity and the Virgin Mary had been urged as the ideals of human and Christian living, the goddesses of love and pleasure had by no means been banished.

Near the end of the Middle Ages the third factor will appear strongly—a woman's liberation. There will be, to the joy and elation of Betty Friedan and Gloria Steinem, worldly women, learned and capable of more than "merely domestic" chores. Their presence will even be felt in the political and economic life of the society—as more than an occasional and exceptional "miraculous" event. It cannot be asserted, however, that this feminine prosperity was more than a brief flurry. Under the influence of the Humanists, antiquity's ambivalence toward woman was revived. As we shall see, from the Minnesingers on, Western European Humanism has been characterized by this ambivalence.

In spite of its antifeminism, the Church did favorably influence the position of woman in many respects. It insisted that woman was neither merely a slave nor the property of the tribe, only changing hands in marriage. However, whether its opposition to concubinage and prostitution was all that effective can be called into doubt when one recalls that fifteen hundred whores set up shop in Basel during the council held there in the 1430s. The effect of this statistic is somewhat spoiled by the fact that when the council was at its height, with from five to six hundred participating, there were scarcely twenty bishops among them and the great mass were not clerics at all. However, the provisions made for the event by way of prostitutes would suggest a kind of hierarchical tolerance of double-standard morality among those concerned with the cause of religion.

Huizinga finds it astonishing that the Church allowed such work as the *Roman de la Rose* to circulate freely, that the Church

> which so rigorously repressed the slightest deviations from dogma of a speculative character, suffered the teaching of this breviary of the aristocracy (for the *Roman de la Rose* was nothing less) to be disseminated with impunity.[2]

It is not inconceivable that Church authorities, then as now, might have reconciled themselves to the inevitability of sexual immorality among the population at large. Thus their opposition would be more in the area of preaching and absolution, less in the area of effective social institutions to protect the disadvantaged female from abuse and exploitation, whether marital or extramarital.

Indeed, Christian theologians generally showed themselves

well aware that the highest of ascetical standards could not be imposed even on a society that thought of itself as Christian. Thus St. Augustine held that legalized prostitution should be allowed, and this position continued to be maintained in the Middle Ages. The argument was that society could tolerate certain evils to the end that greater goods might not be eliminated and greater evils fostered. It is interesting to note that St. Thomas would allow the prostitute to retain her earnings.

A small work attributed to Aquinas, "On the Rule of Princes to the King of Cyprus," comments on some ideas from the political theory of Aristotle. One of the topics is whether soldiers should be allowed to marry and/or to have sexual intercourse. (Sounds a little like the controversies current among coaches and athletic trainers today.) The following is a free translation of this discussion. Some assert that sexual pleasure is to be avoided because it makes the soul (disposition; character) soft (*mollescit animus*—it even sounds good in the original Latin) and less virile. However, against this opinion, Aristotle maintains that warriors and fighters are given over to luxury and pleasure by nature. Further, if men abstain from women, they tend to search out other men; and this is even less desirable than consorting with women. There follows the famous simile from Augustine about the role of the prostitute in society, compared to the bilgewater in the sea or the sewer in the palace. If you remove the sewer, the palace will be filled with filth; remove whores from the world, and it will be filled with sodomy. Thus, in *The City of God,* St. Augustine says that the earthly city has made the use of whores a lawful disgrace and infamy (*licitam turpitudinem*). Aristotle himself explains that sodomy is a vice due to vitiated natures and perverse customs; since such practices are in themselves not properly human delights and pleasures, it is impossible to assign to or find in them that happy middle which is the hallmark of virtue.[3]

Many find this text, especially the sewer simile, degrading to both sex and women. However, it should be noted that the whole situation is rejected as inhuman. Furthermore, such an approach to legalized prostitution does establish a qualitative difference between heterosexual intercourse and, at least, homosexual activity. Admittedly the implications of such a position are not drawn out, but it does indicate a complementarity between man and woman that does not exist between man and other men or animals. Furthermore, sodomy is rejected precisely because it is not a properly *human* pleasure. Hence one would have to conclude that sexual intercourse between a husband and wife was precisely a human act. And again, although the author himself does not draw the proper conclusions, he would at least have posited a very valuable principle for others to work with.

I do not want this to appear to be a personal defense of St. Thomas. That would hardly be necessary since he didn't write this part of the book anyhow. It was written by his disciple, Ptolemy of Lucca, whose style and rhetoric are considerably different from St. Thomas'.[5] In fact, St. Thomas does not use the sewer simile when he refers to the same basic passage from St. Augustine in the *Summa Theologiae*. Furthermore, he only cites that passage in passing, to illustrate the general principle whereby the state can tolerate certain evils to avoid other, greater evils.

In the medieval debates about the nature of marriage an insight was clarified, with great benefit to both marriage and woman: namely, that marriage is essentially constituted by the consent of the partners contracting marriage. Nowadays we are frequently reluctant to speak of marriage as a contract because we don't want to be legalistic. However, even the conclusion that marriage was a contract was already a break-through for both human liberation and matrimonial dignity.

The Middle Ages' understanding of marriage was the result of three major cultural influences. From the later Romans had come the understanding, as we have seen, that marriage was to be entered through the mutual consent of the spouses. The Northern Europeans (Germans, Franks, Celts), on the other hand, contended that marriage consisted in the handing over of the bride—that is, her transferral from the control of her father to the control of her husband. A third factor was the ancient and universal understanding that marriage had not really (fully, essentially) taken place until it had been con-summated sexually. In a sense, this third factor placed the essence of marriage in sexual intercourse. It did not deny consent theoretically, but it emphasized that marriage was a sexual state of life, and therefore could be adequately con-stituted only by sexual intercourse.

In the Church this history was concentrated in the question whether marriage was constituted by consent or copulation. The theory of the Scholastic writers (unlike the tendency of the Fathers of the Church) did not separate sex from mar-riage. Likewise, their Jewish heritage emphasized the family as a procreation and education reality. Hence they were under great pressure to locate the essence of marriage in the sexual act. An additional confusing element was the im-portance attached to the betrothal or engagement by the Northern Europeans. If the betrothal was followed by copula-tion, even though this was severely forbidden, there was a tendency to regard the man and woman as married. This, of course, militated against the consent view, because the betrothal consent was clearly understood *not* to be the matri-monial consent.

The theologians tended to support the consent position;

the canon lawyers the copulation. Was then, in the Church, marriage to be regarded primarily as (1) sexual community; (2) an interpersonal community in which sexual procreation would be part of the spouses' duty but not the essence of marriage; (3) a procreative community in the sense connoted by the popular etymology of Isidore of Seville which claimed that "matri-mony" was explained by the Latin words for that *office* (duty task) by which women became *mothers?*

This dispute was resolved in favor of the consent theory, for even the canonists, in the summation of Gratian, granted that the partners' consent brought about the marriage. However, another dispute immediately arose, using the same terms. Could a marriage which was only consented to, but not sexually consummated, be dissolved? This distinction is made and used even today in the Catholic Church's theology and law of matrimony. It is considered that the actual sexual consummation of matrimonial consent gives that marriage a much greater solidity and permanence than a marriage based "merely" on consent. Nonetheless it must not be forgotten that the marriage which is "only ratified" is as essentially a marriage as one which is both "ratified and consummated." It cannot be nullified simply by the exit of the spouses, but only by a juridical act of the proper authority.

Thus we can see that in the Scholastic era the Church developed the understanding that marriage was the decision of persons mutually consenting to have each other for husband and wife. This was an impressive liberation of both marriage as an institution and the spouses as persons. It means that everything else—parental rights, dowry, engagement rites, even the priestly witness and blessing—is only accessory. Unfortunately this theological clarification did not necessarily induce a similar practice within the population at large. The practice of child marriages for the sake of the state or the family fortune continued, and since they had to be carried out secretly, the problem of clandestine marriages arose. Against this practice Pope Alexander III did not hesitate to levy the penalty of excommunication.

Nevertheless the old understanding which located marriage in the will of the father did not easily and immediately give way. Again, the weight of society's factual condition shows its power to curb a Christian insight. However, the Middle Ages can be credited with the laying of a firm foundation for feminine emancipation from sexual oppression. The consent theory of marriage, once fully understood, would (should I say, will?) eliminate not only child marriages but also rape marriages (that is, it would make illegitimate the custom whereby a male could compel a reluctant maiden to marry him by simply carrying her off and/or having sexual intercourse with her by force). Implicit in this new understanding of marriage is that the human being is to be defined not in terms of sexuality but of personality.

It is difficult to exaggerate the Church's difficulty in trying to secure the dignity of both marriage and woman. This difficulty was based not only on the weakness and sinfulness of the members of the Church but also on the enduring sexual emphasis of any given culture. That preoccupation with venery is witnessed even by so continent a scholar at St. Thomas Aquinas. In the open discussions held in the medieval universities any question, serious or light, could be posed as a challenge to the mastery of the professor. St. Thomas was once faced with the following question: Which is strongest, wine, woman, the king, or truth?[4] He responded by saying that in themselves these four subjects are not comparable since they do not belong to the same genus. However, they can be compared in regard to the effect they have on the heart of man. The heart of man can be changed insofar as it is corporeal, sensitive, and intellectual—the latter being either practical or speculative. Wine is most powerful corporeally. Delectation, especially venereal, is most powerful in regard to the senses. Thus woman is stronger here than the other three. In regard to the practical things of the mind, the king is stronger; in regard to speculative things, truth is the highest and most powerful. St. Thomas concludes that since in this series listing the qualities of the heart of man, each one is subordinate to the one following it, beginning with the corporeal, the truth must be the most powerful thing of all because man's other three qualities are subordinate to the speculative intellect.

This passage is interesting insofar as it shows the obvious influence of Greek philosophy on a Christian thinker: speculative truth is the highest value, higher even than personal relationships of love. But for our purposes it is even more interesting for the light it casts on the simple and uncomplicated way in which woman is related to venereal pleasure. Within the whole universe of values, woman's strong point is to excite the sense appetite of man. That this reflected the factual situation can doubtless be granted without too much qualification. That the saint could accept it so matter-of-factly is, I think, a strong indication of just how overwhelmingly sexist a culture can be.

The Minnesinger culture of the Middle Ages was chiefly in the tradition of courtly love, with its artificial glorification of women; in extolling romantic passion it already presented certain problems to the moral theologian. But the real frontal attack on both marital fidelity and monogamy comes from the lower levels of French literature. This is illustrated by the history of the *Roman de la Rose,* which is the work of two quite disparate writers. The first part, written by Guillaume de Lorris around 1230, describes "the love of the ideal woman. The lover has to deserve his reward . . . by a refinement of the mind."[5] The second half, completed some time before 1280 by Jean de Meung, is a work of blatant realism which disparages all love but the sensual as unnatural.

Among its other admonitions, de Meung's *Rose* contains the following encouragement from the Fool, who also utterly rejects both matrimony and the monastic life: Young maidens should "sell their persons early and dearly." Fear and shame are trifles, as are lying and simulation. The whole of life is to be consumed in the pleasure(-s) of the body. Denis de Rougemont's summary indicates how the earlier "romantic passion" has become a much less romantic and henceforth highly carnal and sexual exercise:

> Jean de Meung, on the other hand, looks upon the Rose as no more than sensual pleasure. A most outspoken realism supersedes Lorris's fiddle-faddle; Platonism gives place to an apology of sensual enjoyment, and emotional fervour to cynicism. The Rose is won by main force. Nature triumphs over mind; and reason over passion.
>
> From Jean de Meung the ancient tradition, according to which passion is to be rejected as "a sickness of the soul," was transmitted to the lower levels of French literature—to *gauloiserie* and the schools of broad Gallic jokes, to controversial rationalism, and to a curiously exacerbated misogyny, naturalism, and man's reduction to sex. All this has simply been pagan man's normal way of defending himself against the myth of unhappy love.[6]

This passage recalls a theme we have been able to trace all the way through our history: the male's disenchantment with woman, of whose sex he demands too much—indeed, the impossible. Since she does not fulfill his phantasies, the male is compelled to degrade her. Hence his longstanding tradition of misogyny. The French (who else?) have a saying which can be adapted to fit here: *qui fait l'ange, fait bête.* We could freely translate, "If you want woman to be an angel (goddess), you will end up making her a beast." This was, as we have seen, the fate of women in Mesopotamia. Elevated to the status of sex and fertility goddess by the longing of man, she is cursed as his drudge and drone in the real world. Obviously we are not far from that famous verse 16 of Genesis 3. Who makes sex divine pays for his crime in slavery. We have also noted that women have traditionally paid the higher price. And the Middle Ages are no exception. As the following citation indicates, the male ego sought to protect itself by magnifying the fickleness and unreliability of women. In this we have an echo of that more ancient tradition which regarded women as both morally weaker and basically nymphomaniac:

> The whole genre of *Les Cent nouvelles nouvelles* and the loose song, with its wilful neglect of all the natural and social complications of love, with its indulgence towards the lies and egotism of sexual life, and its vision of a never-ending lust, implies, no less than the screwed-up system of courtly love, an attempt to substitute for reality the dream of a happier life. It is once more the aspiration towards the life sublime, but this time viewed from the animal side. It is an ideal all the same, even though it is that of unchastity.[7]
> This underlying connexion between *gauloiserie* and an over-refined treatment of love is brought to the surface in a thirteenth-century satire called *L'Evangile des femmes*.
> If chivalry made a mock of marriage from above, *gauloiserie* was undermining it from below. The procedure adopted by the latter is well indicated in the *Dit de Chiceface*. Chiceface is a fabulous monster who feeds only on women who keep their marriage vows and he is terribly emaciated. But his comrade Bigorne, whose diet consists exclusively of submissive husbands, is the very barrel of a fellow.[8]

A peculiar twist is given to the traditional double standard of morality. The poor husband is relieved of responsibility for his failures, however mild and few they have been to begin with, since in any case the female of the species is incurably promiscuous. So, if the male should fail, it is not really his fault. In himself he would be faithful and pure, but how can he escape the cunning and charms of the eternally restless female?

Against such a background the exceedingly antifeminist attitudes and antisexual precepts of late medieval moral theologians like Vincent of Beauvais are much more understandable:

> At the bottom of the intoxicating cup of the *Roman do la Rose* the moralist exposed the bitter dregs. From the side of religion maledictions were poured upon love in all its aspects, as the sin by which the world is being ruined. Whence, exclaims Gerson, come the bastards, the infanticides, the abortions, whence hatred, whence poisonings?—Woman joins her voice to that from the pulpit: all the conventions of love are the work of men: even when it dons an idealistic guise, erotic culture is altogether saturated by male egotism: and what else is the cause of the endlessly repeated insults to matrimony, to woman and her feebleness, but the need of masking this egotism? One word suffices, says Christine de Pisan, to answer all these infamies: it is not the women who have written the books.[9]

The insistence on devotion to Mary as precisely the Virgin also received increased impetus. Against the Minnesinger culture's attempt to understand humanity in terms of sexual recreation, the Church would have felt compelled to assert the values of marital fidelity and virginity. This effort could only compound the already existent antisexual tendencies which had accompanied the Church from the very beginning. Furthermore, the combat against this emphasis on passion and romance as the meaning of human existence could only intensify the praise of monastic continence as the road to salvation.

In his commentary on the Epistle to the Galatians 3:28, St. Thomas Aquinas asserts without reservation that baptism's effects are not different for the two sexes.[10] "For nothing in men could cause discrimination in regard to the sacrament of faith and baptism in Christ." He then comments on the three possible differences which could theoretically be discriminatory. The first, between Jew and Greek, he attributes to rite or religious background; the second, between slave and free man, he refers to state in life or social condition. "The third difference pertains to nature . . . sex makes no difference in regard to participating in the effects of baptism. . . . The reason is that none of these three differences is the source of differentiation in Christ because all the faithful are one in Christ . . . many members and one body, although diverse among themselves. . . . Where there is unity, difference no longer has a place."

However, St. Thomas did not rigorously pursue this concept of unity and non-difference to its logical conclusion. Although he holds that men and women without distinction may share in the effect of baptism, his theology certainly does not provide for their equal participation in Church and society. We shall see this in much more detail in a later chapter when we examine the possibility of the ordination of women to the priesthood. Certainly there sexual discrimination seems to have lived beyond the teaching with regard to equal participation in the effects of baptism—with a vengeance.

We are again faced with the "weight of the fact," and the fact was the social inferiority of women. Although there were reasons aplenty in the Christian tradition to liberate women, the fact is that

> . . . medieval literature shows little true pity for woman, little compassion for her weakness and the dangers and pains which love has in store for her. Piety took on a stereotyped and factitious form, in the sentimental fiction of the knight delivering the virgin. The author of the *Quinze Joyes de Mariage*, after having mocked at all the faults of women,

undertakes to describe also the wrongs they have to suffer. So far as is known, he never performed this task.[11]

So, we may close our considerations on woman in the Middle Ages with the same conclusions we have used for all the preceding chapters and ages. Woman is indeed human, but. . . . No one would have excluded her from the human species, no one would have said she is canine, bovine, or feline rather than human. But that she is really equal in humanity, at least in the *real* world and not only in abstract philosophical and theological definition—that is still a long way off. The ambiguity and ambivalence of woman's status in society continues.

And things do not get better in the so-called modern world. Philosophers generally consider the modern world to have begun with Francis Bacon (1560-1625) and René Descartes (1596-1650). Other scholars prefer to start the modern world somewhat earlier, with the Protestant Reformation. For our purposes the difference is insignificant.

A phenomenon which does span the end of the "Catholic world" and the beginnings of both the Protestant and the modern secular worlds is the witch hunt. Although belief in witches can be called a universal phenomenon, it flared up in Europe especially in the late Middle Ages. The classic witch is, of course, female. Although males can also be witches, the preference for the female is indicated by the general absence of the proper word for male witch in the popular vocabulary. Although everyone knows what a witch is, how

9/ The Modern World: The Reformation Onwards

many know what a warlock is? Art, whether verbal or plastic, has also preferred the female as the representation of the witch. There are various explanations for this, and we have already noted a point where they all converge—the awe and fear mankind (especially the man) has experienced in regard to woman as the source and bearer of life, and blood as the symbol and carrier of life. There is another strange quirk here. Although ancient biology regarded the male as the sole agent of reproduction, the role of the woman apparently still overwhelmed and fascinated him.

In medieval Europe this whole situation was complicated by the mythologies of both the ancient Greco-Roman and the German civilizations and by the biblical condemnations of divination. For medieval man demons were a lively reality. The nearly chaotic social conditions of the late Middle Ages combined with the religious crisis of the corruption of the Church and the ensuing division of the Reformation to provide a fertile field for the witch craze which held sway for almost three centuries. Demon worship was flourishing when Pope Innocent VIII commissioned the Inquisition to intervene in 1484. In 1487 two Dominican inquisitors compiled a commentary on court procedures for the trial of witches, the famous *Malleus Maleficarum* (the Hammer of Witches). Although this book did not contain much that was new, it was characterized by "a notable animus against the female sex."[1] A similar attack on witches was waged by Luther and the other Reformers.

I have included this small section on witches only to illustrate once more how women tend to be victimized, even though such victimizing of women may not have been the original or primary intention of the event. I also think that the preponderance of the feminine in witch-ness is one more sign, albeit negative, of mankind's (especially the male's) awe and confusion in regard to the female sex. This is indeed strange conduct for him who is considered the "lord" and "master." The witch trials gradually tapered off in the second half of the seventeenth century. It is perhaps fitting that in the Austro-Hungarian empire a woman, Maria Theresa, should have brought the persecution of the witches, predominantly women, to an end. She died in 1780, a date which fittingly marks the end of the witch hunts.

The participation of the Reformers in the witch hunts is a good indication that the Reformation will not offer a fundamentally new interpretation of sex and woman. And one could hardly, in all honesty, expect anything new. This was not due to a special animus against women, but to the Reformers' general pessimism in regard to human nature and the human race. Both Luther and Calvin revelled in describing the "totally corrupt human nature" which originated in Adam's (and Eve's) original sin. However articulate and sophisticated such an assertion may have been in the doctrine of these theologians, the practical result will be quite negative in regard to any doctrine of man (anthropology). This pessimism will also certainly influence any and all attempts to describe the interpersonal being of man and woman. In general, however, Calvin is much less unfavorable toward women than Luther—a distinction which may be due more to the different personalities and styles of the two men than to any basic doctrinal differences.

Insofar as one's attitude toward polygamy is a barometer of one's attitude toward women, Calvin fares better than the other Reformers. He regarded polygamy, even in the Old Testament, as unacceptable. He even goes so far as to call the polygamous patriarchs adulterers. On the other hand, although Luther and Melancthon invoked this patriarchal practice to justify polygamy, they did not thereby automatically encourage it.

This position is only logical in view of Luther's general understanding of woman. She is precisely designed for sexual intercourse with the male and for procreation. The spirit of the Middle Ages continues in Luther—woman is designed primarily for domestic duties. Until recently, Germans traditionally described the essence of women with three K's—*Kirche* (Church), *Kinder* (children) and *Küche* (kitchen). However, the emancipation of women in post-war Germany has been remarkable. The American presence in Germany after World War II has contributed not only to the Wirtschaftswunderland (Germany as an economic miracle), but also to the Fraüleinswunderland (Germany as a miracle of feminine beauty and sophistication). I remember, when I was a student in Germany, the dismay of the German male when he would see an American GI carrying a baby or pushing a baby buggy. That was clearly and eternally woman's work!

How far are the current young and middle-aged generations from such a mentality! How far from Luther's understanding that women were basically a remedy for concupiscence (of the male, of course). He did not shrink from referring to them as the medicine or antidote for lust. Of course, even matrimonial sex is not, to the Reformer's mind, good—recall the doctrine of human nature's total corruption. Since even spouses do not engage in sex solely out of *duty* (how delighted Kant, the philosopher of duty, must have been when he read that!), their marital intercourse is not without shame. The original sin and ensuing sexual shame will, of course, weigh more heavily on the woman than the man.

The natural subordination of woman to man, even in Eden, has been intensified in the cursed world after the Fall. Here again the fate of woman is worse, her punishment greater. According to Luther, this is most strikingly illustrated by the pains women experience in childbearing and the dangers in childbirth.

Calvin likewise continues the theme of woman's subordination, which he held already existed in paradise. The difference between Eden and the present world is in the mode and severity of this subordination, not in its presence or absence. The present mode is described in the spirit of Genesis 3:16. Woman is now so related to man that her condition could be described as slavery. Calvin is not nearly as restrictive as Luther in his description of woman's nature or duty. Eve was not only to be wife-mother, but also wife-companion. Calvin does not succumb to that interpretation of Genesis 2 which makes woman both secondary and inferior, an afterthought. Rather, he sees, without her mankind is not complete and fully present. However, this insight in no way leads Calvin to assert the general equality of men and women. Men are by far the more important. They are the leaders, the principal members of society. There is a strong indication of this in Calvin's masterwork, *Institutes of the Christian Religion.* In those sections dealing with the original sin, the reference is almost exclusively to Adam. Explicit reference is made to "the woman (who) was seduced to discredit the word of God by the subtlety of the serpent . . . the Fall commenced in disobedience . . . all men were ruined by the disobedience of one." He continues, "though the transgression of our first parents was not simple apostasy; they were also guilty of vile reproaches . . . so that they cast off the fear of God. . . ." However, later he says, "But we shall not find the origin of this pollution, unless we ascend to the first parent of us all. . . . Thus it is certain that Adam was not only the progenitor, but as it were the root of mankind, and therefore that all the race were necessarily vitiated in his corruption." This is followed by a reference to St. Paul's Epistle to the Romans, 5:12, where Christ and Adam are compared. Generally no reference is made to Eve or to the woman. Calvin attributes the temptation not to Eve, but to Adam's "being seduced, therefore, by the blasphemies of the devil...."[2]

In his developed doctrine, however, Calvin is clear about the role of women. Like minors, they are basically to stay at home. There is also still a strong emphasis on procreation as primarily the continuation of the male lineage. Hence woman is justly punished more severely for adultery. Not only does the adulteress dishonor her husband (shouldn't it work the other way too?), but she also endangers the purity of his posterity. We can see here that the fear of miscegenation is not only racial. In all this, of course, there is at work the ancient biology that attributed all to the male semen and only incubation services to the female. However, there is also an inordinate male egoism at work, which would severely condemn the female participant in a possible confusion of off-spring but would regard the male only as the one deceived.

It is apparent that although Calvin may not have been as beholden to the Scholastic Middle Ages as Luther in regard to women, he was also not very emancipated. The Reformation did introduce one significant modification, the de-emphasis of virginity as *the* preferable life style of Christian women. This was accomplished by the absence of required celibacy for ministers and pastors in the Protestant Churches. Thus women not called to the ascetical life of virginity were enabled to enjoy some influence in their Christian communities. It also served as a disclaimer to that inevitable corollary of the virginal state of perfection, that only by "denying" her normal sexual nature could a woman achieve liberation and/or equal status with man.

However, in this movement away from the virginal and monastic there was also a reinforcement of the opinion that women were indeed meant for husband and home. So, again, it was not a matter of simply trading bondage for liberty. To enjoy greater mobility in one respect meant to give up the greater mobility and freedom of another possible way of life. Such an either-or was not absolutely necessary, but the factual disappearance of celibacy from Protestantism amounted to such a choice.

Although Luther himself did not give up devotion to Mary, Protestantism generally tended to lose Mary as an ideal and consequently as a motive of women's dignity, however inadequately this ideal might have been practiced. Likewise, Calvin emphasizes that "the visible Church (is our) *mother,* (and) how useful and even necessary it is for us to know her."[9] However, since the Church will lose more and more importance in Protestant theology, an analogy of the Church as Mother will also lose its effectiveness as a symbolic liberation of woman.

In general, then, we can say that the Protestant Reformation did not do much to elevate women's dignity and status in society. At least not immediately.

Later on, in the Anglo-Saxon Churches and in the movement known as Pietism, the liberationist text of Galatians 3:28 will be taken very seriously and practiced much more effectively. More than such usually credited causes as Rousseau and the Enlightenment, this particular brand of Christianity helped bring about a greater emancipation of women from second-class status in society. However, Protestantism in general, for all its lip service to the liberty of the Christian, accomplished little for the liberation of women, Christian or otherwise. Its understanding of women can hardly be said to surpass that of the immediately preceding Middle Ages.

The Enlightenment is most famous for its critical spirit. According to the slogan of its most famous spokesman, Immanuel Kant, its goal was to have every person dare to think for himself or herself. However, its own immediate philosophical background did not prepare it to deal with the relationship of the sexes and the dignity of woman. In the philosophy of Descartes a great distinction is made between the invisible thinking substance which is the mind and the extended visible substance of the body. One is tempted to say, "And ne'er the twain shall meet." Well, they do meet, but only barely. One can see immediately that this approach will not be conducive to a holistic or total approach to understanding the human being, whether male or female. As with the Reformers, a deficient general anthropology will make an adequate explanation of the sexual nature of mankind impossible.

What we shall in fact find in all of modern philosophy is basically a repetition of the ambivalent attitude of the ancient world toward woman. There will be a continuation of the anti-body philosophy of Plato as well as the sexism of the Mesopotamian fertility religions. Practically, however, it can all be reduced to the disillusionment man experiences when he demands too much from his sexual partner whom he has made into a goddess, whether explicitly in the ancient or implicitly in the modern world.

We cannot, of course, examine all these sages in detail. So, we shall limit ourselves to certain statements of theirs which have come to be invested with the power of aphorisms and proverbs. That means we shall consider those statements which have been regarded as decisive insights, with permanent historical significance. It will be important to keep in mind that the quotations come from those who are considered the finest minds and thinkers of their generations. They are the ones who are supposed to be able to think precisely and distinguish finely. They are also the ones who are supposed to know more than the rest of the population. Finally, their words both reflect what the human race has thought and is thinking and influence what it will think in the future. We shall see, however, that although they may be more complicated, they are not all that more liberated or advanced.

Males are apparently fascinated by what they perceive to be the verbal unreliability of the female. As Shakespeare said, "Who is't can read a woman? When my love swears that she is made of truth, I do believe her though I know she lies." Is this a long-term reaction to the first recorded message Eve gave to Adam?

Sir Philip Sidney maintains that "no is no negative in a woman's mouth." Of course, since girls have so often been taught that nice girls don't do *that,* they must say no even though they don't remove themselves from the situation in which they must say no. Such negative protestations in regard to sex are also necessary to preserve the male's self-concept as the aggressive hunter.

Some years ago on a train in Germany, I was able to read part of a novel over the shoulder of a fellow (male) passenger. A line caught my eye, as the whole book had obviously caught his attention. The praise of a female lover emphasized one specific perfection: *Man muss sie jedesmal erobern* —that is, "you have to conquer (make, overcome) her every time." Which brings to mind one of my liberated female university students: in her times of need, she was not reluctant to call up male students whom she had favored in their times of need. Needless to say, this took the bloom off the male's sexual experience, because the element of hunt and conquer was missing.

Throughout history there has existed a definite pattern of

marriage by seizure—that is, the marriage is accomplished by the male's abduction of the female. When this no longer happened as a fact, it was continued symbolically in various betrothal and marriage rituals. It is hardly mere coincidence that today the movement known a women's liberation should be accompanied by an increase in the incidence of male impotence, whether temporary or permanent. The traditional male roles as warrior and chief are not readily reconciled with the new role of a female who is also able to be aggressive. That women have not always been *basically* "aggressive," would be hard to maintain, especially since we now know how great the influence of social expectations and conditioning can be. We could therefore legitimately conclude with John Masefield that in a sense "women were liars since the world began." But we would hasten to add that they were placed in such a position by the sexist rules of the male-dominated society. Some sort of prevarication or dissimulation was the only means of survival available to them. Are we again faced with a case of the fact becoming the theory?

From the time of Eve on there has been the lingering suspicion that behind every good (and/or bad) man there is a woman. We have seen how this theme was utilized by the Church Fathers as they tried to excuse Adam and place all the blame on Eve; how they also explained the oppressed status of women in society as a consequence of Eve's sin. The Latin poet Juvenal was certainly carrying on this ancient tradition when he wrote that "there is hardly any activity at all in which woman does not play an initiating role." The same idea has received its classical form in a saying attributed to Alexander Dumas: *Cherchez la femme.* When anything untoward happens, one is counselled to "look for the woman." We had traditionally associated this with the situation of the male divorcing his older spouse for someone new and also with the male who suddenly and mysteriously disappeared. Such events could simply never have happened without the connivance of a female accomplice. After all, the male is ideally the Boy Scout, loyal, trustworthy, and true blue. Any inadequacies on his part must be explained on the basis of the eternal-temptress syndrome—from Eve until our very day.

In our own days this explanation has received a renewal and expansion in regard to those Catholic priests and bishops who have given up their active ministries. It is, of course, often true that the celibate minister has given up his active ministry for the love of————(fill in the blank). However, the idea that she would be more responsible than he is hard to take. Rather than an aggressive, man-eating female, the major agent in such clerical departures would clearly appear to be the moon-eyed and moping superannuated clerical teenager himself.[1] We do not use the same seduction explanation for nuns and sisters who have left the religious life to get married. The sexist nature of the *Cherchez la femme* explanation is clearly emphasized by the nearly total absence of a similar search for the conniving male who would theoretically be involved in the departure of these religious women.

Perhaps as an overcompensation for his insecurity, especially in regard to women, there has been a strong male tradition of deprecatory remarks about the equal humanity of women. Immanuel Kant, perhaps the most famous and influential of all modern philosophers, is famed for his philosophical objectivity. Nevertheless, he could write the following description of woman—its only objectivity would be that it adequately reflects his society's sexist prejudices: "Intellectually woman is the less gifted, morally women are inferior because they want men to pay homage to their charms. Man himself has taste, but woman makes herself an object of taste for another, it does not matter whom." It would be interesting to examine

---

these remarks psychoanalytically, as the expression of a personality who twice lost fiancées because he could not reach a final balance which would make matrimony more appealing than bachelorhood. However, Kant could also assert that "domestic relations are founded on marriage, and marriage is founded upon the natural reciprocity of the sexes. . . . For the same reasons the relationship of the married persons to each other is a relation of equality as regards the mutual possession of their persons, as well as their goods. Consequently marriage is only truly realized in monogamy." However, after such a clear and decisive statement of the equality of men and women, at least in marriage, Kant himself gives us one more example of the weight of the fact. That is, he gives in to the customs of his age as he defends the legal superiority of the husband:

> Hence the question may be raised as to whether it is not contrary to the equality of married persons when the law says in any way of the husband in relation to the wife, "he shall be thy master," so that he is represented as the one who commands, and she is the one who obeys. This, however, cannot be regarded as contrary to the natural equality of a human pair, if such legal supremacy is based only upon the natural superiority of the faculties of the husband compared with the wife, in the effectuation of the common interest of the household, and if the right to command is based merely upon this fact.[5]

It is not immediately apparent how "natural equality of a human pair" and "natural superiority of the faculties of the husband" are able to be reconciled. And Kant gives us no hints on how it is to be accomplished. In fact, his later discussion of active and passive citizenship and the power of suffrage supports the negative interpretation. Among those who enjoy only passive citizenship are the "apprentice, the minor, all women, and, generally, everyone who is compelled to maintain himself not according to his own industry, but as it is arranged by others . . . (they) are without civil personality, and their existence is only, as it were, incidentally included in the state."[6]

Kant maintains that this political inequality is "not inconsistent with the freedom and equality of the individuals *as men*. . . ." However, it is a strange human equality that leaves more than half of the human race in a perpetual state of immaturity as legal and political minors. Such a position is clearly no improvement on earlier cultures which also regarded the female as a perpetual minor, incapable of taking care of herself. For Kant woman is still the domestic creature. The same idea is also very influential in Hegel.

I have always found it interesting that the greatest idealist of all, G. W. F. Hegel, should have found time to become both a connoisseur of wine and the father of an illegitimate child by the daughter of his landlord. It is not a bad idea to keep in mind while reading the profound thoughts of profound philosophers. For all his efforts to overcome the divisions that plagued all previous history and thought, Hegel ends up unable to reconcile and mediate the differences which divide male and female. Although he wished to consummate the history of the world, he remained obliged to it. He did emphasize the necessity of the consent of both parties to be married. Matrimony's "objective source lies in the free consent of the persons, especially in their consent to make themselves one person, to renounce their natural and individual personality to this unity of one with the other. From this point of view, their union is a self-restriction, but in fact it is their liberation, because in it they attain their substantive self-consciousness."[7]

Such an approach to the union of marriage is at least implicitly a major support of the equality of women. Furthermore, Hegel insists that this freely contracted bond of marriage elevates it beyond the transience and fickleness of passion and sexual desire. The important dimension is thus seen to be not the sensuous but the ethical. In this assertion Hegel has clearly surpassed many of his forebears who explained marriage chiefly as a remedy for concupiscence and lust. Moreover, he finds the primacy of marriage in the ethical consent and union, not in sexual pleasure or procreation. Hegel insists on the necessity of monogamy and permanence in marriage, although he does not absolutely disallow divorce. In addition, "there can be no compulsion on people to marry."[8] This latter statement is also applied to people who are already married. However, only a third ethical authority can grant a divorce, and only then when "it is satisfied that the estrangement is total."[9] Given the facts of a history in which woman was subject to the whims of men, such a doctrine of marriage has to be regarded as liberating for women.

Hegel also makes a good beginning in his attempt to explain the differentiation and complementarity of the two sexes. "The difference in the physical characteristics of the two sexes has a rational basis and consequently acquires an intellectual and ethical significance." However, as he proceeds to elaborate on the difference, he falls victim to the traditional and then current sexual division of labor. "It follows that man has his actual substantive life in the state, in learning, and so forth, as well as in labor and struggle with the external world. . . . Woman, on the other hand, has her substantive destiny in the family, and to be imbued with family piety is her ethical frame of mind."[10] Not only is woman thus restricted to the family for her being and fulfillment. Later on she is also restricted within the family, which is founded by the "children (who) have been educated to freedom of personality. . . . The sons as heads of new families, the daughters as wives." It does seem, however, that this headship of the father was to be benign. Hegel continues, "They now have their substantive destiny in the new family."[11] This would certainly imply that both men and women "create" their being and identity together. Furthermore, he objects strenuously to the ancient Roman practice which gave absolute power to the father in family matters. As we have seen, this power extended to the sale and execution of other family members.

Nevertheless he was not able to free himself from traditional sexist explanations of the spheres of being and influence proper to each of the sexes:

> It must be noticed in connexion with sex-relations that a girl in surrendering her body loses her honour. With a man, however, the case is otherwise, because he has a field for ethical activity outside the family. A girl is destined in essence for the marriage tie and for that only; it is therefore demanded of her that her love shall take the form of marriage and that the different moments in love shall attain their true rational relation to each other.
>
> Women are capable of education, but they are not made for activities which demand a universal faculty such as the more advanced sciences, philosophy, and certain forms of artistic production. Woman may have happy ideas, taste, and elegance, but they cannot attain to the ideal. The difference between men and women is like that between animals and plants. Men correspond to animals, while women correspond to plants because their development is more placid and the principle that underlies it is the rather vague unity of feeling. When women hold the helm of government, the state is at once in jeopardy, because women regulate their actions not by the demands of universality but by arbitrary inclinations and opinions. Women are educated—who knows how?—as it were by breathing in ideas, by living rather than by acquiring knowledge. The status of manhood, on the other hand, is attained only by the stress of thought and much technical exertion.[12]

Hegel acknowledges his capitulation to the factual inequality of society in his meditations on world history:

> Against the existence of "classes" generally, an objection has been brought, especially in modern times, drawn from the consideration of the state in its "aspect" of abstract equity. But equality in civil life is something absolutely impossible; for individual distinctions of sex and age will always assert themselves; and even if an equal share in the government is accorded to all citizens, women and children are immediately passed by, and remain excluded. The distinction between poverty and riches, the influence of skill and talent, can be as little ignored—utterly refuting those abstract assertions.[13]

It is not that Hegel rejoices in or even approves of these distinctions—we could say "discriminations"; but since for him all history is the development of freedom, it is not easy to see how his distinction between the real and the abstract can permit their continuation to be tolerated.

I think the longer treatment given to Kant and Hegel is justified because they are so important in the history of philosophy. It is not without considerable value to see that such "great and objective minds" were not able to assert clearly and distinctly the real equality of men and women. It is also important to remember that Kant and Hegel are representatives of the Christian tradition. We may not agree with their explanations of Christianity, but they did intend their philosophies to explain and perfect the Christian understanding of God, man, and the world. Therefore they are not merely philosophers but also "Christian" thinkers. Furthermore, their writings are by and large not tainted by that misogynist rhetoric we have seen so often elsewhere. Consequently they are not so vulnerable to the suspicion that they write out of resentment and frustration born of disappointment with women—which brings us most fittingly to our next author.

It is not surprising that the fundamental pessimism of Arthur Schopenhauer should be reflected in his attitude toward women. One can also "wonder" about the experience of women which would prompt the following assessment:

> Woman is the *sexus sequior*. The veneration of woman is the perfect flowering of Germanic-Christian stupidity, which has led to only one result, to make women so arrogant and disrespectful that one is reminded at times of the sacred apes of Benares, which, knowing their own holiness and invulnerability, permitted themselves any and every excess. Only housewives and girls who want to become housewives should be allowed to exist.[14]

Women should not, however, feel that they have been unjustly singled out for Schopenhauer's disdain. His attitude toward the human race in general was not much different. When his lectures at the University of Berlin failed to outdraw Hegel's audience, Schopenhauer realized even more acutely how fundamentally stupid mankind is. So he withdrew even further from the society of humans to that of his more perceptive poodles, apparently a much more sympathetic audience.

The idea that woman is the later and secondary sex has, as we have seen, a long history. It has been taken up in our day and age. Simone de Beauvoir, the matriarch of current feminist movements, entitled her book on the status of women *The Second Sex*. Friedrich Nietzsche was also a proponent of this view. For him "woman was God's second mistake." Again there is evident that pessimism about the meaning and value of human existence in general. And again, as we have seen so often, a general negative approach to life always has more severe repercussions on the woman. Both Schopenhauer and Nietzsche continue the tradition that would restrict woman's essential being to the bedroom. Nietzsche is also the author of a sentence that could be regarded as typical of the sexist reaction of the male-dominated Christian officialdom to femine inquiries about the study of theology: "When a woman inclines to learning there is usually something wrong with her sex apparatus." I would not want to restrict this attitude to my fellow celibate Roman Catholics. Clearly the same mentality has been at work among both Protestants and the population at large. And the overwhelmingly male faculties of colleges cannot be regarded merely as ancient history.

The generally derogatory attitude toward women usually concentrates and expresses itself in an explicitly sexual declaration. Hence Napoleon quite bluntly stated that "women are nothing but machines for producing children." The legendary Gallic spirit is also obvious in the remarks of the so-called social liberationist Jean-Jacques Rousseau: "All the education of women ought to be in relation to men. Woman is made to give way to man and to put up with his injustices." That is, of course, the traditional pipedream of every red-blooded male. It is also a reasonably adequate description of women's de facto status in society. It very well reflects the tradition of the curse of Genesis 3:16 as well as the (pseudo-) Pauline injunctions that women be veiled and silent. The great French novelist Balzac reflects this whole tradition even more accurately: "The destiny and sole glory of women is to excite the heartbeat of man." "The married woman is a slave whom one ought to know how to put on a throne." Could there be a more apt summary of the status of women in ancient Mesopotamia or the present-day Chicago where Hugh Hefner's bunnies and playmates are cultivated? Such a throne is a very feeble foundation for a lifetime's living. A similar "Woman equals Hausfrau" is obviously the source of Disraeli's very undiplomatic contention that "every woman should marry, but no man." The practical difficulty of such a position cannot have escaped him, and for this reason the remark is all the more valuable. It is clearly the manifestation of that ancient as well as medieval mentality which regarded the male as being "essentially" more equal in the everyday business of living. In the abstract definition of humanity, male and female may be accorded equality. But as soon as this abstract world of essences is left, the equality is also left behind.

This mentality has had its practical application in the legal ability of a husband to sell his wife. Viola Klein reports the 1815 deed of sale of a married woman from a workhouse in Surrey, England. She also quotes Ralph Waldo Emerson's comment in 1856 that "the right of a husband to sell his wife has been retained down to our times."[15] The "absolute" lack of rights on the part of women which could permit such a state of affairs is illustrated by the complaint of a wife whose divorce by her husband spurred her into feminist liberation activity in the mid-1800s. She wrote in a letter to the Queen, in 1855: "A married woman in English law has no legal existence: her being is absorbed in that of her husband."[16] Such a policy does not require the sellability of the wife, but it does allow for it since it effectively deprives the married woman of a being of her own.

From England, too, comes the masculine sentiment: "I expect that woman will be the last thing civilized by man" (George Meredith). In this understanding, woman must be a replica of the male—or she should not be at all. Taking up the theme of woman as mistake or defect, I. A. R. Wylie asserted: "Next to the dinosaur woman is nature's most outstanding failure." Apart from the possible rhetorical extravagance of such statements, there remains the lasting impression of a basic disappointment in woman. She has simply not been able to satisfy man's expectations. And that may not be her fault at all. The root may be almost entirely his faulty expectations.

All of this leads us to the fundamental experience the male has in regard to the female, his general perplexedness. The old and famous saying is by no means entirely awry: "You can't live with them, and you can't live without them." This inability to get women into nice neat categories is incisively expressed by Jules Lemaitre: "Of women one may say whatever one likes; it will all be equally true." That the same statement could not be made of men can be assumed only with great difficulty. I also think that the "equally" is very important. More than any other in the above statement, this word emphasizes the male's puzzlement in regard to his sexually other partner. With his usual perception, Dr. Samuel Johnson noted: "Nature has given women so much power that the law has very wisely given them very little." Not only Dr. Johnson's wonder but also the wondrous resilience of women to have survived for centuries in a male-dominated universe is well expressed in this sentence. Women themselves have been impressed with this same insight, although George Sand may not be the most desirable witness for her sex: "Woman, O Woman, you are an abyss, a mystery, and he who believes he knows you is mad, thrice mad."

It is time to note again that the sexual differentiation of the human race is a particular instance of that more general problem of both philosophy and life—the problem of the one and the many. An entirely adequate understanding of being which is sexual and human is not possible without an understanding of being at all. In other words, we can give a good answer to the question, What is man and woman? only if we can give a good answer to the question, What is it all about? In the real history of the West and Christianity, the understanding of sexual humanity has focused on the woman. Mystics and poets who claim full understanding of being tend to be regarded as madmen. Hence George Sand's observation could be taken literally and not just as rhetorical exaggeration.

Perhaps the most "feminist" of all the modern philosophers was John Stuart Mill. His general interest in social philosophy and his "radical" approach to social problems make his interest in women's liberation quite logical. He helped found the first women's suffrage society in England. We take women's right to vote as a matter of fact, forgetting that in Europe they did not enjoy this right until 1918 in Germany and Great Britain, 1931 in Spain, 1944 and 1945 in France and Italy. Switzerland is still struggling with the problem. According to de Beauvoir, Mill made the first speech officially favoring women's suffrage in the English parliament. This was in 1867. Two years later he published a book entitled *The Subjection of Women.* (It is not out of place to note that this publication and the topic of women are generally absent from the standard histories of philosophy. In passing we can also note that the indexes of philosophy and history of philosophy textbooks generally contain no entry under "woman.") The *Subjection of Women* was written at the suggestion of his daughter:

> As ultimately published it was enriched with some important ideas of my daughter's, and passages of her writing. But in what was of my own composition, all that is most striking and profound belongs to my wife; coming from the fund of thought which had been made common to us both, by our innumerable conversations and discussions on a topic which filled so large a place in our minds.[17]

Mill's general passion for liberty logically embraced women and children. To urge liberty for them meant necessarily to oppose the vested interests of the male, especially as husband and father. A typical passage from Mill's writings illustrates this:

> The almost despotic power of husbands over wives need not be enlarged upon here, because nothing more is needed for the complete removal of the evil than that wives should have the same rights, and should receive the protection of law in the same manner, as all other persons; and because, on this subject, the defenders of established injustice do not avail themselves of the pleas of liberty, but stand forth openly as the champions of power.[18]

In a lengthy passage on the need for universal suffrage, Mill also points out the poor logic which allows women to be equal in humanity, but not, if we may so speak, in the practice of it:

> In the preceding argument for universal, but graduated suffrage, I have taken no account of difference of sex. I consider it to be as entirely irrelevant to political rights as difference in height or in the colour of the hair. All human beings have the same interest in good government; the welfare of all is alike affected by it, and they have equal need of a voice in it to secure their share of its benefits. If there be any difference, women require it more than men, since, being physically weaker, they are more dependent on law and society for protection. Mankind have long since abandoned the only premises which will support the conclusion that women ought not to have votes. No one now holds that women should be in personal servitude; that they should have no thought, wish, or occupation, but to be the domestic drudges of husbands, fathers, or brothers.[19]

The special value of this entire passage is that it illustrates that emancipation in one area does not automatically entail full liberation. Hence, although women were "allowed" to be single, businesswomen, and teachers, they were still not allowed to vote.

I have deemed it fitting to close this chapter on a more positive note. It is an interesting coincidence that the Great Books of the Western World included, in one volume, documents and writings about the American Revolution with its selections from John Stuart Mill. It is a reminder that freedom can only be for all. Abraham Lincoln remarked, "As I would not be a slave, so I would not be a master." And also, "The union cannot long endure half slave and half free." Unfortunately for women (and minority groups in general), action on this insight has been neither instantaneous nor universal. And it still isn't. We conclude our considerations of the past and begin our survey of the current scene with John Stuart Mill's insistence that the logic of liberty requires that all be free. A more fitting transition could not be found.

The immediate background of today's women's liberation scene is provided by two male philosophers who could have been included in the preceding chapter. They are Karl Marx and Sigmund Freud. Although some may wonder when I call them philosophers, I think that there is a sense in which this is the best description of their work. The philosopher is someone who tries to figure out what it is *all* about. That is, he tries to explain things on a very general basis. This is precisely how Marx and Freud occupied themselves. They are somewhat deficient philosophically because they tended to restrict the "all" they wanted to explain. Marx tended to reduce all of being to economics and politics; Freud, to reduce it to psychology and sociology. Their influence is most clearly reflected in a book some have called the bible of the women's lib movement in America, namely Kate Millet's *The*

10/ Women's Lib

Politics of Sex. The "politics," of course, comes from Marx, the "sex" from Freud.

These two authors also illustrate the immense importance of one's general philosophy and ideology in approaching the question of woman's dignity and status in society. As we have said repeatedly: one can only answer the question, What is man/woman? on the basis of one's answer to the more basic question, What is it all about? In the case of both Marx and Freud, the meaning of life is defined by the consideration that the human being must reckon with annihilation at death. The universe is basically a hostile environment in which man must scratch out some sort of existence in the few years allotted to him. Ultimately, then, all talk of liberation must have a hollow ring. Man is inexorably enslaved to death, a master (mistress) from whom there is no escape.

It is noteworthy that Marx's dilemma with regard to freedom should be expressed in an admiration for Prometheus, who stole fire from heaven and whom the gods chained to a rock for ever. "I shall never exchange my fetters for slavish servility," says Prometheus. "'Tis better to be chained to the rock than bound to the service of Zeus." And Marx comments: "Prometheus is the noblest of saints and martyrs in the calendar of philosophy."[1]

The Marxist approach to the liberation of women must be seen in terms of his understanding of alienation and private property. Alienation remains one of the most popular terms in contemporary religious and psycho-sociological literature. When contemporary authors write about the meaning of human existence, an important element in their discussion is always man's alienation or separation—from himself, nature, and mankind. Sometimes alienation from God is also included. The great difficulty with this term is its capacity for expansion. It can be applied—and is—to almost everything. In Marxist theory alienation and private property always go hand in hand. Hence alienation will logically cease when private property ceases.

The exploitation of women with respect to private property has been documented by a variety of books in recent years. A thoughtful reading of such literature, even as it involves the law of the twentieth century, will indicate that Marx's contention was not entirely off the mark. Woman has indeed been regarded as the property of the male, especially of her husband. Logically, then, according to Marx, she would be in a state of alienation; she would not "belong" to herself; she would lose her identity in being caught up with that of her husband. Logically, too, in this system, man and woman are alienated from each other. The whole of society is judged to be in a state of alienation, separation, and hostility.

Philosopher that he was, Marx described this state very well. But his remedies for this pathological condition share the same philosophical characteristics: they don't *do much.* Lenin was the revolutionary.

Marx's theory is also reflected in the theories of those famous ideological bedfellows, Jean Paul Sartre and Simone de Beauvoir. For both of them the concept of the "other" is negative. Sartre goes so far as to say, "Hell—that's the other (person)." And de Beauvoir emphasizes that the history of the West is the history of how the male has regarded the woman as the "other" one. She has been made into a object (objectified), inferior and subordinate to the male. In the index of her *The Second Sex* "woman as other" has twenty-seven listings—more than any other item. The significance of this concept is best summarized in the following passage:

> History has shown us that men have always kept in their hands all concrete powers; since the earliest days of the patriarchate they have thought best to keep women in a state

of dependence; their codes of law have been set up against her; and thus she has been definitely established as the Other. This arrangement suited the economic interests of the males; but it conformed also to their ontological and moral pretensions. Once the subject seeks to assert himself, the Other, who limits and denies him, is none the less a necessity to him: he attains himself only through that reality which he is not, which is something other than himself.[2]

I have emphasized this idea because it is an illustration from another source that the fundamental philosophical problem of the one and the many is very much at work in describing the relation of the male and female. I do not think that either Sartre or de Beauvoir offers much help in the way of a solution. In general their philosophy is unable to deal with the question of the one and the many, unity and diversity. Consequently they are ultimately impotent in solving the problem of sexual diversity and unity. They illustrate in a striking way that one's understanding of being in general determines how well or poorly one understands beings in particular. Furthermore, like Marx both Sartre and de Beauvoir are so limited in their understanding of being that they end up being only sociologists or psychologists. Thus they lose the perspective necessary for a final solution or understanding of the sexual being of the human being. In fact, if anyone were even minimally logical and took Sartre's general understanding of being seriously, he would voluntarily cease to be at all.

The influence of Marx on women's lib writers has generally been positive. He has provided them with the revolutionary motivation that they have nothing to lose but their chains. He has also provided them with certain ideas and categories which enable them to describe the plight of woman in past and present society. Almost alone among Marxist devotees they still urge his solution to the problem of alienation. In this view all reality can be reconciled, as Richard Schall puts it, by the positive elimination of all alienation, especially natural alienation. This meant that the so-called normalcies of nature had to be positively overcome in order to attest to man's identification of all being with himself. While Marxist movements themselves have ended up almost by accepting the validity of the original Aristotelian normalcies, the more radical contemporary philosophies are still enamoured of Marx's notion that the overcoming of natural sexual forms is the most positive and direct way to discover all being and transform man.[3]

This desexualization approach to the solution of sexism is unmistakably present in the women's lib movement. We shall return to the subject later on. Thus we can see that however impractical his theories might be, Marx has been the inspiration for many who want, in the words of Marx's eleventh thesis on Feuerbach, "not only to describe the world, but to change it."

The same cannot be said of Freud. He could be called an inspiration only if there is such a thing as negative inspiration. Perhaps no other writer so incites the hostility of women's libbers. For all his originality, there is a sense in which he was still committed to the idea that woman is a sort of defective male. As de Beauvoir points out:

> Freud never showed much concern with the destiny of woman; it is clear that he simply adapted his account from that of the destiny of man, with slight modifications. He admits that woman's sexuality is evolved as fully as man's; but he hardly studies it in particular. "The libido is constantly and regularly male in essence, whether it appears in man or in woman." He declines to regard the feminine libido as having its own original nature, and therefore it will necessarily seem to him like a complex deviation from the human libido in general.[4]

However, it is the "anatomy is destiny" approach to women that arouses greatest hostility. This remains the case even though Freud himself developed a highly complicated theory "of bisexuality, as though the individual were neither man nor woman, but both at the same time, only rather more the one than the other."[5] He cautions that psychological and anatomical explanations share the same ambiguity. The one, unfortunately, does not clarify, but only applies or reinforces the other.

Even in such an enlightened and emancipated writer we can still see how influential is the *fact* of society. This is so even though Freud himself is aware that "we must take care not to underestimate the influence of social conventions, which also force women into passive situations. The whole thing is still very obscure." He adds, "You are now prepared for the conclusion that psychology cannot solve the riddle of feminity."[6] It is interesting to note that the *female* is the riddle. This is but one more confirmation of a fundamental attitude. Although Freud wanted to "free" people from the superstitions and restrictions of the past, he ended up explaining them.

This is, of course, the great disadvantage of psychoanalysis. Much less a real therapy than a philosophical enterprise, it is utterly dependent on description of factual occurrences, as Freud himself confesses: "It is in harmony with the nature of psychoanalysis that it does not try to describe what women are—that would be a task which it could hardly perform—but it investigates the way in which women develop out of children with their bisexual disposition."[7] Here is an admission that although he will act like a philosopher, he will so narrow the scope of being that the world and humanity will be dwarfed. This is already a severe limitation of any possible liberation and freedom. Furthermore, in this statement we again see at work the temptation of the philosopher to confuse the fact to be explained with the theory explaining it. Woman's factual status in society is not only explained by

Freud, some even say he justifies it. One of his latest works, *New Introductory Lectures on Psycho-Analysis,* contains statements as misogynist as any we have seen thus far seen, among pagans or Christians, ancient or medieval.

In Freud's theory of human being, major roles are played by such concepts as libido, oedipus complex, and penis envy. In fact, each of these major categories is favorable to the male, indicating and reinforcing male superiority and preferability. Although, according to Freud, no sex can be assigned to libido (the basic energy of human life), "nevertheless the phrase *feminine libido* cannot be possibly justified. It is our impression that more violence is done to the libido when it is forced into service of the female function. . . . Nature has paid less careful attention to the demands of the female function than to those of masculinity." Consequently biology has endowed the male with the power to initiate the sexual encounter, while the female need only cooperate to some extent. Women are given to both vanity and modesty in order to "compensate for their original sexual inferiority." The choice of objects by girls is "according to the narcissistic ideal of the man whom the girl would have liked to be."[8]

Apparently Freud has not really gone beyond the ancient theory of Aristotle and the medieval theory of St. Thomas that woman is passive and therefore a deficient (defective) male. Perhaps this is not his motive, not what he wants. But it is what he *does.* Thus for Freud: "The only thing that brings a mother undiluted satisfaction is her relation to a son. . . . The mother can transfer to her son all the ambition which she has had to suppress in herself, and she can hope to get from him the satisfaction of all that has remained to her of her masculinity complex."

Freud also imitates his sexist forebears in that he extends the inferiority of the female from her "nature" to her ethics.

Thus "it must be admitted that women have little sense of justice, and this is no doubt connected with the preponderance of envy in their mental life." Furthermore, at the age of about thirty a man seems youthful and still full of promise, "but a woman of about the same age frequently staggers us by her psychological rigidity and unchangeability."[9]

Freud closes his chapter with a disclaimer. His presentation has been only fragmentary and applies to "women only in so far as their natures are determined by their sexual function."[10] Even Freud admits that human beings are not merely sexual. However, his protest is not very impressive when viewed against the description of feminine human being we have just examined. It is not unjust to regard Freud as one more member of that ancient and illustrious club of philosophers and theologians who started out to explain the bisexual nature of humanity but ended up justifying the sexist status of society.

Marx and Freud are not usually considered "Christian" authors. Nevertheless they deserve our attention here, for they both grew up in a "Christian society" and reacted negatively against it. Freud is especially important because he clearly shows that almost thirty centuries of Judeo-Christianity had not been able to establish clearly and universally the equality of men and women. Against this historical backdrop people wonder whether we have really made any progress at all. It would not do to assume that it is only in the machismo-dominated cultures of South America or the Mediterranean world that woman is still subject to second-class citizenship. Even in the United States in 1974 woman is still the weaker sex legally. As of this writing:

> In California the testimony of a woman who has been raped is insufficient and must be corroborated.
> In Ohio women are not permitted to work as bellhops, pin setters, public utility meter readers.

In Georgia women are prohibited from working in retail liquor stores.

In Alabama every married female applying for a driver's license must use her husband's surname.

In several states a husband can shoot his adulterous wife in a so-called "passion shooting" and the law will countenance it or look the other way, but a wife shooting her adulterous husband is charged with homicide.

Even more inequitable is the fact that the Social Security law awards a more generous package of benefits to a man who has worked his entire life than to a woman.[11]

Even the Christian Churches do not seem to be able to apply the principle of sexual equality across the board. Thus in 1974 the Episcopal Church has still declined to ordain women to the priesthood—the rebellious attempt of four Episcopal bishops in the Philadelphia area to ordain eleven women only serves to highlight that Church's general reluctance. In June of 1974 the Southern Baptist Convention "ordered (women) back to their kitchen, their nurseries, their pedestals, any place but the decision-making councils and positions of leadership in the Church." The reason for this is, of course, biblical. That is, it is God's will and revelation. In the words of Rev. Richard Jackson, "We must recognize that God has intended man to be the spiritual leader, both in the home and in the Church. And when they're willing to do that, the women will be glad of it."[12] And thus the convention rejected a proposal which requested that at least one-fifth of the total membership of official boards and agencies of the denomination should be women. They also tabled a resolution demanding equal pay and the elimination of discrimination against women in employment generally.

In Roman Catholicism women have only recently and reluctantly been allowed into the sanctuary, and then hardly in overwhelmingly significant roles. (Perhaps, however, we really shouldn't regard this as so insignificant, since as we earlier saw, in this century they were sometimes not even allowed in the choir.) In a later chapter we shall examine the possibility of women's ordination to the priesthood in more detail. But it is worthwhile noting here that highly placed Churchmen still argue against the ordination of women on the most esoteric grounds. One cardinal is fond of repeating, "If God had wanted women ordained, then he would certainly have had his divine Son Jesus ordain that perfect flower of womanhood, His Mother, Mary." I mention this here both as a caution and a consolation. A caution, because it clearly notifies us that it is not always prejudice against women which results in discrimination. Sometimes it is lack of theological thought. It is a consolation for exactly the same reason.

Against this secular and churchly background the contemporary women's liberation movement, in all its diversity, can be seen as a basically justified phenomenon. There is, of course, more than enough that is trivial and oppressive in this movement. But no movement is ever all pure. Furthermore, it is clear that one of the most severe effects of discrimination is the difficulty the discriminated-against have in being reasonable and objective about their condition and its improvement. A history of suppression and rejection is not exactly the best preparation for a measured, moderate, and realistic approach to a new order of justice and equality.

Certain critics among women's lib spokespersons take great delight in deploring the inane women who inhabit the world of television, especially in the advertisements. It is certainly true that by and large TV's portrait of woman is hardly inspiring. But, then, has anyone looked very closely at the portrait of the male? His whole being seems to be taken up in avoiding suicide while shaving; trying somehow to spice up his otherwise totally drab self, so that he might possibly catch the attention of a lady; having his entire day ruined because the coffee is no good. One could go on forever. Admittedly the heroes of night-time television are predominatly male, but so are the bad guys. Here, of course, television is faced with the problem of whether to mirror or to try to modify the society environing it. Since its chief concern is financial profit, the choice is hardly matter for agonizing.

There is, furthermore, the problem of woman as sex object. This objection is raised with regard to society in general, but especially television and movie entertainment, and perhaps even more especially advertising. I do think that the most unrelentingly sexist programs on television are, first of all, "Hee Haw" and secondly, that of the more sophisticated hill-billy, Dean Martin. In the language of the male on the prowl, those shows know what women are for. And they do seem to reflect Genesis 3:16 much more than even the various beauty pageants. However, in the long run I don't know of any thoughtful and busy person who pays that much attention to television, especially the commercials (except to wish that they were over).

Another triviality is the objection to the ending "man" to designate certain agents, like spokesman, fireman, etc. I know of no case where the accent is on the "man": the accent is on the action being performed. To substitute "woman" for "man" in such words won't accomplish much. Of course, it won't hurt much either. When one writes a letter to a company and uses the salutation "Dear Sir," who ever thinks a "Sir" is going to open and read it? It seems to me that such usage is clearly a stylization, not a sexist assertion of male domination. I wonder whether such efforts to de-sex words don't really end up restoring and re-emphasizing sexism in our contemporary society. I think the replacement of "man" with "person" (spokesperson) is really out of place. The word person is a precise attempt to emphasize the dignity of the human being. Its use to describe the agents of ordinary and everyday occupations is another case of inflation. And the inevitable consequence of inflation is devaluation, whether of money, words, or concepts. If one doesn't like "man" at the end of words, one shouldn't restore sexism by substituting "woman" or devalue important concepts by substituting "person." Try "ist" or "agent" or something, but don't abuse words which have much more important functions.[13]

An oppressive dimension within the women's lib movement is the call for abortion on demand. There is no doubt that pregnancy has been the male's ultimate weapon in the war between the sexes. To keep a woman barefooted and pregnant has been the classic way to keep a wife safe and secure within the confines of the home. I do think, however, that a movement dedicated to liberation cannot logically adopt a position of free and open abortion or abortion on demand.

A very general reason against such a program is simply that liberation and freedom demand a high degree of responsibility and discipline. Only the most naive think an open abortion policy is for the benefit of those few tragic pregnancies resulting from rape or incest. Open abortion is primarily for the irresponsible.[14]

Even more to the point for a movement which expressly wants to liberate the oppressed is the fact that abortion is a severe, in fact, an irremediable oppression. This is a denial of rights which cannot be redressed. And it is certainly inflicted upon the most defenseless of all human life. What is most disconcerting about the typical justification of abortion by certain women's libbers is their use of basically the same arguments used by men to justify the oppression of women—namely, that they just aren't (quite) human. "It's just a fetus" is no more compelling an argument than "It's just a woman." At least I hope it's not. The argument appears in various ways. The fetus is not human; it is not an independent life; it is not a person; it can't think; it can't take care of itself; it can't relate interpersonally—and on and on. But the foregoing pages should be a warning to us about these "arguments," since every one has been used previously to explain woman's place and to keep her there.

What is really at play here is the age-old strategy of using a third party to get one's revenge or freedom. Here the woman uses the unborn child to avenge herself on the male. In a way she is only being consistent. Since impregnation has traditionally been the male's ultimate weapon, to terminate and destroy the impregnation would be the woman's ultimate weapon. However, it ill behooves a liberationist to use the destruction of an innocent third party for either one's own liberation or the conquest of the opponent.

One important point has to be made about these elaborate liberationist justifications of abortion. Most women get an abortion for one simple reason: convenience. That is a straightforward, if not a completely acceptable, justification. It is left to the intellectuals of the women's liberation movement (and really concerned ministers of religion anxious to be "relevant," whether Judeo-Christian or Secular-Humanist) to spin the fantastic theories of abortion as liberation. Celebrities such as movie and sports stars also get into the act, but that can usually be chalked up to their general need for exhibitionism. What they all seem to forget, or conveniently ignore, is that the real oppressor against the woman is not the baby but the impregnating male. An abortion would be at best a pyrrhic victory. It can destroy the evidence of the male's victory, but cannot nullify it. I do not think the women's liberation movement serves itself well by using abortion as a tool or weapon in its battle against a sexist society dominated by males.

What such a broad pro-abortion position can really indicate is both an antihuman and antifeminist attitude. To treat abortion as a symptom of despair and rejection of the human in general is beyond the scope of this book. However, one need only examine the statements of the pro-abortionists to see that they are embarrassed by the fragile and unimpressive beginnings of human life. Thus the fetus is called merely a random mass of cells, merely a part of the woman's body, etc. All of these attempts to denigrate the fetus end up, of course, denigrating all of human existence. "In our beginning is our end" is, after all, much more than a pious platitude.

What is much more interesting for our purpose, however, is the antifeminism contained in the open-abortion mentality. During a lecture at the University of Evansville in the Spring of 1974, Dr. Kenneth Vaux of the Institute of Religion at the Texas Medical Center in Houston reported the following facts. Daily pregnant women come to the Center for a pregnancy test to determine the sex of the child they are carrying. Also daily, three or four women whose child is female apply for an abortion on that very ground alone. As Dr. Vaux notes, there has been no protest whatsoever from any women's liberation spokesman (I think in this case the only adequate ending is "man"). However, if there is a more intensely antifeminine and inhumane sexist practice than this. . . .

This antifeminism is also more generally discernible among women's lib authors. Their disaffection for the restricted status of women does not always seem to avoid extending itself to women themselves or to womanhood itself. While I was teaching at St. Louis University School of Divinity I assigned book reports on major women's lib books. The seminarians read basically de Beauvoir, Friedan, Millet, and Greer. A general impression given to these readers was that

---

the authors did not like women and did not enjoy being women. I would not expect this impression to be the last word, but I do think it is reliable. It is indicative of a serious problem among the most vocal advocates in the women's lib movement. The problem or disease that has no name may not be boredom with housewifery, as Betty Friedan asserts. It could easily be a discontent with being feminine at all—and ultimately, with being human.

This mentality can lead to two unacceptable expectations. One is flight from the wicked sexist world, withdrawal into oneself—a sort of sexist solipsism. This is illustrated in many of Helen Reddy's songs, whose fame increased when she accepted her Grammy with a statement, reminiscent of an earlier feminist's advice to a discouraged protégée, "Pray to God. She will help you." Ms. Reddy's songs tend to feature such lines as "Leave Me Alone" (repeated untold times), "No one bending over my shoulder, No one whispering in my ear," "You and me against the world," "Living in a world of make-believe."

However, much more destructive of bisexual human being is the unisex philosophy which has grown out of the protest against the exploitation of one sex in our sexist society and history. There is a tendency for some to advocate the elimination of bisexuality in order to eliminate sexual discrimination. Of this approach Kate Millet's *Sexual Politics* is a prime representative. However, as her latest book, *Flying,* clearly indicates, Ms. Millet's problems are much more profound and widespread than a sexist society. I am somewhat reluctant to make such a statement because there is a deplorable tendency to refute positions by rejecting people. However, I also think it is important to keep in mind that people's own peculiar personal problems often do rearrange their analysis and solution of social problems. Others have made similar observations in regard to Ms. Millet. One of her most incisive critics has been Irving Howe:

> I suspect, however, that what troubles Miss Millet is not merely the injustice of sexual discrimination but the very idea of sexual difference. For all that she is so passionate an advocate of the cause of women, she shows very little warmth of feeling toward actual women and very little awareness of their experience. Freud speaks in his essay on "Femininity" of the woman's "active pursuit of a passive function," and Miss Millet finds the phrase "somewhat paradoxical," thereby revealing a rather comic ignorance of essential experiences of her sex, such as the impulse toward the having of children. Indeed, the emotions of women toward children don't exactly form an overwhelming preoccupation in *Sexual Politics:* there are times when one feels the book was written by a female impersonator....[15]

In a way there is a confirmation of Freud's penis-envy theory in the theories of and persons of people like Kate Millet. If they can't have exactly what the male has, and has had, they don't want anything. Just in passing, we must note that not only some women's libbers are of such opinion. Famous male authors like Jean Genet and Henry Miller share the same approach. It probably has much more to do with the arrogance of the intellectual than with either sexual differentiation or discrimination. As Paul Valéry acutely observed, the egoism of the "thinker" has trouble tolerating the existence of anyone else at all.[16] This is a good point to keep in mind when reading women's lib literature, since the authors will tend to be "intellectual" in this pejorative sense.

Whether women's lib advocates want to be free and equal or whether they want to be male is not always clear. Certainly Betty Friedan appears more than willing to exchange one meaningless situation (according to her judgment, housewifery) for another equally meaningless one—the successful male, middle-executive mortgaged to suburbia and indentured to his corporation. Perhaps more than anyone else Ms. Friedan gives the impression that liberation means being able to be as aggressively competitive and commercial as any WASP robber baron. She also illustrates the typical middle-class woman's liberation ideal—to forsake the kitchen and nursery for a job. The job always seems to be in the executive boardroom of General Motors or Exxon. But how many jobs like that are there? It is difficult to see that she offers prospects of any real human or personal improvement. She seems to be a victim of the "grass is always greener on the other side of the fence" mentality.

In this context it can be noted that it has been said of Gloria Steinem that she has always envied men. Consequently, she has always tried to be like a man and be accepted like a man. Like Friedan, Steinem seems to accept as most desirable the prevailing cultural values. Thus business success is desirable above all else. It is the chief, if not the only, criterion by which a meaningful and fulfilled life is to be measured. Ms. Steinem also provides another instance of what I judge to be the antifeminism of some women's libbers. Although, as one of my seminarians pointed out, some libbers may be understandably upset by beautiful women, Steinem, as befits an ex-bunny, has to try to make herself unattractive. Now, I must admit that I have not been able to see Ms. Steinem all that frequently— a few television talk shows, photos in the papers and journals. What has impressed me is that she doesn't try all that hard. There are the glasses, the rather jejune coiffure, minimal cosmetics, and the sort of mourning clothing— indeed all that. But I still get the impression that she doesn't want us to forget that she did make is as perhaps the second most exalted sex symbol of our time— a Playboy bunny (I take it for granted that the Playboy playmate is the most exalted). It would be invidious to apply to

Ms. Steinem the argument used against St. Augustine in regard to the change he underwent between his "profligate" youth and his stringent later life, namely there is nothing worse than a reformed drunk, smoker, lecher, or sex symbol. So, we won't.

This same "unfeminine" antifeminism has been noted by Midge Dector.[17] She remarks that women's lib members try to make themselves unattractive. Hence they don't use cosmetics, they don't shave their legs, they don't wear bras. Ironically, according to Ms. Dector, many men found the braless state to be seductive. Hence, what was intended to be a means of repulsion and rejection became one of encouragement and invitation. Ms. Dector not only finds the movement anti-male and lesbian; she has also detected that more general hostility to women we noted above. "Members of the movement don't seem to believe there are many competent women." This judgment is perhaps a reflection of their own self-concepts. "Now members of the women's liberation movement have given them [women] a crutch so they can say that all women's problems are caused by men and society." She also finds in the movement in general that "irresponsibility" we noted in the abortion-on-demand position: "[Woman] has the right to be as unformed, as able to act without genuine consequences, as the little girl she imagines she once was, and longs to continue to be. . . . It is the response, not to the experience of exploitation, but to the discovery that to be in charge of oneself also requires the courage to recognize the extent of one's fragility and dependence on others." Hence Midge Dector would also find the movement not innocent of that solipsism noted earlier in regard to the songs of Helen Reddy.

I cite this criticism at length, not because it has to be the pure truth, but it points out that the desire to liberate can in fact enslave. As Jesus said, not everyone who says Lord, Lord will be saved. And not everyone who cries freedom, freedom really wants it either. The same syndrome can be seen in various minority groups, especially in the intellectual spokesmen. What always impressed me so favorably about Whitney Young, Junior, was that he could have made it in the system. Nevertheless, he chose to work for the liberation of minorities. In other words, he did not depend on his opposition to the system for his success and livelihood. His life was not a negative "being against." One certainly does not get the same impression from many spokesmen in the various liberation movements.

The same negativity occurs frequently, for example, among my brother (male) priests. They delight in bemoaning authoritarian, unfeeling, and generally benighted bishops. Whereupon they take a firm stand for liberty by proclaiming, "Whatever the Bishop wants me to do, wherever he wants me to go." In my own diocese a few years ago a really concerned priest summoned up sufficient rage to produce a manifesto entitled "The Priest as Nigger." Of course, that was the in-thing to say in those years. But it is difficult to imagine a more unniggerly existence than that of the Roman Catholic clergy, to be a member of which I delight in. Most of us are more like the dauphins of royal France than the "slaves" of the inner city. However that may be, it brings me to another point about freedom and responsibility. It does seem to me that of late priests have been more prone to moan about their lack of freedom than to enjoy and use the freedom they really do have. It is a combination of "the grass is greener elsewhere" mentality and the fear of risk and responsibility we have seen among women's libbers.

I intended this little detour on priests to illustrate a particular point: people in even privileged positions can perceive themselves to be oppressed. But even more so, people can overlook the advantages and opportunities they do enjoy in the present because they are so preoccupied with the conditions of the past. Thus, many women's libbers bemoan the life of the housewife as a slavery and drudgery which allow no opportunity for self-development and social involvement. They forget that we live in the 1970s A.D., not B.C. Technology has certainly made the workload of woman both as wife and mother different from what it was three generations ago. It might just be—I personally do not doubt it at all—that the homemaker has much more opportunity to be involved in meaningful and fulfilling activities—outside and inside the home—than the "working" woman.[18] That is, as long as one does not fall victim to the Friedanesque pipedream which assumes that every job outside the home is a vice-presidency. I do not wish to appear as an advocate of the old Hausfrau-equals-fulfillment school. The point I want to make is that today's Hausfrau, especially in the middle class, might just have the choice position in society. But she has to be perceptive enough to realize it and responsible enough to actualize it. Unfortunately, among the vocal women's lib advocates there is no trace of such awareness. Again, one really has to wonder whether they want to be economically and socially equal to the male, or whether they simply want to be male. Is Germaine Greer's passionate identification with all things male really typical? We can hope not. But how often does the vocal advocacy within the women's lib movement not seem to confirm Freud's contention that woman's basic characteristic, her nature, is to be envious of the male?

What this all indicates is that we must be very discriminating in regard to the women's liberation movement.[19] Simply to reject it would be to abandon it to the excessive influence of the forces we might find least acceptable. It would also be to lose a possibly valuable tool in the achievement of equality for men and women in all domains of public life. I say "possibly valuable" because there is obviously so much inane and unproductive posturing and prancing within the movement that will accomplish nothing—except the temporary emotional relief of the professionally enraged. However, in a movement as broad as women's libe there will be many effective programs in which our participation can help eliminate injustice and nurture a just social order. For all Christians this must be seen as a means of making always more real Paul's proclamation that in Christ all hostility and barriers and divisions have been overcome—especially between male and female. The women's lib movement, for all its freaks and foibles (if we Catholics can accept both error and sin within our holy Church,[20] certainly we can tolerate a less than immaculate women's liberation movement), offers a framework in which the goals proclaimed by Vatican II can be furthered:

> Since all men possess a rational soul and are created in God's likeness, since they have been redeemed by Christ, and enjoy the same divine calling and destiny, the basic equality of all must receive increasingly greater recognition.
> True, all men are not alike from the point of view of varying physical power and the diversity of intellectual and moral resources. Nevertheless, with respect to the fundamental rights of the person, every type of discrimination, whether social or cultural, whether based on sex, race, color, social condition, language, or religion, is to be overcome and eradicated as contrary to God's intent. For in truth it must still be regretted that fundamental personal rights are not yet being universally honored. Such is the case of a woman who is denied the right and freedom to choose a husband, to embrace a state of life, or to acquire an education or cultural benefits equal to those recognized for men.[21]

A fundamental contribution Catholics (and others, of course) can make to the liberation of women is to provide a more positive content to the liberation. Like other liberation movements, the women's is very eloquent about the *negative from which* they want to be freed. But they are not nearly as eloquent and precise about the *positive to/for which* they want to be freed. However, as Karl Rahner pointed out long ago, it is the "for what" of freedom that is all-important.[22] More recently the same point has been made by a *Newsweek* columnist, Anne Taylor Fleming, who asks, "Up From Slavery— To What?"[23] Here we must recall the Marxist dilemma we noted at the beginning of this chapter—Is Prometheus any "freer" when he is bound to the cliff as Zeus' prisoner than when he was bound to the god's service? We can say, then, that Catholics can provide a double service to any liberation movement, and hence to women's lib.

First of all, the long and rich history of the Church can be a caution that the millennium and golden age are not just around the corner. One's expectations must be reasonable. Otherwise the subsequent disillusion can evoke a worse state of slavery than that from which one has just been liberated. Second, the Church can try to emphasize the need for definite content in the new liberated state. As we have seen in other liberation movements, it is very easy to "burn this place down" —at least in oratory. But it is much more difficult to describe an effectively just social and economic order. Likewise, the goals of many women's libbers are frequently exceedingly vague. Goals such as equal pay for equal work, equal job opportunity, equality before the law are reasonable, definite, and attainable. But when one speaks of liberation from "the chains of my womanhood, of being free to celebrate the new me, free to escape the prisons and molds of the past, to experiment"—just what does that mean? Likewise, how far does woman's "right to privacy" actually extend? In the mouths of some advocates, this right is hardly distinguishable from the ancient Roman father's absolute power, his *patria potestas* which enabled him to do anything he wanted. When a woman is supposed to be able to do with her body what she wants, what is the difference between that statement and simple anarchy, or a sexism from the female instead of the male?

In conclusion we can say that the status of women in today's society still suffers from certain historical injustices. Against these injustices we must all strive. It is worthwhile, however, to recall once more the observation of Jesus: sometimes the condition subsequent to liberation from demonic forces can be worse than the prior state.

It is important that we keep constantly present in the world, and more specifically in the women's lib movement, the Judeo-Christian conviction that human being is male and female from the very beginning. And above all that this bisexuality is both the gift of God and the image of God. This does not mean that any particular cultural form of human bisexuality has to be preserved or canonized. It does mean that the negative relationship—the curse resulting from sinful conduct and described in Genesis 3:16—cannot be tolerated in any way. The goal Christians can propose for bisexual living is contained in their two most fundamental theological doctrines, the Trinity and the Incarnation. In these doctrines God has given his answer to the tormenting dilemma of the One and the Many, and what he has revealed of his own inner life is a mystery to enjoy. The trinitarian doctrine of three persons, each wholly possessing the one divine nature, yet distinct from each other owing to the relations among them—the Son is not the Father, nor is the Holy Spirit the Father or the Son—shows us that "many" does not necessarily mean hostility or strife, that "one" does not mean the suppression of distinction and monotony. Long before the current "dancing god" silliness of a Sam Keen, theology had described the being-in-one-another of the divine persons with the word perichoresis, which comes from the Greek word for "dance." The word is important because it suggests the joyful celebration which the exchanges of the divine persons within the Godhead resemble. The same word, perichoresis, is used in Christology to describe the perfect coming together of the divine and human in Jesus.

Not only is the divine being in itself such that we may venture to speak of God in terms of the dance, but his relationship with the world is so much an encounter of love between the One and the many that God and mankind can be thought of as dancing together. This understanding can be traced all the way back, a least in general, to the basis for St. Paul's doctrine that the marriage of husband and wife is both within and in the image of the union of Christ and the Church. Frequently the sexes have been described as "opposite," their relationship as the "war of the sexes." For Christians this is intolerable. The practical vocation of Christians, whether married or single, is to see to it that men and women live together not in war, but in a dance of joy and celebration. We should imagine how Adam and Eve must have leaped and danced when they first discovered each other, that they were bone of bone, flesh of flesh, that they were meant to be one flesh.

In the Christian tradition any discussion of the rights, humanity, and equality of women must face the question of the possibility of ordination to the priesthood. Just as I write the final version of this chapter, eleven women have been ordained to the priesthood in the Episcopal Church in Philadelphia. The television news account featured Charles V. Willie in an impassioned imitation of Martin Luther King's famous oration, "How long, O Lord . . . ?" It was applied to the problem of the personhood of women deprived of priestly ordination.[1] Even in an age accustomed to rhetorical overkill, that was too much. If women depend on ordination to the priesthood for certification or confirmation of their personhood, they are in bad trouble. In fact, one of the difficulties encountered in excluding women from the ordained priesthood has been the dignity of woman. That is, the theologians and

---

11/ Can Women Be Ordained Priests?

canonists have found it hard to exclude women because the woman Mary has been regarded as enjoying the greatest holiness and therefore the greatest dignity of *all* human beings, both men and women.

According to Professor Willie, exclusion of women from the priesthood was a form of "oppression" by which they were compelled to "remain on the periphery of full participation in the Church." Now that is nonsense. Full participation in the life of the Church in no wise depends on ordination to the priesthood, as the long list of unordained martyrs, confessors, virgins, and just plain old ordinary saints amply manifests. The purpose of priestly ordination is much more circumscribed and moderate. The more proper question, which the oratory of the preacher in Philadelphia missed, is whether the Church has had any good theological reasons to exclude women. That is what we want to consider here.

This question has become really urgent only in the last few years. It is not only the "traditional" and "high" Churches like the Roman and Anglican which have been reluctant in regard to the ordination of women. According to Elsie Gibson,[2] the first woman ordained—Antoinette Brown in the Congregationalist Church in 1853—was not ordained without great struggle. The Methodist Church granted women the local preachers license in 1919. Although Methodists allowed women to be ordained in 1924, they did not grant them equal rights of placement until 1956. Only then, as members of the Annual Conferences, did ordained women have access to the same security as ordained men. The first woman's ordination in the United Presbyterian Church, USA, took place in 1956. Lutherans ordain women in Scandinavian and Germanic countries. Since 1970 the Lutheran Church of America and the American Lutheran Church have ordained women. The Missouri Synod, however, still declines to ordain them.

This recent history marks some progress. However, it must be noted that to be ordained in a Congregationalist Church is not really very momentous, since in the theology and self-understanding of the Churches in the Congregationalist tradition, the ministry is of less than major importance. The same is true to a greater or lesser extent of the Methodist and Presbyterian Churches—in fact, even of those Lutheran Synods which do ordain women. But theologically women will have achieved this goal only when the Roman, Anglican, and Orthodox Churches ordain them. These are the "Catholic" Churches in which ancient traditions, both in doctrine and practice, are of great importance. Only when these Churches accept the ordination of women will the factual ordination of women be significant.

That is why the Philadelphia happening is not all that important. I don't think one need go as far as the *young* (that was an artful choice!) priest-spokesman who said, in response to the ordination of the women, that "the Church did not gain eleven priests today, it did lose three bishops!" However, anyone who is even vaguely acquainted with Church history knows that it is not all that difficult to find a few bishops who will do almost anything. The case in Philadelphia is not helped by the fact that the ordaining bishops were retired. It must be noted, of course, that (at the most recent National Assembly of the Episcopal Church in 1973) only a voting technicality made the Philadelphia situation possible at all. Possibly the Church will ultimately decide that this ordination was indeed valid, although illicit. Thus it seems that the Anglican Church may have come to the conclusion that women can be ordained to the priesthood.

What about the Roman Catholic Church? As recently as 1953 the most complete and up-to-date theology textbook covered the whole question in one page. Citing canon 968,

#1 of Church Law, it concluded that "woman is incapable of receiving the Sacrament of Holy Orders."[3] It judged this conclusion to be a doctrine that belonged to the "Catholic doctrine of the faith" insofar as the episcopate and priesthood were concerned, but only "certain" in regard to the diaconate. In this context "belonging to the Catholic doctrine of the faith" and "certain" are technical terms in theology. They are attempts to describe the degree of certainty any given doctrine or theological idea enjoys in the Church. According to Volume 1 in the same series, "Catholic Doctrine" means a "truth which is taught in the whole Church, but is nevertheless not always infallibly proposed." "Certain" means a "truth which is certainly acknowledged in theological schools as being necessarily connected with revealed (truths). This connection can be virtual or teleological or presuppositional."

In sum, this textbook would regard the exclusion of women from the priesthood as being almost absolutely necessary. The only reason the exclusion is not absolute is that no solemn magisterial definition by either the papacy or an ecumenical council has made it so. Special mention is made to exclude both deaconesses and abbesses from participating in the sacrament of holy orders. Their "ordinations" are at best sacramentals or blessings. As we shall see later, this entire exposition is ill-founded and quite unacceptable. It is a prime example of that sexist, biased reading of history that knows what the facts must be because it knows what the theory demands. The entire argument is based on 1 Corinthians 14:34-35 and 1 Timothy 2:11, as well as the fact that the Church's tradition has rejected the ordination of women, both by heretics and within the Church. As I have said, this entire subject occupies one page.

What is more surprising is the complete absence of the question in a four-volume summary of theology in the twentieth century, published in Germany and France in 1970. Neither in the section on the "Sacrament of Holy Orders" (III, 274-277) nor in the section on the "Family and Status of Woman" (I, 52-55) is the subject even mentioned.[4] Perhaps this absence serves to support Sister McGrath's contention that "affirmative action in this regard has been gathering momentum during the past five years in Europe and the United States."[5] The question we must now ask is whether this momentum is really going to take the action anyplace.

First of all we should examine the question whether a real, true, and factual equality of women with men can be maintained if only men are allowed to be ordained. Some have suggested that the example of St. Paul returning the slave, Onesimus, to his master, Philemon, is pertinent here. They maintain that this is an argument which at least allows, even if it does not demand, the exclusion of woman from the priesthood without thereby endangering her dignity. That is, just as Onesimus could continue as a slave to Philemon, his free master, but both would be equally Christian, so can women continue to be excluded from the priesthood but still be equally Christian. Or, if St. Paul can call Philemon and Onesimus "dear brothers, even blood brothers as well as brothers in the Lord" (v. 16), why can't men and women be brothers and sisters even if only the male can be ordained? The more theoretical background of this position is that true equality in dignity does not require egalitarian sameness in every function and position.

This is an artful argument, but it is hardly convincing. The point St. Paul makes is really that even a slave can share in the grace of the reign and kingdom of God proclaimed by Jesus Christ. It in no way states that slavery is good or acceptable or that slaves should continue to be slaves. That this was not immediately and explicitly clear to the early

Church does not mean it is not true. We must again recall that Christianity is not revolutionary. It is able to give new meaning to older realities by asserting that sovereign reign belongs to God alone. That is, human realities, however old, traditional, and powerful are not able to nullify the rule of God. However, that must not necessarily be taken as an approval or encouragement of these older realities. How could one argue that the new reality expressed in Galatians 3:28, "neither male nor female, slave nor free," should not find any factual expression in society? Admittedly this condition, in all its simplicity and purity, belongs to the eschatological state. But this "present evil world is passing away." We pray every day that God's kingdom come. How could the Church, then, simply restrict St. Paul's words to the other world?

As we also have seen, the early Church's expectation that the world would soon end gives it a particular approach to the realities of the world. This approach need be taken neither as a paradigm for later generations nor as a perpetual mark or quality of the Church. We must also keep in mind that Jesus treated no one as a slave. As we have seen in earlier chapters, his treatment of women was astonishingly egalitarian. Finally, Jesus preached frequently and urgently against "lording" it over one another—that is a pagan practice. Hence no Christian can legitimately use the slave-master relationship to justify or perpetuate any idea or practice.

Some argue against the ordination of women on the grounds that women don't have to be just like men in every consideration in order to be equal. That is certainly true. But that does not prove that women cannot or should not be ordained. To my knowledge no one has proved that women's ordination would make them identical to men. Thank heavens.

On the other hand, a reason is frequently advanced in favor of the ordination of women that is equally off the mark. Some, like G. Tavard and L. Swidler, advocate the ordination of women, at least partially, in the hope of a "Second Spring of the Church":

> Then in ringing terms Tavard states what I have also thought and written for years—namely, that to apply the feminist revolution to the church renewal would tap the greatest potential resource of energy and launch the most profound and widespread renewal of the church possible: the liturgical reforms, the canonical adjustments, the institutional updating that have taken place in the last few years . . . will be looked upon as elementary in comparison with the infinitely more thorough self-reform implied in the accession of women to the full freedom which they should enjoy in the church.[6]

I am sure that such sentiments endear Mr. Swidler to Mrs. Swidler. I don't know to whom they might endear Father Tavard. Perhaps in his case they can best be attributed to a certain Gallic fervor. In any case, throughout our long history we have often been promised a renewed and flourishing Church or society as soon as some reform or other has taken place. After the horrid cancer of slavery had been abolished, a golden age of brotherhood was to ensue. And what did we get? After women would finally have gotten the vote, the evils of male sexist politics were to have been eliminated. And what did we get? After the antisexual tabus of Victorian prudery had been removed, we were to return to the delights of the innocents in the garden of paradise. And what did we get? Has anybody checked the incidence of venereal disease, prostitution, illegitimacy, and abortion lately? After we would have elected more women to governmental office, we would experience a decrease in assertive, aggressive, and power-wielding public officials. Has anybody watched Bella Abzug lately? And after the reforms of the Second Vatican Council, what a flourishing of the Christian life and Church there was to be—worship, spirituality, priestly ministry, ecumenism, social justice, etc.!

And what do we have? Still a pilgrim Church, still a sinful and holy Church.

On these grounds I simply cannot buy the expectations of Tavard. I do not mean to adopt the professional pessimist's gloom-and-doom attitude. Certainly every one of the reforms mentioned above has been desirable, and has been productive of good results for individuals and society, especially for the formerly oppressed groups. But the reform of any society, unfortunately perhaps but nevertheless, proceeds in such giant steps only in the minds and books of reformers. The real world has been much more recalcitrant. The real Church, as we have seen, is too often too much like the world it wants to redeem rather than the redemption it wants to proclaim. No, a new golden age of the Church is not a legitimate reason for the ordination of women, especially since neither Jesus himself nor the Apostolic Church was able to bring into existence such a golden age, three verses from the Acts of the Apostles notwithstanding. Nor is the hope of a Second Springtime of the Church a reason. As we saw in *Hermas,* the Church is a very, very old woman. She has endured and will endure without the undue romanticism of the wishful dreamers in her bosom.

There is only one legitimate reason for the ordination of women—the absence of any compelling theological and ecclesial reasons against it. Here we can leave out of account all the so-called psychological and sociological questions of whether the "people" are ready for it. If such ordination is theologically tenable, then the only possible course of action is to prepare the people. If it is not, then one needn't worry about it. I also want to state quite clearly that I am fully aware that the people are often much less unready than the pastors (at whatever level of the hierarchy).

Our investigation must, then, turn to the history of the Church to see whether the fact that women have indeed not been ordained means that their ordination is impossible.

The fact is very striking: they have *not* been ordained to the priesthood, apparently not a single one.[7] Almost equally impressive is the general stand taken by the teaching authorities of the Church: they seem to have closed ranks against women's being ordained to the priesthood. However, it is noteworthy that whereas there is no solemn declaration or definition to this effect on the part of the extraordinary magisterium of the Church, local synods, councils and ordinary papal pronouncements offer an abundance of testimony against the ordination of women.[8]

In the earliest history of the Church, that is, until the Council of Nicaea (325), a distinction was made between women who were deaconesses and widows and men who were deacons. Since the women were not entrusted with liturgical functions they were not ordained, they did not receive the imposition of hands. Explicit note was made of the fact that they did not present the offering, as the deacon does. According to Hippolytus, ordination through the imposition of hands was restricted to the clergy who participate in the liturgical service. The nineteenth canon of the Council of Nicaea states that deaconesses do not receive the imposition of hands and hence are to be reckoned among the laity. These stipulations are important, especially for later considerations, because they indicate an understanding of holy orders which is essentially liturgical or sacramental.

Later on, however, deaconesses as well as male clerics were ordained. According to the *Apostolic Constitutions,* women were ordained like male deacons, by episcopal imposition of hands and prayers. In canon 15, the Council of Chalcedon (451) also speaks of a formal ordination of the deaconesses. The Emperor Justinian I (527-565) numbered deaconesses among the clerics. Nevertheless, no hierarchical functions were attributed to the deaconesses. They did not bless, nor did they perform the normal duties of the priest or deacon. Their service was basically that of porter and anointing of women in baptism.

As Peter Lombard indicated, the Scholastic era generally regarded baptism and maleness as the presuppositions for ordination. Interestingly enough, theologians of early Scholasticism were willing to accept as valid the ordination of baptized male children even if they were only one day old. This is interesting because, as we shall see later, a frequent argument against the ordination of women has been that they are congenitally immature. We have already seen that the tendency to regard women as perpetual minors is very old. This viewpoint was very influential in restricting women from public office in both civil and ecclesial society.

In the theology of high and late Scholasticism the general opinion was that only males could be ordained. However, Johannes Teutonicus admitted that some theologians did maintain that every baptized person can be ordained. St. Bonaventure says that the general opinion is that women may not be ordained legitimately. However, he continues, there is some doubt whether they cannot be validly ordained. His own view, which he considers to be in accord with the safer and better informed opinion of the scholars, is that women cannot be ordained. St. Thomas' position we shall examine later, in greater detail. Let it suffice here to note that he regards women as incapable of ordination.

An interesting position is taken by John Duns Scotus. He traces the incapacity of women for ordination all the way back to the will of Christ. His reason: the Church could otherwise never have deprived women of an office to which they were entitled, and which could negatively affect the salvation of both the women themselves and other people. Thus St. Paul's prohibition in 1 Timothy 2:12 is not merely his own private opinion. It is based on an ordinance of Christ himself. Among his supporting arguments, Scotus cites a traditional one, namely, that Christ did not ordain his mother, Mary, who surpasses all other women in holiness. Likewise, he notes, nature supports the Church's position in that at least after the Fall woman is subject to man. Genesis 3:16 again!

Since the Council of Trent all theologians have maintained that the recipient of holy orders must be male, and that this requirement is of divine origin, not a matter of ecclesiastical or human law. The Church does not have the power to dispense from this requirement. Hence, any attempted ordination of woman would be invalid, null and void from the very beginning. H. Tournely emphasizes explicitly that the exclusion of women from holy orders is a positive divine ordinance, one which is, however, in keeping with the feminine nature of women. In this post-Tridentine era the exclusion of women from the priesthood proper is extended to the so-called minor orders, which are not sacramental. Although some few oppose this exclusion, the general opinion of the theologians affirms it. The admission of male children to ordination is generally declared valid, although some theologians, following Saints Thomas and Bonaventure, make an exception for the episcopacy. The basis for this exclusion is that the bishop is primarily an overseer, someone with jurisdiction. Such an ordination must be deliberately chosen to be valid.

This brief history[9] indicates the state of the question at the time of the Second Vatican Council. The documents of this council contain no clarion call for change. In fact, the problem is not even explicitly mentioned. However, some Council Fathers did speak on the topic of the role of women in the

Church. One of the most forceful statements came from Archbishop Paul J. Hallinan of Atlanta, Georgia. He said that "the Church has been slow in denouncing the degradation of women in slavery and in claiming for them the right of suffrage and economic equality . . . women in many places and in many respects still bear the marks of inequality."

He also made the following proposals, which are perhaps more striking because of what they don't say than because of what they do say:

> That the Church define the liturgical functions of women so that they could serve as lectors and acolytes, and, when properly prepared, also, as they once did, in the apostolic office of deaconess. They could thus, as deacons do, administer certain sacraments.
>
> That the schema should include them in the instruments to be set after the Council to further the lay apostolate.
>
> That women religious should have representation in those matters which concern their interest, especially in the present and post-conciliar agencies.
>
> That every opportunity should be given to women, both as Sisters and as lay women, to offer their special talents to the ministry of the Church. Mention should also be made of women who are not married. Because of the universal call to women (in *De Ecclesia*), they also promote family values by witnessing in their own way to this universal vocation.[10]

What they don't say, of course, is that women can be ordained to the priesthood.

At the conclusion of this council Pope Paul issued closing messages to various groups of people. To women he said:

> And now it is to you that we address ourselves, women of all states—girls, wives, mothers, and widows, to you also, consecrated virgins and women living alone—you constitute half of the immense human family. As you know, the Church is proud to have glorified and liberated woman, and in the course of the centuries, in diversity of characters, to have brought into relief her basic equality with man. But the

hour is coming, in fact has come, when the vocation of woman is being achieved in its fullness, the hour in which woman acquires in the world an influence, an effect, and a power never hitherto achieved.[11]

The question forces itself upon us. Can the Church be said to have liberated and glorified women if it universally excludes them from the public and official ministry of the Church? Furthermore, will the achieved fullness of woman's vocation include ordination to the priesthood?

Already in 1945 and again in 1956 Pope Pius XII had dramatically described the changed social status of woman and her expanded opportunities:

> As children of God, man and woman have a dignity in which they are absolutely equal; and they are equal, too, in regard to the supreme end of human life, which is everlasting union with God in the happiness of heaven.
> ...there is no field of human activity which must remain closed to woman; her horizons reach out to the regions of science, politics, labor, the arts, sports; but always in subordination to the primary functions which have been fixed for her by nature itself.[12]

Now the question has become even more urgent. Does the universal exclusion of women from the priesthood in the past mean that there is a "field of human activity which must remain closed to women"? Is there a "subordination to the primary functions . . . by nature itself" which would exclude her from holy orders?

Pope John's voice can also be reckoned among those who at least call for a re-examination of the ordination of women. In his 1963 Encylical *Pacem in Terris* he noted that women were leaving a de facto state of subjection:

> Since women are becoming ever more conscious of their human dignity, they will not tolerate being treated as mere

material instruments, but demand rights befitting a human person both in domestic and in public life.

Thus in very many human beings the inferiority complex which endured for hundreds and thousands of years in disappearing, while in others there is an attenuation and gradual fading of the corresponding superiority complex which had its roots in social-economic privileges, sex, or political standing.

More important, however, is a sentence which comes very early in that encyclical:

> Human beings have the right to choose freely the state of life which they prefer, and therefore the right to set up a family, with equal rights and duties for man and woman, and also the right to follow a vocation to the priesthood or the religious life.[13]

The crucial question, then, is whether the "right to follow a vocation to the priesthood" extends to all "human beings" and then whether these "human beings (who) have the right to choose freely the state of life which they prefer" includes women as well as men?

At first glance one might feel overwhelmed by the negative evidence against an affirmative answer to this question. It could easily seem that woman has been excluded in all times and places, by all authorities. However, as we have seen, theology itself has never been content to recite the facts. It has always sought the reasons for the facts. And so it must seek today. The primary question is not only whether women have been denied access to holy orders, but also why. And that is the question we must now answer. We shall restrict ourselves to the theological or doctrinal reasons.

As we have seen already, a frequent argument is that Jesus did not ordain Mary. This argument can be found at least as early as Epiphanius of Salamis (315-403):

> If God had wanted women to be priests or occupy any other

office in the Church, then Mary would certainly have had to have been a priest.... But he did not want it. She was not even commissioned to baptize. Otherwise Jesus would have done better to be baptized by her than by John (the Baptist.)[14]

Many theologians maintain that consequently no woman can ever be ordained. However, just because Mary did or did not do something can hardly be normative for the rest of the Church's history. Mary did not do many things which the Church allows and even calls upon women to do. As we have seen, at the time of Mary there were many reasons against a woman's being ordained to the priesthood. But the most important refutation of this argument is that it clearly misapprehends the nature of priesthood and holy orders. That Mary is the holiest of all Christians is no adequate reason for her to be ordained. The priesthood, or holy orders, is neither a guarantee nor a sign of personal holiness. Nor is it a reward or honor from God. It is a particular vocation within the whole body of the Church. It is hard to figure out why anyone would even want Mary to be ordained. She had certainly done her part already. Besides, it was not Jesus who "ordained priests" in the early Church, it was at best Peter and his associates acting with the authority Jesus conferred on them. The argument that Jesus ordained the apostles to be priests at the Last Supper is simply not tenable. Such an argument confuses many different offices and gifts in the early Church. It is based on both a reading of Scripture and a theory of holy orders which do not, in my opinion, conform to either the historical or the theological realities and data. Finally, if those theologians who use Mary as the model or paradigm are going to be logical and consistent, they should argue in the following manner: If Mary, who is holiest of all, was not ordained priest, then no one should be ordained priest. Otherwise they can only invoke Mary's womanhood as the reason she was not ordained. In point of fact, that is the only reason ever given.[15] But the question is precisely whether *women* can be ordained; or negatively, whether there is anything essential about woman which would make her incapable of holy orders.

A second, and very frequent, reason is that God is male. Therefore the priest, as his representative, must also be male. The origin of this argument, which we have already touched upon above, is in the reference to God as Father and in terms of the subsequent use of masculine pronouns to refer to God in Sacred Scripture and elsewhere. We shall consider the theological question of God the Father in detail in the next chapter. So it can suffice now to emphasize that for the Judeo-Christian tradition God's being has always been thought of as superior to man's being. In fact, God is basically indescribable, he is beyond all human categories. This is basically the meaning of the assertion that God is invisible. The attribution of either or both sexes to God in a direct and univocal way is clearly and completely unacceptable. In fact, it can be argued, as we have seen, that one of the Hebrew's greatest efforts was to avoid the Mesopotamian sexualization of God. What Genesis wants us to understand is that bisexuality is a gift which comes from God, not a punishment, not a trick, not a divinity itself. The ability to procreate which is provided by this bisexuality enables man to be the image and likeness of the God who creates. Since this human being as God's image is both male and female, God cannot be designated as male in opposition to female. Hence an exclusively male priesthood cannot be based on the concept of an exclusively male God.

A third argument is similar to the preceding. Since Christ was male, the Christian priest, as his sacramental image, must be male. Even a theologian as wide-ranging in his thought as

St. Bonaventure used this argument. The difficulty with it is, however, Why limit such a restriction of women to the sacrament of holy orders? Some theologians have maintained that women cannot validly baptize, though they will, most oddly, allow unbaptized males to baptize. Strange indeed! But the basic point here is that women are called to hear the word, to receive the Holy Spirit, to bear witness, to live as virgins, resist temptation, suffer persecution, endure martyrdom, receive the sacraments. We know that they have been teachers, even and already with St. Paul. We know that they have been ordained as deaconesses, indeed in a rite identical to that of the deacons. The question then arises, if they are so generally able to be *alter Christus,* why must they be excluded from participation in the sacrament of holy orders? The only reason advanced, once again, is that they are female and Christ was male. But why can they do all those other "male" Christian things—and not precisely this one?

In connection with the above, a fourth and similar argument is advanced. The Church is our Mother, the baptismal fount is her womb. Thus the priest as the minister of the sacrament must be male. Here, again, is a case of an exaggerated and one-sided sexual symbolism. Proponents of this argument do not seem dismayed by the presence of males in the *mother* Church. But whoever heard of a mother who was about half male? No puns please. In any case, the adequate father or spouse for the mother Church would be Jesus, not the individual priest. At best, this argument reverts to the prior one about Jesus the Priest who is male. At best that is one of the worst arguments in favor of the exclusion of women from the priesthood. Also implicit in this argument is the understanding of the priest as primarily a sacramental agent or minister. This way of thinking about the priest is not wrong, but it is by far not the only way. And it is also not the best.

The celebration of the Eucharist is indeed the greatest function of the priest. But only because it is the greatest act of the priestly people and Body of Christ. This does not, however, require that the sacrament of holy orders or the ordained ministry of the Church be explained primarily in terms of sacramental power or function.

In connection with this argument we can mention two more sub-arguments. They are really variations on all the above themes.

One argument claims that the male is the generator of life. Thus the priest, as the agent of God, who is the prime giver of life, must be male. The application is then made to the Church insofar as it is the sacrament of Christian life in general, and then to the seven sacraments as the channels of divine life.

Almost nothing is right with this argument. First of all, the male is not alone the generator of life. Only an unreconstructed ancient and medieval biology could maintain this viewpoint. Today we know that the man and woman are equally necessary for the "generation" of human life. In any case, this view also entirely omits or forgets that God is trinity, so that man can at best reflect in some quite inadequate way the life-giving power and being of God. Furthermore, once again: God is not male in distinction to female. According to Genesis 1:27 it is only the male and female together who reflect the divine nature in creation. Finally, it is not the male as such who is the minister of the sacraments; it is the baptized member of the Church. Whether beyond baptism there is also a sexual stipulation for the ministry of the sacraments is precisely the question we are considering.

At this point the theology of the bridegroom of the Church can be broached. Traditionally the priest, more precisely the bishop, has been described as the bridegroom of the Christian community, especially the diocese. It is indeed true that the Church is described as a bride. But the bridegroom is Christ. However, the proponents of this argument urge that this fact, namely that Christ is the Church's bridegroom, should be included in the sacramental representation provided by the priest. Hence, since Christ is male, the priest thus representing him must also be male. Implicit in this position, however, is the assumption that the maleness of Christ is a principal element in his role as mediator and savior. That has never been proven and, of course, cannot be.

Apart from this, one cannot press the image of the bishop as bridegroom of the diocese too far. Bishops very readily move from diocese to diocese. But, if the image of bridegroom is to be insisted on in a univocal way, then this practice would be not only reprehensible (as some sort of ecclesial adultery), it would be impossible.

Here as elsewhere an obvious symbolic characterization must be taken for the affirmative and positive insights it gives us. It must not, however, be made into an exclusive explanation. Furthermore, it must always be insisted that all ministers in the Church, even the sacramental ones, only represent and manifest Christ insofar as they can. Thus they need in no wise be the totally and exclusively adequate re-presentation of Christ. In fact, they cannot, fortunately for them and all of us.

Finally, it must also be recalled that Jesus describes his love for mankind not only in male metaphors but also in female, as when he uses the image of the mother hen (Matthew 23:37). If the people who urge the bridegroom argument in favor of a male priesthood are going to be consistent, they should also urge a female priesthood on the basis of the Jesus' hen simile. Furthermore, those who argue that women are essentially receptive and therefore are not suited for the priesthood, which is essentially an active and presiding office, must contend with Jesus' own self-concept as the one who is totally and unreservedly receptive to the Father. In any of the typologies of male and female characteristics this degree of receptivity (passivity, even subjection) could only indicate a fundamentally feminine dimension in Jesus' person.

It is clear, however, that what is the basis of all these arguments, at least implicitly, is the understanding that woman's inferior status of subjection makes her incapable of representing Christ and God, who are thought of as male. However, we know that God is not male, and that Christ's sex was not essential or primary in his role as mediator and redeemer.

We shall now examine the other member of this argument, the presumed status of subjection in which women exist.

The most important exclusionary reason in the history of theology has been the subordinate status of woman. Technically woman is described as being in *statu subjectionis,* in a state or condition of subjection (to man). That is, her status in society is inferior and subordinate to the status of the male. She may be equal to man in regard to the individual soul; she may also be equal to man in the sight of God. But in the society of human beings she is not equal. She occupies a lower position. Christianity did, indeed, modify this viewpoint which it received from its forebears. But it was not able to overcome it purely and simply.

Since the priest-bishop is the leader (official) of the Church, and since women are in a subordinate and secondary state of subjection, they cannot be considered capable of being ordained to the priesthood. It is important to note immediately that the argument is not about women's suitability—whether they are apt, fitting, suitable, good-risk candidates. No, they are judged and declared simply *incapable.*

At this point we must recall the whole historical investigation we made earlier in the book. The consequences of all this for woman in the Church are not difficult to draw. How can an inferior be a superior, how can a subject be a presider? In a word, how can a woman be a presbyter, an overseer? These terms for office in the Church clearly indicate some sort of pre-eminence in the society of the Church.

St. Thomas asks explicitly whether the feminine sex impedes the reception of holy orders.[16] In accord with his customary method, he starts with three arguments which support the opposing answer. He then invokes an authority to oppose those affirmative reasons. Of course, his chief authority is 1 Timothy 2:12—women may neither teach in church nor tell men what to do. He also refers to 1 Corinthians 11:6 which requires a woman either to wear a veil or have her head shaved. St. Thomas obviously does not consider this last argument to be decisive or even very important. I have cited it here, however, because its presence in St. Thomas' argument indicates the general tendency.

St. Thomas argues that women are excluded from the valid reception of holy orders. Hence even though everything else be done correctly, the attempted ordination of a woman would be null and void precisely because the presumed recipient was a woman and therefore incapable of receiving this sacrament. Again we should emphasize that this has nothing to do with the candidate's suitability, holiness, or intention or with the minister's power or jurisdiction. Just as one cannot baptize a rock or a poodle, so one cannot ordain a woman. Why?

> Every sacrament is a sign. Consequently every sacrament requires not only the thing itself, that is, the grace conferred in the sacrament, but also a sign of the thing (the particular grace). For example, the sacrament of extreme unction requires a sick person so that the need for healing be signified. No pre-eminence of position or status can be signified in the

feminine sex since woman has (is in) a state of subjection. Therefore she cannot receive the sacrament of Holy Orders.

St. Thomas then proceeds to refute the affirmative reasons he had cited at the beginning of the article. The first is based on the Old Testament (2 Kings 22:14): women were prophets, and the prophet is superior to the priest. Hence there is no reason to prevent the ordination of women. St. Thomas does not treat the matter of superiority, he distinguishes prophecy and priesthood:

> Prophecy is not a sacrament although it is a gift of God. Hence prophecy does not require a *sign*ification of grace, but only the grace itself. And since woman does not differ from man in what pertains to the soul as such—in fact, sometimes a woman is better than many men in the things of the soul— therefore a woman can receive the gift of prophecy and other such gifts. But she cannot receive the sacrament of Holy Orders.

St. Thomas then concludes his argument with a reference to Deborah, who was a judge in the Old Testament. Of her he says that "Deborah was an official in temporal things, not in sacerdotal concerns, just as today women can enjoy and exercise temporal power." He uses the word *dominari,* which clearly reflects lordly power. With this statement, however, St. Thomas does not only conclude his argument. He weakens it!

If woman has no pre-eminence of status, how can she exercise temporal power, since such pre-eminence is required for civil as well as ecclesial office? His explanation for woman's status of subjection is universal and unqualified. This is evident in his commentary on 1 Corinthians 14:34, which enjoins women to be silent and subject.

> Hence, since teaching bespeaks precedence and presidency

(a sort of foremanship) this office does not befit those who are subject. The reason why they are subject and do not preside (lead) is because they are deficient in reason, which is the most important quality for leadership. Thus, in the *Politics* the philosopher (Aristotle) says that government breaks down (is corrupt) when the rule passes to women.[17]

In his commentary on the same verse St. Thomas defends the right of women to prophesy. Here as elsewhere he distinguishes two moments of prophecy: revelation and its manifestation. Women are not excluded from revelation. However, they are excluded from the public announcement of this revelation, which St. Thomas calles preaching (proclamation). This is a public and official act in the Church! Hence women are not capable of it. They may make their revelation known privately. However, this is not preaching, but only announcing.

Now, it is difficult to see St. Thomas' logic in excluding women from office in the Church if he allows them office in the state. And he does allow the latter. If, however, the status of subjection is disqualifying for the one, it should also be for the other. The principle is the same. Furthermore, against the objections of some theologians St. Thomas does allow woman the power to baptize.[18] It is not clear how such an exception can be made and the general principle of women's incapacity and subject status still be maintained.

In any case, it is important to keep in mind that St. Thomas was strongly influenced by Aristotle's biology. Hence for him woman is deficient and inadequate in comparison to the individual male. However, in relationship to mankind she is not something that has gone awry. Rather she has been purposefully designed by nature. Nature, however, depends on God, who is the universal author of all nature. St. Thomas says explicitly:

> According to Sacred Scripture it was necessary for woman
> to be created as help for man. However, she is not, as some
> have said, help for any work other than generation. For any
> and all other work a man can be helped more adequately by
> another man.

St. Thomas also indicates that there was a subjection before the Fall. This was not an exploitative subjection, but one
whereby "the presiding member uses (orders, arranges) the
subjects for their own convenience and good." "In such a subjection the woman is naturally subject to the man because he
has greater powers of reason and discretion."[19]

St. Thomas understands St. Paul's command that women
be veiled (1 Corinthians 11:10) to indicate that "she is not
immediately subject to God, but that, in addition she is also
subject to man." In sum, "man is more perfect than woman,
who is also less able to resist and overcome temptation."

However, in the same context (1 Corinthians 11:6) St.
Thomas defends the right of religious women to shave their
heads, in (apparent) contradiction of St. Paul's admonition:

> Insofar as they take the vow of virginity or widowhood,
> Christ thus becomes their spouse, they are elevated to the
> status and dignity of men in that they are freed from sub-
> jection to men and immediately united to Christ.[20]

Here we meet again that theology developed in the patristic
age: virginity, not baptism, accomplishes the liberation of
woman from her state of subjection and inferiority to the male.
Not baptism, but virginity undoes the "curse" of Genesis 3:16.
The question would have to be put to St. Thomas, Could not
at least these virgin-women be capable of priestly ordination?
Apparently they no longer linger in that state of subjection which
makes them incapable of the status of pre-eminence which in
turn made them incapable of being ordained.

Again, in all this one must keep in mind the influence of

that ancient biology which regarded women as defective males. If one does not accept that biology, then one is automatically freed of one objection to the ordination of women.

However, there remains the objection which is really ultimately an application of the above biological argument, namely that women are socially inferior and subject. Hence they cannot be ordained, because the priesthood is a superior and presiding office. It could be objected immediately that the New Testament strongly objects to "lording it over." Hence, although the priest may have been elevated in one sense, he is nevertheless commanded to be as the servant of all.

However, we can more directly deal with St. Thomas' argument because there were women who enjoyed authority and jurisdiction in civil society. And, as we have seen, he knew it. How, then, could he insist that woman can be only a subject, without any pre-eminent status and hence without jurisdiction or ruling power? Furthermore, the Church's ritual includes a blessing for the Queen which speaks of her as participating in the ministry of the Bishops. In the civil sphere she exercises an office similar to that of the Bishops. Like them she is a defender of the Church.

The question then arises, did women likewise enjoy and exercise power and authority in the Church? That is, did women have and exercise spiritual jurisdiction in the Church? Although some still want to dismiss the possibility, the evidence is overwhelming in favor, not merely of the possibility, but of the historical fact. The best source is Joan Morris' *The Lady Was a Bishop*.[21] She has not hesitated to subtitle the book "The Hidden History of Women with Clerical Ordination and the Jurisdiction of Bishops."

Early in the book she gives the thesis of her entire investigation:

> Many women are known to have been heads of double com-

munities of men and women in early Christian times, both on the Continent and in England, such as the well-known case of Hilda of Whitby.

The subjects of study in this book—the quasi-episcopal abbesses—can be looked on likewise as continuing the accepted custom of apostolic times. A great number of communities headed by abbesses with independent jurisdiction exempt from bishops were spread throughout Italy, Spain, France, Germany, Poland, Austria, England, and Ireland.

We can conclude that to have women overseers *(episcopae)* of churches and Christian communities was a common practice from apostolic times and that it continued throughout many centuries and was only very slowly suppressed.[22]

The bulk of her book is taken up with the documentary evidence to support her thesis. Her survey shows "the great numbers of women's monasteries that held independent jurisdiction. It gives an idea of what this jurisdiction entailed: abbesses with independent jurisdiction had all the duties of a bishop with regard to ecclesiastical and civil administration in a diocese, which in their case was called a separated territory."[23] The abbesses had spiritual and temporal jurisdiction, which in Canon Law was termed *nullius diocesis* or *praelatura nullius*. This status did not entail a priestly ordination, even though abbesses had a form of ordination. Latin terms like *nullius diocesis* and *praelatura nullius* indicate that there is a "jurisdiction" or a "jurisdictional area/sphere" within the Church that is not subject to the "normal" jurisdiction of the local bishop. The technical term which describes this is "exemption." That is, the monastery, convent, or other religious institution is exempt or removed from the normal authority of the local bishop. This exemption has understandably been a cause of displeasure on the part of most bishops. In fact, it was one of two topics most suggested by the bishops for discussion at Vatican II. They, of course, meant the exemption of male religious orders, and they meant to abrogate or at least severely modify it.

What Joan Morris has been able to show is that women's religious orders and their institutions enjoyed the same jurisdictional exemption for a great part of the Church's history. In fact, it was not until 1874, under Pope Pius IX, that the last exempt women's community, of Las Huelgas, Spain, lost its exemption. It is also interesting, as Morris notes, that "when Pius IX decided to withdraw this right of jurisdiction, he did not have the courage to write directly to the abbeys."[24] She also asserts that "Pius IX took away the right of the Spanish Abbesses to exemption on the grounds that with the change of regime the system was no longer in keeping with the new democratic ideas. At that time democracy did not include women, so one half of the human race was left out."[25]

This case is also valuable because it shows the influence secular events have on "Church" policy and doctrine. The demise of the exempt monasteries was aided by the French Revolution, which suppressed their communities and expropriated their property, thus depriving them of their economic base of independent operation. The Napoleonic legal code subordinated wives to their husbands with a vengeance. More important for our question was the concordat with the Vatican. This effectively compromised the possibility of independent abbeys, whether male or female. Only Las Huelgas, of all the previous exempt women's orders, had been able to survive all this.

A much earlier secular, and negative influence on the jurisdiction of women in the Church was the Renaissance:

> It was only after the twelfth century when there was a slow return to Greco-Roman culture reaching its zenith during the Renaissance that the service rendered by abbesses was looked upon as wrong. The example of Bossuet's enforced domination over the Abbey of Jouarre was a flagrant contradiction of the earlier Christian ideal of monastic freedom.

> The dislike of women having any right to rule shows that the
> whole idea of what it means to rule had become repaganized.
> Administration was no longer considered a service but a right
> of dominion, a right to lord it over another, which was the
> pagan idea of government and not the Christian one of hum-
> ble service.[26]

This brings us back to our original topic, St. Thomas and
the problem of women's capacity for jurisdiction. He was not
entirely unfamiliar with the data Morris has presented. For
example, he knew terms like *diaconissa* and *presbytera,* the
feminine gender forms of deacon and elder (a word often used
for priest). He dismissed their significance by explaining that
"deaconess" is someone (female) who participates in any act
of the deacon, like reading the homily in church. "Elderess"
is a widow, since "elder" (presbyter) is the same as senior
(older). He says explicitly of abbesses that "they do not have
ordinary prelature, but as if by commission, because of the
danger of men living together with women."[27]

What such a distinction can accomplish is not at all clear.
A parallel text does not shed much light on the problem. In
reply to an objection that "some women do seem to have the
power of the keys (a metaphor for jurisdiction), for example,
abbesses who have spiritual power over their subjects,"
Thomas answered that

> Woman, according to the Apostle, is in a state of subjec-
> tion, and therefore cannot have any spiritual jurisdiction, be-
> cause, as the Philosopher says in the *Ethics* (Bk. VIII),
> civility (the civil order of society) is corrupted when dominion
> and rule are exercised by woman. Hence woman has neither
> the key of (Holy) Orders nor the key of jurisdiction. But
> some use of the keys is commissioned to the woman, as, for ex-
> ample, the correction of the woman subject (to her), because
> of the danger which could threaten if men and women lived
> together.[28]

Already Suarez noted the difficulty of the distinction made

by St. Thomas between the use and possession of the keys. How can one use a power if he (she) does not have the power? Furthermore, as we have seen, St. Thomas himself, in opposition to his own state-of-subjection principle, admitted that women do have and exercise civil or secular jurisdiction. The exclusionary and incapacitating principle is apparently not absolute.

I have spent considerable space on this idea because it is really *the* argument against the ordination of women. As should be readily evident, it can operate only on the basis of certain suppositions which are no longer operative today. Furthermore, it does not appear to be consistent in itself.

Most important, though, is the fact that it once again shows the importance or the weight of the fact. In fact there were no women priests; in fact there had not been any; in fact there could not be any. But the third fact is not a fact, it is a conclusion. (Thank you, Perry Mason.) Hence its value is only as good as the basis on which it is reached. As we have noted before, in theology the material fact is never sufficient. An argument is conclusive only because of the formal reason given. In this instance the formal reason is the state of subjection which makes women incapable of jurisdiction. However, there were exceptions to this incapability in both the civil and ecclesial societies, as we have seen. What kind of fact is a fact that isn't even a fact? And what kind of a proof or argument is one based on such a non-fact?

It's not all that complicated. What is really at work here is the same process we have seen so often before. Because men already knew that something couldn't be so, they could not see that it already was so. This is the only possible clarification for the argument and distinction proposed by a man of genius and geniality such as Thomas Aquinas. The facts were there, but they did not fit the theory. Hence some explanation must be found. His solution was in the distinction between possession or endowment with jurisdiction and use of or commission to exercise jurisdiction. On any other subject, that would not have been accepted as logical at the University of Paris.

Furthermore, active in Thomas' argument is the desire to protect the great authorities of St. Paul and Aristotle. However, as we have seen, St. Paul's statements restricting women do not have to be considered as everlasting universal principles. Both St. Paul and Aristotle had to deal with cultures which by and large took a dim view of women, generally for inadequate reasons—religious and philosophical, biological and sociological. In point of fact, however, the Christian Church, without being entirely aware of it, had greatly transcended the limitations imposed by both the Hebrews and the Hellenists. Women had in fact been delivered from their presumed state of subjection—by baptism, faith, the service of Christ, the vow of virginity. This is why the theory no longer fits the fact and not because people in a state of subjection can possess and exercise jurisdiction and enjoy public office. They probably can't.

It was the fact that had changed, even though the Church was not entirely aware of it, even though the Church had not drawn all the legitimate conclusions—just as Paul hadn't. The fact was and is that women are not in a state of subjection, either naturally or supernaturally. The doctrine of creation means that they are equal in being, the doctrine of redemption means that they are equal in grace. As St. Paul noted, in Christ there is neither male nor female. It behooves the Church not to arrange its life and practice in any way that would obscure Christ.

There is another theological "fact" which should be mentioned here because it helps us understand how women could have enjoyed the "power of jurisdiction" but not the "power of holy orders":

> From about the twelfth century on, a distinction is made in the episcopal office between the *ordo* and *jurisdictio*, i.e., between the power of ordination and the power of governing. The power of ordination is, then, particularly related to the "true body of Christ" in the holy eucharist in which the priest, by virtue of the *ordo*, consecrates the bread in holy Mass while the power of jurisdiction is said to be related to "the Mystical Body of Christ."
>
> It should be noted that because of this view medieval theology denied that episcopal consecration was a separate degree of the sacrament of holy orders, since in the ordination of the priest the full power of eucharistic consecration was conferred, to which nothing could be added. Today, in the light of biblical and patristic studies, we consider this distinction, if not insignificant, at least insufficient.[29]

In the *Concilium* article from which the foregoing extract is taken, Ratzinger is primarily interested in the relationship between the pope and the bishops from a pastoral point of view. The interest of the passage for our thesis is the way in which the power of ordination and the power of governing tended to restrict the power of holy orders to the sacramental action of the Church, especially the celebration of the Eucharist. Jurisdiction, then, referred strictly to the "administration" of the Church as the People of God. Through his power of jurisdiction the bishop was ruler, administrator of Church order, property, personnel, etc. The power of orders, on the other hand, became increasingly identified with the role of minister of the sacraments, and especially celebrator of Mass. Indeed, sometimes priests did not even have enough power of jurisdiction to preach, which was considered a jurisdictional act. As the breach widened, it almost amounted to two different "offices" in the Church. Of course, the bishop had the power of orders as well, so that the parallel with the case of women enjoying the power of jurisdiction but not the power of holy orders cannot be exact.

At this point we need to recall what we have already discussed in a different context, namely the bearing of the concept of ritual purity on the female sex. This idea that woman was "unclean" was not restricted to the Near East but has continued in various ways down through Christian history. According to a statement attributed to Pope Sixtus I (116-125) only men consecrated to the service of the Lord may touch the sacred vessels used in the liturgy. These men must be consecrated to the service of the Lord. The inference that women are excluded was attributed to the pope by a later age. However, for our purposes this later date is perhaps more important than papal authority. For it shows that this anti-feminist bias was long-lived in the Church. A similar decree is attributed to Pope Soter (166-174), although it too comes from a later date. It is very important because Gratian included it in his very influential compilation of Church law in 1142. At a synod held at Laodicea in Phrygia between 343 and 381 it was ruled that women were excluded from the altar area of churches. The Council of Saragossa ordered the separation of men and women in church. Since this council was directed against the Priscillianists, who apparently had women priests, one could expect a condemnation of that practice. However, there is none.

The Synod of Nimes (394), also against the Priscillianists, spoke of the ordination of women, "which the order of the Church clearly does not allow, because it is against good custom, practice and morals." The reason for this prohibition is of great interest—it simply isn't done in a good, healthy society.

In 494 Pope Gelasius wrote against women who serve at the altar and perform all that which is reserved for the male sex. In 578 or later women were forbidden to receive the Eucharist with their hands. Neither might they touch the altar cloth. Bishop Haito of Basilea (807-823) forbade women to approach the altar. Even women consecrated to God were not to participate actively and closely in the sacred liturgy at the altar. Women were basically excluded from the sanctuary.

From the year 829 come two reports that indicate that women are to be excluded from active participation in the celebration of the liturgy because their presence would provide carnal temptations. Women are also told to stay in their place (that is, outside the sanctuary) because of the inadequacy and weakness of their sex.

Here we have the combination of two "feminine defects" which provide the practical basis for the exclusion of women from the sanctuary and hence from the priesthood and hence from public office in the Church. First, woman is ritually unclean—hence she is unworthy, and therefore to be excluded from the most sacred place and action. Second, she is both weak and seductive—hence she is dangerous, and therefore equally to be excluded. There are many other texts which could be adduced to illustrate this latter reason. However, the classic text, both precise and succinct, has come from St. Thomas. In response to the question whether women have also received the grace to communicate wisdom and knowledge he distinguishes, as he is wont to do, between private (basically in the home) and public (in church). They may, of course, teach privately, but not in church. There they must be silent. Why? "Lest the spirit of (male) man be stimulated to lust."[30]

In this same article St. Thomas again asserts that "there is no sexual difference insofar as the grace of prophecy means a mind illuminated by God." And he cites Colossians 3:10 as follows: "Putting on the new man who is renewed according to the image of the one who created him: there is neither male nor female."[31] But in the whole article St. Thomas decisively invokes Genesis 3:16 and the state of subjection to man in which woman now finds herself. Hence she may do certain things in private which she is incapable of doing in public. All this because she is subject to man, in a state of submission. And for him public official activity belongs to prelates. St. Thomas is not unaware that in fact many men are also subjects, but still act officially in public. He resolves this apparent contradiction by distinguishing between this male subjection, which exists by virtue of some accidental condition, and female subjection, which exists by virtue of the nature of her sex.

On this basis we can see why St. Thomas, and generations before and after him, would be reluctant to admit that women could share in the public administration of the Church's life. This is what the sacrament of holy orders is all about. The distinction between order and jurisdiction intensified the concentration of the sacrament of holy orders in the celebration of the sacraments, especially the Eucharist. The uncleanness, weakness, and seductiveness attributed to woman made her exclusion from the active ministry of the Eucharist easier, if not imperative. Since office in the Church tended to be thought of primarily and principally in terms of the eucharistic ministry, it was also possible not to reckon as real Church officials those women who obviously had powers of jurisdiction without, at least apparently, any power of orders to confer the sacraments. This is the best explanation of St. Thomas' attempt to explain how women could have the "use" of the power of jurisdiction without having the power itself.

We are faced once more with the weight of the fact. And the fact is the sexist ideology which has been so dominant in Western society and culture. This ideology was so strong that even when in practice women did enjoy great power and office in the Church, in theory it was not—and perhaps could not—be admitted.

In sum, many activities and positions in the Church were at one time forbidden to women. Among these forbidden activities were touching sacred vessels, entering the sanctuary during the liturgy, speaking, reading, or singing in the public liturgy, baptizing, distributing Holy Communion, taking the altar cloths directly from the altar instead of receiving them from male clerics at the edge of the sanctuary, giving the liturgical vestments to the priest. And on the same grounds as for these restrictions woman was declared incapable of priestly ordination and ecclesiastical ordination. However, since all of the above listed actions formerly forbidden are now allowed, one can also only ask once again, "Why this one exception, namely ordination to the priesthood?"

The answer will be twofold. First, the Church has never ordained women. But as we have seen, the Church had never done many things which it does do now. Second, women cannot be ordained! But that is the question, not the answer. Theologians say that this "doctrine" belongs to the doctrine of the faith. But they do not say which doctrines would be wiped out if women were ordained. There is, of course, only one: namely the "doctrine" that says women cannot be ordained. But again, we must insist that that is the question, not the answer.

Unless one accepts the position that women are by the very nature of their sex in a state of subjection, by virtue of both the creation and the Fall, and unless one accepts the position that in the case of the Fall this sin-caused subjection somehow escaped the efforts of Jesus' redemption, one cannot find support for the exclusion of women from the sacrament of holy orders and the priesthood—not in the Bible, not in the magisterium of the Church, not even in the writings of theologians.

Some argue, finally, that because the Apostolic Church *did not* ordain women the later Church also *can not*. The reason given is that the Apostolic Church provides the foundation for the later Church. Hence, although some practices might not be absolutely—purely theoretically—necessary, they have become unalterable because of the normative practice of the Apostolic Church. One example offered is the language of the New Testament. Certainly in some abstract, theoretical sense it did not have to be Greek. But it was, and this cannot be repealed or reversed. All that is certainly true. But it is not equally clear that the language of the New Testament and the ordination of ministers to the service of the Church can be grouped together in the same class. Clearly the language of the New Testament is a once-for-all-times choice. But even in this respect the Church has allowed translations, and indeed for a long time gave precedence to the Latin translation over the original Greek. The most important objection to this point, however, is that it does not adequately designate which elements of the freely acknowledged normative status of the early Church are absolutely normative.

As we have seen, all of the reasons given for the exclusion of women from the sacrament of holy orders and the jurisdiction of Church office are at least as old as the Apostolic Church. Hence its practice would basically be no more compelling than these reasons. Furthermore, although it had many occasions when it could easily have done so, the Church's official and extraordinary magisterium has never given a solemn and irreformable definition excluding women from the sacrament of orders.

Finally, as Tertullian once said, "Christ did not say 'I am the custom.' He said, 'I am the truth.'" Consequently we may and must also say that the custom of the Church has been not to ordain women. However, this custom does not exhaust the truth. The truth, as this chapter indicates it, would be that the Church does not *have* to ordain women; but also that there is no compelling doctrinal or theological reason why it cannot ordain them if it so chooses.[32]

At this point we can ask whether there are any reasons favoring the ordination of women in the history of the Church and theology. As we said earlier, the only really adequate reason for the ordination of women would be the absence of any prohibiting theological reason. We have seen that there are no such prohibiting reasons. In general we must be very careful about ascribing certain traits or characteristics exclusively to either man or women. With this caution we shall now list a few items from the Judeo-Christian tradition which would favor the ordination of women.

First of all, this tradition insists that all salvation and being, whether in the creation or the redemption, is the entirely free gift of God the Creator to his creature. Since everything is a gift, it would be fitting that both men and women share all significant ways of mediating and representing this gift throughout time and space. This bisexual representation could be a powerful aid in preventing an overestimation of the ability of either sex. It would seem almost inevitable that the restriction of office in the Church, especially the priesthood, would lead to a preferential status of that group to which it was restricted. And this would automatically lead to an obscuring of the universal gratuity of God's gift of being.

Secondly, I would like to turn the Marian argument in favor of the ordination of women. If a *public* act in the history of salvation like being the mother of the Messiah could be performed by a woman, it is difficult to see why a woman should be restricted from performing other public acts in the continuation of that history. Without entering into the doctrinal complexities of Mary as Mediatrix of All Grace, it is possible to say that it is exceedingly difficult to think of a mediatorial act greater than Mary's motherhood. Hence, even in the theology which emphasizes the priest as mediator, the concept of Mary as a mediatrix would be more of an incentive to ordain women than to exclude them. By this argument I in no wise want to assert that Mary was ordained a priest or that she in any way shared in the sacrament of holy orders. What I want to assert simply is that the life and vocation of Mary offer incentives in favor of women's inclusion among the priestly officials of the Church.

As we have already noted, Jesus himself referred to his person and mission in feminine imagery. The analogy of the hen (Matthew 23:37) serves to provide the balance with respect to an understanding of Jesus' role in exclusively male terms. This is a strong reinforcement of the frequent parables and images where the kingdom of God is compared with "typically" feminine activities. Indeed, we must see in Luke's parable (15:8-10) about the woman searching for the lost dachma a feminine God the merciful Father. If Jesus was not afraid to allow the feminine image to stand for or represent him and his divine Father, then the Church need not be reluctant to do the same thing. This does not prove, of course, that women have to be ordained. It does, however, prove that the Christian tradition does offer substantial symbolic support in favor of their ordination.

Furthermore, although St. Paul frequently refers to himself as the Father of various churches (I Corinthians 4:14 and others), he is also able to speak of himself in very feminine terms: "My children, I must go through the pain of giving birth to you all over again" (Galatians 4:19). It should also not be overlooked that St. Paul never refers to himself as the bridegroom of any particular church nor to any church as his spouse! The public activity of officers in the Church must consequently be regarded as having a "feminine" as well as "masculine" imagery. If the "father" can also be "mother," why cannot the "mother" also be "father," especially since the minister is only the representative of God and Christ? God is certainly not a male, and Jesus hardly saved us precisely by virtue of his male sexuality.

More recently Vatican II has also spoken of bishops and priests in terms of feminine imagery. In the Decree on the Bishops' Pastoral Office in the Church (13): "In propounding it (Christian doctrine), bishops should manifest the Church's maternal solicitude for all men, believers or not."

This passage recalls a classical theme from theology, namely that where the bishop is, there is the Church. A whole theological tradition has seen the bishop as the embodiment and representation of the Church. If, then, the Church is bride and mother, the bishop must also be wifely and motherly. That is, the bishop must be representative not only of the bridegroom but also of the bride. Under these circumstances it could only be capricious to restrict the representatives in holy orders to the male sex.

The Decree on the Ministry and Life of Priests (6) asserts that "the Church community exercises a true motherhood toward souls who are to be led to Christ." This is the section entitled "Priestly Functions." Although this pasage does not assert the feminine dimension of the priesthood as clearly as the preceding document, it does remind us that insofar as the ordained priest is in a special way the representative of the Church, it would be fitting to have women priests insofar as the Church community is truly maternal. To make such a suggestion is not to succumb to sexism in reverse. It is, rather, the attempt to avoid the sexism that is implicit and inherent in the exclusive ordination of our one sex. If God is willing to have men and women in his image and likeness, it hardly seems fitting that the Church should decline to have men and women in its sacramental ministry.

God the Mother is a phrase that can still bring people up short. They find it odd, strange, baffling. It makes them uneasy. When I have used the phrase in talks or sermons, I have noticed not only initial shock but also some nervousness. Is God's dignity being assaulted when he is called "Mother"?

However, in reality "God the Mother" should sound no stranger than "God the Father." The ease with which we accept the latter designation of God is perhaps a good indication of how unseriously we take it and of how prone we might be to misunderstand it. What do we really think when we pray, "Our Father"? Many have thought of an old man with a long white beard, thanks to the artwork in churches and religious books. The beard was to help us understand the eternity of God, which was almost inevitably thus confused with antiquity.

12/ God the Mother

We can also wonder whether the male picture of God the Father, with or without beard, has not also produced a mistaken idea of what is meant by the Fatherhood of God. First of all, it does not mean that God is sexually male rather than female. As we have seen, both the Hebrew and Christian traditions have insisted that God is beyond all such creaturely qualities. Hence, God is not only not male, he is not sexual at all. If God is not even Father, why suggest that we speak of God as Mother? Simply because, as we noted earlier in this book, we have to use "human" words when we speak of God, or we cannot speak at all. Of all human words "father" and "mother" are among the most important and most precious.

Let us examine the meaning of the Fatherhood of God more closely. It may give us some help in understanding the Motherhood of God. (I almost said *his* Motherhood. That, however, is not as unacceptable theologically as it is grammatically.) First of all, God as Father is not to be understood as a wrathful, vengeful, authoritarian, capricious, divine tyrant who delights in ordering people around.

This is a favorite theme with certain writers today, even some theologians who apparently perceive themselves to be oppressed. Their sense of oppression seems to concentrate itself on traditional and institutional authority, especially paternal authority. This is all generally included under the rubric "patriarchal." In this view, fatherhood is fundamentally oppressive, restrictive, anti-libertarian.[1] It must have been such an "understanding," if not experience, which gave birth to Mary Daly's misbegotten and silly book, *Beyond God the Father: Toward a Philosophy of Women's Liberation.*[2] Admittedly women have been generally oppressed in the patriarchal societies, religious and civil, which have existed until now. What Ms. Daly (whom grimness is not far removed from that of Jane Fonda) offers, however, is oppression for everybody, male and female. What lies *Beyond* (Mary Daly's) *God the Father* is the fascism of the dyspeptic feminist intellectual who wants a world created in her image and likeness. As Margaret O'Brien Steinfels pointed out in her review of Ms. Daly's book, a new religion is being proposed here.[3] Although this is supposed to be a liberating religion, it is, perhaps unwittingly, nothing more than a reinstatement of the patriarchal imperialism under a new name.

If God the Father is neither male nor authoritarian nor patriarchal, what does the description mean, if anything at all? Primarily it means that God is the source of life and being. God is called Father not because he is male, but because he is not impotent or sterile. Even among humans one is called father, not because he is male, but because he has been the source of life and being for others. This title is applied to God for the same reason.

It is important that God be called Father because of the other dreadfully unacceptable possibilities. First of all, God as Father is personal, not an impersonal force of nature like the wind, sun, rain. As personal, God is both knowing and loving. Hence God is not a blind force of nature. And neither is God the blind necessity of fate or chance. It is in opposition to these possibilities that God is called Father, not in opposition to woman or mother.

The designation of God as Father further emphasizes that God is not a deistic God. That is, God does not produce something and then leave it, to survive on its own as best it can. Of course the human race, especially woman, has regularly experienced the oft-departing male, as Chris Connors has sung so well: "He was a good man as good men go, and, as good men go, he went." To call God Father, however, is to emphasize that God stays and takes care of the beings to whom he has given life.

Finally, in the Christian experience God is not only a lordly father, he is an affectionate one. This is indicated by the fact that when Jesus called God his father he used the word *abba*:

> Abba ("my father") is in fact derived from the chatter of children. When a child has begun to "eat bread" (i.e., soon after it has been weaned) it learns to say *abba* and *imma*. Although *abba* was no longer restricted to children's talk in Jesus' time, it nevertheless remained a familiar word with which no one would have dared to address God. No Jew ever called God *abba*, yet the evangelists record that Jesus always called God *abba*, "my Father" (except for the cry from the cross, Mark 15:34). We have thus established the emergence of a completely new manner of speaking which at the same time reflects a most profound new relationship with God.[4]

This does not turn the image of God into that of a cosmic Santa Claus, but it does emphasize that for Christians it is always better to be than not to be, because the source and creative center of being is benign and personal. We are not the playthings or the mistakes of blind necessity or capricious chance.

To call God Father is fundamentally to emphasize the graciousness and meaningfulness of human and all created being. For this reason God could just as well be called Mother. However male and female might ultimately be distinguished, they are both equally able to share in and represent God's nature and being as a caring, capable, loving, and affectionate source of being for others. God, whether as Father or Mother, is not offered as an oppressive and tyrannical elder or someone bigger and stronger. The symbol is rather of one who makes it possible for others to be at all, and especially to be free and to flourish. There are those who are against any sort of "parental" symbolism for God. For example, in her review of Mary Daly's non-book, Carol Christ says, "We may not need a divine mother, but a divine sister would be nice."[5] This kind of nonsense recalls the recent solemn, but fortunately shortlived, Death of God fad, which wanted to keep Jesus the Brother but be freed of God the Father. One would think that these anti-authoritarian devotees had never heard of Cain, Joseph's brothers, or even sibling rivalry. From the point of view of the question, What is it all about?, we do not have a choice between God the Father/Mother and God the Brother/Sister: we have the choice between God the Father/Mother and blind necessity, fate, chance; the exploitative gods of the Greeks, Roman, Mespotamians, etc. Furthermore, such advocates seem to be totally unaware that the Christian understanding of being allows the triune God to be both Father and Brother. Jesus has revealed that God is both fatherly and brotherly. Since the spirit of this God is poured out indiscriminately on both men and women, young and old (Joel 3:1-5 with Acts 2:14-21), Christians can firmly maintain that in the Christic being there is neither male nor female (Galatians 3:28). Can anyone else offer a comprehensive theory of being which offers such fundamentally equal and positive existence to the whole world, but especially to bisexual humanity?

In point of fact, as we have already seen, the Bible does offer support for the understanding of God as Mother. Already in Genesis 1:27 we are forcefully told that when God's being is shared outside himself, it is reflected in a being that is both male and female. To restrict God to male designations would be, then, completely capricious.

Furthermore the prophet Isaiah does not heistate to compare God to a woman, indeed precisely to a mother:

> Thus says Yahweh, your redeemer,
> he who formed you in the womb:
> I, myself, Yahweh, made all things (44:2).

This is not to sexualize God, but to emphasize that the various behaviors which are experienced by human beings and attributed to either sex are all manifestations of the powerful care God gives to all the being of which he is the source. A personal source is called father or mother, equally. And so, if God can be called Father, he can also be called Mother.

The most extensive description of the feminine in God is, as we have seen, in the Wisdom literature. In Proverbs (8, 9) Wisdom is not only personified but precisely as a woman who gives instruction. Furthermore, although she is created, she is created before all God's other works. Consequently she is able to accompany God in his continuing work of creation. She is the hostess of a banquet which offers life. Ecclesiasticus (24), for all its antifeminist bias, goes even further. Wisdom is still a creature but an age-old one. This Wisdom is identified with the divine Spirit who hovered over the waters in the act of creation (see Genesis 1:2) and with the pillar of cloud in the desert during the Exodus (see Exodus 13:21). In the oldest texts this pillar is the manifestation of the presence of God. Wisdom is also the worship of Yahweh in the Holy of Holies. Indeed, Wisdom is the covenant of the Most High God. Wisdom's "divine" nature is again emphasized by her association with Eden, and the inability of mankind, from beginning to end, to "grasp her entirely . . . to fully comprehend her" (v. 28).

The book of Wisdom (7) takes the understanding of Wisdom to its heights. Here Wisdom is a "breath of the power of God, pure emanation of the glory of the Almighty . . . reflection of the eternal light . . . image of his goodness . . . she can do all . . . and over Wisdom evil can never triumph" (7:22-30). This passage clearly emphasizes the divine character of Wisdom, to whom are attributed qualities normally reserved for the divine.

From these texts we can and must definitely conclude that it is legitimate to speak of God in feminine as well as masculine terms. In our particular time it is not only possible but desirable, and may even be necessary. Necessary not only in order to provide balance for the previous overemphasis on male attributes, but also to develop positively our understanding of God.

The psalms also hint at a feminine way of describing God. Not only does Yahweh say, "You are my son, today I have become your Father" (Psalm 2:7). He also says, "Royal dignity was yours from the day you were born, royal from the womb" (Psalm 110:3). The Latin text is even more direct: *ex utero genui te* requires the active voice and must be translated, "from the womb I have given you birth." These psalms are used in the traditional midnight Mass at Christmas.

This theme is also present in St. John's gospel. In the prologue (1:18) Jesus is described as "the only Son, who is nearest to the Father's heart" according to the Bible of Jerusalem translation. The Revised Standard Version says, "the only Son, who is in the bosom of the Father." I think that this latter translation is preferable. The Greek word is *kolpos,* which can be translated "womb" as well as "bosom." The images connected with this word tend to have feminine overtones or connotations.[6]

Finally, we should recall once again that Jesus himself used the unequivocally feminine term "hen" to refer to his person and mission. This would have been even more startling in his day than ours, although men still seem tend to think of themselves as roosters and the world as their barnyard.

What is important is not, of course, to prove that God is a woman; that would be as much of an aberration as to prove God is a man. The point is, rather, to indicate that the Judeo-Christian tradition understands God in such a way that (1) God's being is imaged in both human males and females and (2) both Father and Mother, as terms describing human being and experience, can be applied to God.

As we have seen, the sexist nature of male-dominated societies has furthered the God-Father image and hindered the God-Mother image. Here the influence of the old biological understanding that the male was the only active agent in generation cannot be overemphasized. Especially in the Hebrew tradition, great emphasis was laid on God's power and his ability to produce being and to rule. This emphasis, in conjunction with the ancient biology, would almost necessarily nullify the possibilities of developing the God-Mother image.

However, this idea has been present in the theology of the Church and can be traced back at least to St. Bernard (1090-1153). In the fourteenth century the English mystic Mother Julian of Norwich developed the idea in her *Revelations of Divine Love.*[7] In chapter 57 she asserts that "our Savior is our true Mother in whom we are endlessly borne; and never shall we come out of him." God is both our Mother and our Father.

Mother Julian explains the motherhood of God in terms of the Trinity:

> I beheld the working of all the blessed Trinity. In which beholding I saw and understood these three properties: the property of the Fatherhood, and the property of the Motherhood, and the property of the Lordship—in one God.
> And thus, in our making, God almighty is our kindly Father; and God all-wisdom is our kindly Mother: with the love and goodness of the Holy Ghost; which is all one God, one Lord.

However, the divine maternity is focused on the Second Person of the Trinity, the Son who is also the Father's Word,

because it is through him that all things are made. In this
sense the Word is the divine womb whence is born the world
of creation as well as the renewed world of grace.

> And furthermore, I saw that the second Person, who is our
> Mother substantially—the same very dear Person is now be-
> come our Mother sensually. For of God's making we are
> double: that is to say, substantial and sensual. ... And the
> second Person of the Trinity is our Mother in kind, in our
> substantial making—in whom we are grounded and rooted;
> and he is our Mother of mercy, in taking our sensuality.
>
> Thus Jesus Christ, who doeth good against evil, is our very
> Mother. We have our being of him, there, where the ground
> of Motherhood beginneth; with all the sweet keeping of love
> that endlessly followeth. As truly as God is our Father, so
> truly is God our Mother.
>
> He (God the Father) willed that the second Person should
> become our Mother, our Brother, and our Saviour. Whereof
> it followeth that as truly as God is our Father, so truly is
> God our Mother.
>
> And thus is Jesus our True Mother in kind, of our first mak-
> ing; and he is our true Mother in grace by his taking of our
> made kind. All the fair working and all the sweet kindly
> offices of most dear Motherhood are appropriated to the sec-
> ond Person.

In a series of contrasts between human and divine motherhood, Mother Julian points out the superiority of Christ's:

> This office (the service of the mother) no one might nor
> ever could do to the full, except he (Christ) alone. We know
> that all our mothers bear us to pain and to dying; a strange
> thing that! But our true Mother Jesus, he alone beareth us to
> joy and to endless living; blessed may he be!
>
> The mother can give her child to suck of her milk. But our
> precious Mother Jesus, he can feed us with himself; and
> doth, full courteously and tenderly, with the Blessed Sacra-
> ment.
>
> The mother can lay her child tenderly on her breast. But our
> tender Mother Jesus can lead us, homely, into his blessed
> breast, by his sweet open side; and shew us there, in part,
> the Godhead and the joys of heaven.

No better summary of this doctrine of the motherhood of God can be given than Mother Julian's own summary:

> This fair lovely word *Mother*, it is so sweet and so kind in itself, that it cannot truly be said to any nor of any, but to him and of him who is very Mother of life and of all.

We shall let this suffice, since our purpose is not a history of the theology of God as Mother. It is enough to have shown that even in the male-dominated history of the Jewish and Christian religions it has been possible to speak of God in feminine and motherly terms. (In this regard I think that it is especially interesting to note the ease with which Mother Julian is able to use the masculine pronoun "he" with the noun "Mother." This is a beautiful example of the androgynous mentality which we have found to be so desirable.) Although this practice has not been extensive, it has been present and has not been officially or theologically rejected as unorthodox or heretical. In the era of women's liberation it offers us the opportunity to deepen our understanding of God and the occasion to redress whatever discrimination women have suffered insofar as they were declared not to be in God's image.

At this point the question necessarily arises as to what is specifically male and what is specifically female. In regard to this question there has been both a traditional division of qualities and an intense opposition to the proposed division by various women's lib spokesmen. The division has attributed activity, aggressivity, independence, and similar qualities to the male; passivity, dependence, and obedience to the female. A most typical example of this division has been the assertion that women cry more readily than men. The difficulty with this kind of division of attributes is that it more adequately describes the education and expectation society has traditionally provided for its younger members than it does any kind of immutable nature. Girls are expected, if not encouraged, to cry; boys are almost forbidden to do so.

To this kind of male-female distinction women's lib representatives rightly and strenuously object. They contend—although here they exaggerate—that women have become what they are solely because men have made them this way. However, that the plight of women has not been so unrelentingly miserable is amply documented by the constant complaints men have registered throughout history, namely that women are anything but pliable, obedient, and suppliant. What men may have pined for and daydreamed of, women have apparently been quite reluctant to provide.

It is precisely for this reason that a male must resort to rape. Rape is much less an expression of the male's actual power and dominance than it is of his sense of insecurity and impotence. Rape is a particular brand of violence. Violence is the expression of weakness and frustration; it is the last resort of one who has not been able to get his way and is unable to express himself by other means. As such, rape is hardly "patriarchal," in an exclusively male sense. Rape can be committed equally by the female, although its physical expression will be different. Deplorable though its incidence in our society is, the preoccupation with rape among certain women's lib circles is puzzling. One is at times tempted to think that the motive is envy, a sort of ultimate manifestation of penis envy. For example, Mary Daly's reaction to rape is itself rapist. It is as violent and destructive as any act of male rape. Likewise, her description of phallic morality's basis in Rape, Genocide, and War sounds more like a complaint of one who has been deprived of the exercise of this morality than of someone who really rejects it. Perhaps we can learn from another oppressed and powerless victim of phallic morality that the victim frequently uses the tools of his oppression against his oppressor. Thus the oppressed Eldridge Cleaver revenged himself, the raped black man, by raping the white man's women. It is not difficult to read Mary Daly's position as the white woman's equivalent response. I had often heard of the preening male ego, but not until I heard Gloria Steinem (on Dinah Shore's morning television show) speak about it did I realize that the preening female ego is as much a reality and source of opposition.

However traumatic and injurious the rape of the female might be, it is precisely as such a testimony to the woman's power to resist the desire and ability of the male to make her whatever he wants her to be. It is not being supercilious to regard rape as a negative sign of woman's own ability *not* to be the clay out of which the male would fashion her to his own image and likeness. It is for this reason that our laws and court procedures have to be revised, namely to give the victim of rape more adequate protection. It would be a tragedy if the courts were to award the rapist the victory which the raped woman had denied him. Women likewise must remind themselves that conquest by rape is also possible for women in their own way.

At this point we can sum up by saying that is not adequate to distinguish male and female characteristics by either (1) the active-passive axis, which has been traditional since at least Aristotle; or (2) the charge that woman is emotional, the male is rational (a position frequently expressed in the dictum that the wife is the heart of the family, the husband the head); or (3) the rapist-rapee axis which is advocated by certain women's lib groups today. For some women's libbers this last is the only possible male-female relationship, especially in the sexual sphere. Also unacceptable is that simplistic Freudian school which claims that anatomy is destiny, and then proceeds to accept as anatomical practically the entire historical and socio-economic status of women.

There have been many other modern attempts to provide a typology of the sexes. Such attempts as the Terman "test" to record male and female responses to identical stimuli (for example, the same word) must be approached with extreme caution. They do indeed record typically different responses; but the basis of these responses is not some pure female or male "nature." As we remarked above, these tests are basically "measures" of the de facto education and social conditioning which have been provided for the younger generation.

The best general survey and critique of these attempts is provided by F. J. J. Buytendijk.[8] He is aware of the difficulty of distinguishing the nature, manifestation, and existence of any being, but especially of the human being. Although he is a male and although one may not agree with all his positions, only the most thoroughly sexist female chauvinist could accuse him of being a sexist male chauvinist.

Woman has been described as pure passivity (Fichte), masochistic suffering (Deutsch), receptivity (Schleiermacher). A more contemporary attempt has been to exaggerate the aspects of development and adaptability. Thus de Beauvoir and Merleau-Ponty have tried to describe woman solely as a "becoming" or "an historical idea." In practice this opinion would almost reduce woman to that concept noted earlier, namely that woman is only what man has made of her. At least it would make her extremely vulnerable to such an idea.

A favorite description has been the "eternal feminine," which emphasizes woman's receptivity, her non-aggressiveness, her greater emotionality, her predilection for the beautiful. People who dislike this idea describe it sarcastically as the "Woman on the Pedestal" approach. It is questionable insofar as it tends to accept as eternal what may have been the exceedingly temporal conditions of any given society. There is also the contemporary attempt to regard woman as the male's playmate (the bunny). As Gloria Steinem has shown, though, it is possible to bust out of this mold. Modern contraceptive devices prevent this position from being a simple reversion to the pre-Christian fertility cults of the Mesopotamians. It has the further difficulty, in such a contraceptive and antibiotic age, of reducing the male to the same status. And given the diverse sexual natures and capacities of the male and female, this is going to work to the disadvantage of the male. The increasing incidence of impotence among young "modern" and "liberated" males, which we have pointed out earlier, is a decisive demonstration of this male disadvantage.[9]

Neither is it sufficient to assert, according to the social scientists Betty Friedan cites so gleefully, that "being a woman was no more and no less than being human."[10] The question still remains, for such a "discovery" does not explain what it means to be human. Thus this explanation suffers from the vagueness and lack of content inherent in all such "human" and "humanization" explanations. Furthermore, it doesn't even get to the problem of what man or woman as such is. Even if woman (or man) is human, the question still remains why humanity is bisexual.

A last unacceptable explanation of woman is an equally unacceptable explanation of man. I refer to the practice and/ or theory of unisex. This is apparently an attempt to explain the difference by acting as if there weren't any. It is a sort of secularized version of that gnostic and encratic contention we saw in an earlier chapter. It solved the problem by turning the female into a male. This tendency is another instance of how people try to solve the problem of the one and the many, of unity and diversity, by suppressing or eliminating the plurality and diversity.

The Christian solution proposes that the male and female are indeed different, but equally human. They are neither interchangeable nor expendable. The Christian solution is then faced with the difficulty of describing this difference. A fundamental starting point is provided by the readily apparent anatomical or sexual difference between man and woman. According to William and Nancy McCready:

> Sex role identification is also developed through socialization. Such identification is the set of symbols that the individual uses to locate himself or herself in the relative social positions of "male" and "female." A minimum definition of male and female is provided by the human biological system, but the personal definitions of masculine and feminine are more complicated learned behaviors.[11]

Some differences inherent in this minimal definition are elaborated by L. Cervantes:

> Less obvious but equally relevant is the fact that every cell of a female's body is distinguishable from every cell of a male's body because of differential chromosomal content. Modern findings show the differential functioning of hormones in influencing masculine aggression and initiative and feminine receptivity and propensity to nurture. Woman's blood has a greater white corpuscle content with consequently greater self-healing capacities. The greater viability of the female is evident at every age of life, from the fetal stage to senility; it is offset by a sex ratio of birth of roughly 105 male to 100 female births. Woman's metabolism is anabolic rather than catabolic, thus differing from the male's. Her total nervous system is of greater sensitivity excepting the nerve centers in the genitals. The fact that a woman possesses about one-half the oxygen capacity, one-half the muscular capacity, and a less rugged bone structure than a man tends to place a woman at a disadvantage in physical activities. Consideration of skeletal and muscular structure, skin and hair texture, subcutaneous disposition of fat, rate of bodily growth, or any other of the gross secondary characteristics of the sexes makes

it apparent that women differ from men physically in more than reproductive mechanisms.[12]

This starting point could easily evoke the protest that I have succumbed to Freud's "Anatomy is destiny." Or that I am reducing woman to a baby machine, imprisoning her once again in the kitchen and nursery. That is, of course, not the case at all. But that kind of reaction is important because it reveals a mentality which is extremely negative in regard to human reproduction. In fact, it regards pregnancy as basically a punishment of the woman.

In this connection it is important to note a strange anomaly in our supposed utterly materialistic society, namely a disparagement and rejection of the body that would delight the heart of any Platonist or Gnostic. This does not manifest itself so much or so exclusively in prostitution and sexual exhibitionism as the various and sundry preachers would claim. Sexual irregularities have been with us, apparently, forever. After all, prostitution is supposed to be the world's oldest profession. While the prostitute and the female stripper may have their own psychological problems, and although they are severely subject to male exploitation, they do in their own way make men pay, if not beg, for what they (the males) consider theirs by right. From certain viewpoints, at least, these two professions are no more exploitative than many others. In general "jobs" require the male or female to provide his or her body in the service of someone else. Whether one does this as a miner, trucker, athlete, waiter, professor or whatever, it is not merely Marxist to suggest, from one aspect, a parallel between these professions and the world's oldest.

The real devaluation of the human body is most obvious in the propaganda of the pro-abortionists. For them the "human" is located solely in the will or choice of the human agent.

That is why they can so freely advocate woman's right to choice as the basis of open-abortion policy. That is also why they can completely ignore the human status of prenatal human life: such bodies, in this view, are not human; they are nothing but random masses of cells. This attitude is most strikingly manifested in a pro-abortion advertisement which was given to me just today. The advertisement is, of course, a plea for open abortion-on-demand. The front page of the advertisement is a picture of a (pregnant) woman being strangled by two babies, the hangman's rope and noose being provided by the umbilical cord. As I mentioned above, for these people pregnancy is obviously seen as a punishment. Such a mentality has dire consequences not only for prenatal humanity; it also bodes ill for all human life which does not meet certain qualifications. Consequently we may soon expect a major push to legitimize a more active practice of euthanasia and the disposal of other "defectives."

Now, the point I am trying to make is not concerned precisely with the morality of such practices but with the fact that in them bodily existence counts for almost nothing. It is for this reason that some people protest too violently when it is suggested that any explanation of the precise "natures" of men and women must begin with their biological and bodily reality. If one regards pregnancy as punishment and degradation, such a starting point is bound to be unacceptable. It is interesting that these people do not seem to regard the female's "submission" to the male by whom she is impregnated as a degradation. If they wish to protect women from this sort of thing, one would think that they would emphasize their right not to become pregnant. By the time an abortion is necessary the "damage" has already been done—woman has "submitted," whether freely or by force.

The context in which the Christian must urge his own position on this: namely, that man and woman, who are from the earth (the meaning of Adam, *adamah* in Genesis 2:7; 3:19), are in their very bodily being in the image and likeness of God. Their bodily reality is as much a gift as their "spiritual." Furthermore, this bodily reality with its procreative capacity is a decisive dimension in man's being in the image and likeness of God. The Hebrew tradition emphasized the power of God, and this power was most manifest in his creation of other beings.

Again, this is not to reduce human beings to reproductive agents. It is simply to emphasize the fundamental fact that the corporeal reality of humanity is not a trivial and incidental appendage to the human person. In fact, against the negative protests of some women's libbers it can be argued that such an approach to male-female differentiation is actually in favor of the woman. Just this morning (August 13, 1974) on NBC's Today show Barbara Walters asked anthropologist Ashley Montagu whether he thought women would ever achieve total equality with men. He replied that he thought they would. But he also added that it would be a step down, since women are basically "superior to men in intellect, longevity, resistance to disease and disorders." The reason for this superiority he described as "genetic qualities, not learned behaviors." The basis is the presence of two X chromosomes in women, while men have only one. As Nipsey Russell once remarked, "Women are bound to be stronger than men. You don't see any busloads of widowers touring Europe."

The question automatically arises, If this is so, then how did women get into the depressed state we have recorded in this book? I really do think that the answer is very easy, although some women's libbers like Rosemary Ruether have developed highly complicated theories.[13] (I suspect that these theories are intended more to flatter the author's vanity than to explain the problem. In more than one instance I also think that these elaborate explanations, concentrating as they do on man's consciousness, are simply further attempts to avoid the corporeal reality of human being.) In any case, in the same interview Montagu's remarks suggest the adequate explanation. It is simply that the male has been basically bigger, heavier, endowed with a more powerful musculature. He has been able, therefore, to impose his will on the less strongly structured female.

The subjugation of women, then, has not been due to a male plot or conspiracy.[14] It is simply a manifestation of the age-old experience of the biggest guy on the block. He gets his way, but not only with women: the other males are equally vulnerable, although not in the same way. Here we must mention again that oppressed groups have a tendency to take themselves too seriously because of, and precisely on the basis of, their oppression. This is readily apparent with Blacks, but also with Indians and women—and even the young. There is a tendency to think that one is being oppressed precisely because of color, sex, age. That is not entirely wrong, but it is not the whole story. One has only to think what would happen if there were no Blacks available—would that mean that no one would be discriminated against? The answer is, of course and simply, no. In all discrimination and oppression a most significant element is availability. Worldwide experience indicates that if no Blacks, Indians, or women were readily available, another group would soon be found to serve their function. Consequently oppressed groups must be discriminating in their appraisal of the discrimination which they have suffered. Otherwise—and this is the point—they can easily end up more oppressed in their "liberated" state than they were in their earlier oppressed state.

To apply this to the question of women's liberation means

to acknowledge the fact that men have oppressed women, and precisely through marriage and pregnancy. However, the cause of the oppression was the male's superior physical force, in conjunction with a false understanding that "might makes right." I think it is always difficult for the more physically powerful not to think that they are the "more right." Consequently women would be well advised not to depreciate their own bodily and sexual nature because they have been abused in the past. If women insist that they are just like men, identical, then they fall backwards into that opinion of St. Thomas Aquinas which said that as helpmates women are good only for sexual activity and reproduction. For anything else a male is better off with another male.

Women would be shrewd and farsighted to insist that there is something distinctive about them, that their sex is not a lesser and deficient male misdevelopment.

For a time the prevailing tendency was to explain everything female in terms of social and cultural conditioning. In the 1930s this was clearly the position of such anthropologists as Ruth Benedict and Margaret Mead. However, as Montagu indicated, this viewpoint can easily be overstated. Although the human being is exceedingly malleable and formable, he/she does not start from zero. The human person does begin with a pre-given human, corporeal nature.

More and more today even the anthropologists are acknowledging the importance of that corporeal nature. Among these anthropologists must be included, to the surprise of many (and the disgust of some), Ruth Benedict and Margaret Mead. For example, F. J. J. Buytendijk writes:

> In starting from existence therefore, from being in situation, we must never forget that the human being always finds himself bodily in the world and that the body itself is a situation whose meaning must be understood. This meaning forms itself

within the process of existence which is realized primordially through movements (of the body). These are rather varied, but the field of variation is fixed by the biological constitution which forms the basis of perceptions and of possible activities, the pre-existential ground of the range of meanings which is formed through encounters with things and with other persons. These encounters begin with earliest youth and are effected by the body.

Because of a difference between the constitution of girls and of boys each of the sexes integrates itself in a reality which is different from the beginning.

We conclude then that there exists a world original to the woman, which results from an innate dynamic difference between the sexes. However small the difference may be, it has effects which are more important in that our culture and our educational methods which exert their influence from the cradle tend to accentuate the virility of boys and the femininity of girls.[15]

This is not to be understood as a simple capitulation to the pattern of male domination or a return to the patriarchal society's subordination of women to men. Rather, it is the serious attempt to allow men and women to be and become what their particular natures allow and enable them to be. It is not to deny that men and women also have a common nature and experience. It is an attempt to take seriously the differentiation of men and women which is grounded in a real sexual distinction. Current emphasis, consequently, is not so much on "absolute and total equality." This frequently ends up being a plea for the unisexual identity of men and women, and consequently an oppression of both. Rather, the current call is for equality of opportunity, the removal of all sexual biases and barriers which prohibit otherwise qualified women from enjoying a variety of opportunities.

This approach respects fully the equal humanity of men and women without taking an exploitative advantage of their specific differences. However, neither does it overlook or try to suppress these differences. As German scientist August W.

von Eiff insists, "There is no identity of the sexes, and one should not make a man into a woman and vice versa."[16] He bases this judgment on specifically different cerebral structures in men and women. He goes on to insist, however, that specific behavioral patterns of men and women still have enormous latitude.

The question could arise, Why such an emphasis on preserving and furthering the sexual differences of men and women? First of all, we would have to insist that the intent is not to preserve and further the differences as such. The point is to preserve and further *men* and *women* as such, who are in reality sexually differentiated. In an age when past injustices and oppressions are being redressed, it is worthwhile to insist that the remedy is not to uproot the wheat with the weeds. Although we may not yet know what is precisely "masculine" and what is precisely "feminine," we are now in a position to begin such an investigation seriously and without the old prejudices.

We are, in a word, able to begin seriously the quest for an androgynous understanding and practice of human being. However, as the word itself indicates, we must then take care neither to assume men and women are the same nor to discard hastily this or that quality as not characteristic of one or the other sex. Today we have the opportunity to allow men and women to be men and women without oppressing either one on the basis of sex. This is true of both the society and the individual. Many of the qualities once attributed absolutely and purely to one sex or the other are now seen to be possible and desirable for both.

In this context we can speak of the relation of male and female being as the quest for wholeness. Just as it is only in their diversity that the two sexes are the image and likeness of God, so is it equally only in their togetherness that they are that image and likeness. In this sense they long for each other. They want to emulate each other because they are incomplete without each other. Hence we can say that Freud's intuition was not entirely awry when he spoke of woman's penis envy. However, his explanation is completely unacceptable, at least partly because he was not enough of a philosopher and therefore could not deal adequately with the question, What is it all about ? In the spirit of Genesis 3:16 Freud interpreted the longing of the female for the male as a curse, with oppressive results for woman. However, we know that it does not have to be that way. Hence we may legitimately suggest that the penis envy precisely as described by Freud is indeed the result of sin, and that it is thus oppressive. However, there is another sense in which such an "envy" need not be negative. The great scholar of comparative religion Mircea Eliade provides some interesting data in this connection. In certain primitive tribes part of the rite of initiation is the practice of subincision, which follows circumcision. The purpose of subincision is to give the male neophyte the appearance of possessing the female sex organ. The intent is to establish the human being, who as male is only half, in a state of symbolic totality. The "divine" is always total, hence "composed" of both sexes:

> The androgyne is considered superior to the two sexes just because it incarnates totality and hence perfection. For this reason we are justified in interpreting the ritual transformation of novices into women—whether by assuming women's dress or by subincision—as the desire to recover a primordial situation of totality and perfection.[17]

In this conection I must confess that I am constantly amazed by the inability of the very vocal women's libbers to capitalize on the theory of womb envy which Karen Horney developed.[18] Betty Friedan does remark, "If reproduction were the chief and only fact of human life, would all men today suffer from uterus envy?"[19] This sentence ("chief" and "only" can hardly be equated) itself indicates the hostility such people have toward pregnancy and motherhood. I have noticed in some of my "liberated" and "liberationist" female college students a positive embarrassment at being able to be mothers. It seems that they almost want to confirm Freud's assertion that a constitutive element of woman is her envy of the male. However, Horney's theory maintains that there is in the male an envy similar to the penis envy in women. It is the male's envy of the womb and the life-giving capacity located there. Her theory is by and large free of all the negative overtones of Freud's. It reflects the idea of totality found in both the primitive and the Genesis traditions. That which is one in the Creator God is plural and diverse in creatures.

This, finally, is why we must be vigilant lest the real distinction of the sexes be suppressed or exploited. Although no one is one hundred percent pure masculine or feminine, there is a real differentiation which allows some of us to be women and some men. In the Christian tradition the simultaneous unity and distinction of bisexual human being has been related to the triune God in whom one nature is totally possessed by each of three distinct persons. To return to chapter 1 of Genesis:

> God created man in the image of himself,
> in the image of God he created him,
> male and female he created them (v. 27).

"Male and female he created them": what is one in the Creator is plural in creation; human nature is twofold. And so it is evident that a unisexual humanity would be a hideous distortion of God's creation; so, too, would be a humanity in which male and female were radically separated with respect to the nature they possess in common, and so inimically opposed to each other. It is the androgynous style of being and living which makes the bisexual nature God created come alive.

Earlier in this book we noted how the word "perichoresis," which describes the being-in-one-another of the persons in the Godhead, is the Greek word for "dance." Thus, if the life of man and woman is to be the reflection on earth of the inner life of the Creator, their delight in one another must likewise be a dancing together in love. In a word, we must live androgynously because *together* man and woman are the image and likeness of God, created thus by God in the very beginning.

NOTES TO CHAPTER 2

[1] The importance of the Bible for women in regard to their traditional status in society and their desire and struggle was clearly understood and emphasized by one of the pioneers in the feminist movement. At the end of the nineteenth century Elizabeth Cady Stanton organized a group of women to study the Bible precisely insofar as women were treated, whether by inclusion or exclusion. The result was a commentary entitled *The Woman's Bible*, published in New York by the European Publishing Company in 1898. Mrs. Stanton was prompted to this biblical study by her frequent confrontations with the Christian (chiefly Protestant) clergy, who never failed to remind her of "woman's place." They generally based this place in the Sacred Scriptures. Her point is still pertinent, even in our so-called post-Christian and secularist age. "So long as tens of thousands of Bibles are printed every year, and circulated over the whole habitable globe, and the masses in all English-speaking nations revere it as the word of God, it is vain to belittle its influence" (p. 11).

Several informative papers on *The Woman's Bible* are included

Notes

in Joan Arnold Romero (ed.), *Women and Religion: 1973* (Waterloo, Ontario: Waterloo Lutheran University, 1973).

[2] E. A. Speiser, *Genesis:* Anchor Bible, 1 (Garden City: Doubleday, 1964), p. xliv.

[3] J. L. McKenzie, *The Two-Edged Sword* (Milwaukee: Bruce, 1956), p. 76.

[4] Ibid., p. 95.

[5] "The Historical Roots of Our Ecologic Crisis," *Science*, 155 (March 10, 1967), pp. 1203-1207.

An equally obtuse interpretation of the biblical understanding of woman, both in the Old Testament and in St. Paul, is given by Dena Justin in an article digested from *Natural History*, February, 1973. She says: "When we reach the Old Testament, the female principle has disappeared from the genesis of the universe. Indeed, woman herself becomes a supplement to the male. God fashions Eve from Adam's rib. Even her name attests to the demeaning nature of her origin." Obviously totally unaware of the Wisdom literature, the author continues by showing that she also does not know how to interpret Genesis 3:16, which she apparently understands to be God's command and description of how things are to be rather than the "curse" which describes how things are because of sin—how they are, then, precisely not to be. This article was digested in *Intellectual Digest* under the title "The Downfall of Women," October, 1973 pp. 90f. An equally unacceptable interpretation of Genesis was given by Judith Plaskow Goldenberg on the NBC special, *Of Women and Men*, which I have discussed in Appendix I. It is interesting that so many of these feminist interpretations of Genesis insist on making God the rival of both Adam and Eve, but still allow this rival of even Adam somehow or other to be allied with him in the oppression of Eve. Strange bedfellows, these sexist males, human and divine.

[6] *Genesis*, p. 17.

[7] *The Two-Edged Sword*, p. 95.

[8] A. M. Dubarle, *Le péché originel dans l'écriture* (Paris: Cerf, 1958), p. 64.

[9] J. L. McKenzie, *Myths and Realities* (Milwaukee: Bruce, 1963), p. 173.

[10] *Understanding the Bible* (New York: Sheed and Ward, 1962), p. 61.

[11] Paul Gaechter, *Maria im Erdenleben* (Innsbruck: Tyrolia, 1954), pp. 124-126.

[12] George Tavard, *Woman in Christian Tradition* (Notre Dame: University of Notre Dame Press, 1973), p. 18; Sister Albertus

Magnus McGrath, *What a Modern Catholic Believes about Women* (Chicago: Thomas More Press, 1972), p. 15.
[13] Roland Murphy, "The Concept of Wisdom Literature," in J. L. McKenzie (ed.), *The Bible in Current Catholic Thought* (New York: Herder and Herder, 1962), p. 54.
[14] *Woman in Christian Tradition*, p. 20.
[15] Ibid., p. 25.

NOTES TO CHAPTER 4

[1] J. L. McKenzie, *Dictionary of the Bible* (Milwaukee: Bruce, 1965), p. 149.
[2] Richard Kugelmann, "The First Letter to the Corinthians," in Raymond Brown et al. (eds.), *The Jerome Bible Commentary* (Englewood Cliffs: Prentice-Hall, 1968), p. 265 (51:49, 50).
[3] *Schriften Zum Neuen Testament* (Munich: Kosel, 1971), p. 286.
[4] *Der Brief an die Epheser* (Dusseldorf: Patmos, 1957), pp. 250-252.
[5] Ibid., p. 252.
[6] M. Zerwick, *Lettera agli Efesini* (Rome: Citta Nuova, 1965), pp. 152-153.
[7] McGrath, *What a Modern Catholic Believes about Women*, p. 37.
[8] Tavard, *Woman in Christian Tradition*, p. 34.

NOTES TO CHAPTER 5

[1] *The Parables of Jesus* (New York: Scribner's, 1963), pp. 174 (note 2), 52.
[2] *The Shepherd of Hermas*, trans. by J. Marique in F. X. Glimm et al. (eds.), *The Apostolic Fathers* (Washington, D.C.: Catholic University of America Press), pp. 239-240.
[3] Vision II, 2, 3; ibid., pp. 238-239.
[4] Vision II, 4; ibid., p. 240.
[5] *The Letter of St. Clement of Rome to the Corinthians*, trans. by F. X. Glimm in *The Apostolic Fathers*, pp. 9, 17, 19.
[6] This and the excerpts which follow are quoted from *The So-Called Second Letter of St. Clement*, trans. by F. X. Glimm in *The Apostolic Fathers*, pp. 66, 74.
[7] P. de Labriolle, *La crise montaniste* (Paris: 1913), pp. 551-568.
[8] *De cultu feminarum*, I, 1; cited by F. J. J. Buytendijk, *Woman* (New York: Newman, 1968), p. 60.
[9] Cited by J. Quasten, *Patrology*, II (Utrecht: Spectrum, 1953), p. 34.
[10] For a development of this idea see my article "Mariology and

the Christian's Self-Concept," *Review for Religious,* 31 (May, 1972), pp. 414-419.

[11] Cited by J. Quasten, *Patrology,* I (1966), p. 211.

NOTES TO CHAPTER 6

[1] *What a Modern Catholic Believes about Women,* p. 5.

[2] Cited by Buytendijk, *Woman,* p. 66.

[3] Tavard, *Woman in Christian Tradition,* p. 240, note 7.

[4] Ibid., p. 108.

[5] A paper delivered at the Los Angeles convention of the American Academy of Religion. See *Women's Caucus—Religious Studies Newsletter,* 1 (Fall, 1972), p. 6.

[6] *Patrologia Latina,* 17, p. 239.

NOTES TO CHAPTER 7

[1] *Patrologia Graeca,* 12, p. 296.

[2] *The So-Called Second Epistle to the Corinthians,* in *Apostolic Fathers,* pp. 72, 73.

[3] *Conciliorum Oecumenicorum Decreta,* edited by G. Alberigo et al. (Freiburg: Herder, 1962), p. 6.

[4] Joan Morris, *The Lady Was a Bishop* (New York: Macmillan, 1973).

NOTES TO CHAPTER 8

[1] *The Waning of the Middle Ages* (Garden City: Doubleday Anchor, 1954), p. 334.

[2] Ibid.

[3] St. Thomas Aquinas, *De Regimine Principum,* 2d rev. ed. by Thomas Mathis (Rome: Marietti, 1948), ch. xiv, pp. 82, 83.

[4] St. Thomas Aquinas, *Quaestiones Quodlibetales,* 8th rev. ed. by R. Spiazzi (Rome: Marietti, 1949), question xiv, article 1, p. 232.

[5] Denis de Rougement, *Love in the Western World* (Garden City: Doubleday Anchor, 1957), p. 178.

[6] Ibid., pp. 178-179.

[7] Huizinga, *The Waning of the Middle Ages,* p. 111.

[8] de Rougement, *Love in the Western World,* pp. 190, 191.

[9] Huizinga, *The Waning of the Middle Ages,* p. 127.

[10] *Super Epistolas S. Pauli Lectura,* I, 8th rev. ed. by R. Cai (Rome: Marietti, 1953), *lectio* ix, pp. 605-607.

[11] Huizinga, *The Waning of the Middle Ages,* p. 127.

[1] Herbert Thurston, "Witchcraft," *Catholic Encyclopedia*, XV (New York: Appleton, 1912), p. 676.

[2] *Institutes of the Christian Religion*, 2 vols. (Philadelphia: Presbyterian Board of Christian Education, 1936), I, p. 270.

[3] *Institutes*, II, p. 273.

[4] Could anyone reading the true romances of John A. O'Brien (ed.) *Why Priests Leave* (New York: Award Books, 1969), get any other impression? I would not apply this description to all priests who left the active ministry to marry—after all, some of my best friends have. But it must be recalled that just because one falls in love does not mean he must marry. After all, we are not Mesopotamians.

[5] *Introduction to the Science of Right;* Great Books of the Western Word, 42 (Chicago: Encyclopedia Britannica, 1952), pp. 419, 420.

[6] Ibid., p. 434.

[7] *The Philosophy of Right;* Great Books of the Western World, 46 (Chicago: Encyclopedia Britannica, 1952), p. 58.

[8] Ibid., p. 61.

[9] Ibid., p. 62.

[10] Ibid., pp. 59, 60.

[11] Ibid., p. 62.

[12] G. W. F. Hegel, *The Philosophy of History*, p. 134.

[13] Ibid., p. 222.

[14] Cited by Buytendijk, *Woman*, p. 65.

[15] Ibid., p. 67.

[16] Cited by Julia O'Foolain and Lauro Martines (eds.), *Not in God's Image* (New York: Harper Torchbook, 1973), p. 326.

[17] John Stuart Mill, *Autobiography* (New York: Columbia University Press, 1969), p. 186.

[18] John Stuart Mill, *On Liberty;* Great Books of the Western World, 43 (Chicago: Encyclopedia Britannica, 1952), p. 317.

[19] Ibid., pp. 387, 388.

NOTES TO CHAPTER 10

[1] Karl Marx, "Foreword to Thesis: The Difference between the Natural Philosophy of Democritus and Epicurus," in *Marx and Engels on Religion* (New York: Schocken, 1964), pp. 14, 15.

[2] *The Second Sex* (New York: Bantam, 1965), p. 129.

[3] *Human Dignity and Human Numbers* (Staten Island: Alba, 1971), p. 170.

4 *The Second Sex*, pp. 34, 35.

5 *New Introductory Lectures on Psycho-Analysis;* Great Books of the Western World, 54 (Chicago: Encyclopedia Britannica, 1952), p. 854.

6 Ibid., p. 855.

7 Ibid., p. 855.

8 Ibid., p. 862.

9 Ibid., p. 863.

10 Ibid., p. 864. How "Freud's entire theory of sexuality is built from a masculine model" is well set forth by Richard Gilman in "The Fem Lib Case against Sigmund Freud," *New York Times Magazine*, Jan. 31, 1971, p. 11. He continues: "In psychoanalysis, maleness is the norm and femaleness an incomplete or, even worse, deficient aspect of it." And there is such a tendency today to dismiss Aristotle and Aquinas as benighted ancients and medievals!

11 Lloyd Shearer, "The Weaker Sex Legally," Intelligence Report, Parade Supplement, *Evansville Courier and Press*, May 12, 1974, p. 4.

12 Marjorie Hyer, "Baptists Order Women to Nurseries, Out of Church Leadership," *Louisville Courier-Journal and Times*, June 16, 1974, p. B, 9.

13 The possible extremes in regard to this question can be seen in the desire of various Church groups to eliminate sexist language and imagery not only from traditional hymns but also from the Bible. David Anderson, UPI religion editor, published a short report on the undertakings of the Lutheran Church in America, the National Council of Churches, and the General Assembly of the Presbyterian Church. He notes that expense deterred one major re-writing project. Perhaps filthy lucre will save us from this kind of idle project. It would be most desirable to avoid sexist imagery in the future, but there is really no serious reason for Christians to try to re-write and thus re-create past history. We can leave that kind of revisionism to the Marxists and Secular Humanists, since they, unlike Christians, have no means of dealing with failure, past or present. As usual, William Buckley's acerbic pen is worth some attention: "That there are grown people in the world who go around saying things like 'chairperson' is testimony not to bisexual attempts to create equality, but to trans-sexual resolutions to sound stupid" ("On the Right," *Dubois County Daily Herald*, July 16, 1974, p. 8. I saw the above-mentioned report by Anderson in the same paper, July 26, 1974, p. 8).

14 This is also the the opinion of the eminent black theologian C. Eric Lincoln, "Why I Reversed My Stand on Laissez-Faire Abor-

tion," *The Christian Century*, XC (April 25, 1973), pp. 477-479.

[15] Irving Howe, "The Middle-Class Mind of Kate Millet," *Harper's* (December, 1970), p. 124.

[16] See further on this, note 3 of chapter 12 below.

[17] Midge Dector, *The New Chastity and Other Arguments against Women's Liberation* (New York: Coward, McCann and Geoghegan, 1972). The quotations are from an article by Patricia Rice, "Women's Lib: Is It Based on Fear?" *St. Louis Post-Dispatch*, October 8, 1972, section 1-121.

[18] Oliver Jensen, "Women Have More Options than Men," *The Evening Times* (Trenton), May 24, 1971, p. 9, is of the same opinion. He does not mean, of course, that women have achieved perfect parity. But his comments also indicate that certain women's libbers do not want equality with men, they want to be men.

[19] Certainly Mrs. Edward Mills takes the wrong approach when she oversimplifies: "The women's liberation movement is anti-God, anti-Catholic, anti-family and anti-woman." The keynote address to the Diocesan Council of Catholic Women's national convention, reported in *The Message* (Evansville, Indiana), July 5, 1974, p. 3.

[20] See my book *Holy Church, Sinful Church* (tentative title), to be published in 1975.

[21] The Pastoral Constitution on the Church in the Modern World, n. 29, *The Documents of Vatican II*, ed. by Walter Abbott, S.J. (New York: America Press, 1966).

[22] Karl Rahner, *Schriften zur Theologie*, II (Einsiedeln: Benziger, 1954), p. 98.

[23] *Newsweek*, January 21, 1974, p. 14. It should be noted in passing that religious women (nuns and sisters) in the Catholic Church have not entirely avoided the "grass is always greener on the other side of the fence" attitude. It seems that frequently the more vocal and acerbic spokes-sisters forget that the traditional religious orders provided women with job opportunities which were not generally available to their secular counterparts. Apart from those institutions conducted by Catholic religious women, how many women were presidents of colleges, chief administrators of hospitals, heads of social and welfare agencies, principals of grade and high schools, etc.? I do not mean to imply that these religious women entirely escaped reference to the male hierarchy of the Church. But it does need to be recalled that the virginal (celibate) religious state of life did offer access to many of the executive positions for which so many women's lib advocates still pine in the secular world.

NOTES TO CHAPTER 11

¹ *Evansville Courier*, July 30, 1974, p. 1. As I write this foot-
note (August 15) NBC radio news has just announced that the
ordination of these eleven women has been declared invalid by the
House of Bishops of the Episcopal Church. This judgment means
that there are still no women priests in either the Anglo-Catholic
Church or Roman Catholic Church. However, a final decision has
been postponed until the next convention of the entire Church.
² Elsie Gibson, *When the Minister Is a Woman* (New York: Holt,
Rinehart and Winston, 1970), pp. 17 ff.
³ J. A. Aldama et al., *Sacrae Theologiae Summa* (Madrid: BAC,
1953). The section on holy orders is by F. Sola. Our topic is treated
on pages 709 and 710, but the treatment occupies the equivalent of
only one page. In Volume I of the same series M. Nicolau and J.
Salaverri explain the theological notes on pages 7 and 8. A comprehensive survey of the historical background of the canon restricting ordination to men is provided by the doctoral dissertation
of Ida Raming, *Zum Ausschlus der Frau vom Amt in der Kirche*
(canon 698 #1), University of Munster, Catholic Theology Faculty,
1969. She traces especially the legal history of this prohibition from
the first explicit formation in canon 44 of the Synod of Laodicea
(which was held between 347 and 381). This canon forbids women
access to the altar. It has also served as the basis for later juridical prohibitions and for most of the theological prohibitions of
the ordination of women.
⁴ H. Vorgrimler and R. Van der Gucht, *Bilanz der Theologie im
20. Jahrhundert*, 4 vols. (Freiburg: Herder, 1970).
⁵ *What a Modern Catholic Believes about Women*, p. 107.
⁶ Leonard Swidler reviewing *Woman in Christian Tradition:*
"Two Christian Views of Women," *National Catholic Reporter*,
March 29, 1974, p. 17.
⁷ Haye van der Meer, *Priestertum der Frau* (Freiburg: Herder,
1969), pp. 60, 109, 126.
⁸ Ibid., p. 112.
⁹ For this brief survey I have used Ludwig Ott, *Das Weihesak-
rament*, in Herder's *Handbuch der Dogmengeschichte*, IV, 5 (Freiburg: Herder, 1969).
¹⁰ Vincent Yzermans (ed.), *American Participation in the Second
Vatican Council* (New York: Sheed and Ward, 1967), p. 202.
¹¹ *The Documents of Vatican II*, pp. 732, 733.
¹² *Acta Apostolicae Sedis*, 37 (1945), p. 285; 48 (1956), p. 782.
¹³ *Pacem in Terris* (April 11, 1963), nn. 41, 43, 15.
¹⁴ Cited by van der Meer in *Priestertum der Frau*, p. 16.

15 Ibid., p. 187.

16 *Summa Theologiae*, 4 vols. (Rome: Marietti, 1948), *Supplement*, question 39, article 1.

17 St. Thomas Aquinas, *Super Epistolas S. Pauli Lectura*, Vol. I, pp. 402, 403 (*lectio* vii on 1 Corinthinas 14).

18 *Summa*, III, q. 67, a. 4.

19 *Summa*, I, q. 92, a. 1. See also his commentary on 1 Corinthians 11:9 (pages 345-348, *lectio* ii in work cited above in note 17).

20 See work cited above in note 17, p. 347.

21 Joan Morris, *The Lady Was a Bishop* (New York: Macmillan, 1973).

22 Ibid., p. 3.

23 Ibid., p. 23.

24 Ibid., p. 99.

25 Ibid., p. 104.

26 Ibid., p. 56.

27 St. Thomas Aquinas, *Summa, Supplement,* q. 39, a. 1.

28 Ibid., q. 19, a. 4.

29 Joseph Ratzinger, "The Pastoral Implications of Episcopal Collegiality," *Concilium*, I (January, 1965), p. 27.

30 *Summa*, II-II, q. 177, a. 2.

31 St. Thomas here refers to Colossians 3:11, although the words he cites resemble Galatians 3:28 more than Colossians. This provides the occasion to mention a little known fact. Some important manuscripts indicate that the Colossians text also contained a reference to the disappearance of the male-female dichotomy in 3:11. It would certainly fit both Pauline doctrine and the context of that verse. This possibility adds support to the contention that St. Paul was not nearly as restrictive in regard to women as the possibly emended texts of his writings would have us believe.

32 Just because there are no theological reasons prohibiting the ordination of women does not mean it is necessarily advisable to ordain them. The recent Episcopalian experience is a good reminder of this. After all, the precise purpose of ministry (priesthood) in the Church is the good order of the Church. This concern can be traced all the way back to the primitive and apostolic Church. In spite of the phantasies of some, even the Corinthian experience is a vivid testimony to the need for "structural" and "institutional" order and office in the Church. Only on this basis may anyone be admitted to or excluded from holy orders. Since the Church's life and mission are not restricted to those in priestly or hierarchical office, it is difficult to see why anyone *has* to be a priest or bishop for the sake of the Church. The clericalists of both the left and

right do not seem to understand this. Of late this situation, strangely enough, has worsened on the side of the presumably liberated left.

One night in the Spring of 1974 I happened to tune in to a David Susskind program dealing with the possibility of ordaining women to the priesthood in the Roman Catholic Church. It was hardly an inspiring session, but what particularly amazed me was the inclusion of Rosemary Ruether among the panelists. Given that this was intended to be a Roman Catholic discussion, Dr. Ruether's presence was hard to figure out. She has explicitly and repeatedly described herself as a "post-Roman Catholic" (see, for example, *Commonweal*, 90 [1969], p. 64)—whatever in the world that might be. I suppose that she was included by David Susskind for the same reason that she had been hired by Harvard University as the Stillman professor of Catholic Theology. That reason is the abiding disaffection of the liberal Christian and Humanist intellectual for the precisely and specifically Roman Catholic. Or is she, perhaps, the token woman theologian or token post-Roman Catholic Theologian or even the token post-Roman Catholic woman theologian? Since she can hardly be called (Roman) Catholic in any recognizable sense of the term, it would have to be one of the other three. What is basically unacceptable about people like Doctors Ruether and Mary Daly is that they spend so much time and effort complaining about the position of women in a patriarchal society, when and although they have their own special positions only because they are women. Of course, there's nothing like having your cake and eating it too, and even having a patriarchal society pay for it. Dr. Ruether has since returned to Howard University.

Anyhow, although many of the advocates of women's ordination are precisely the kind of people who would scare anybody out of ordaining women, that is no real reason not to ordain them. Because on that basis we would also have to stop ordaining men.

[33] The sacramental principle extends from creation all through salvation history in Christianity. We may legitimately use the word "sacrament" to describe Adam and Eve as the visible "image and likeness" of the invisible God in this world. It could only be capricious to exclude woman from the particular priestly sacramental representation of God's saving action in the world if God himself has chosen to be "represented" by both men and women.

NOTES TO CHAPTER 12

[1] For some pertinent remarks on this anti-authority dimension of modern man and theology see J. B. Metz, "Kirchliche Autoritat im Anspruch der Freiheitsgeschichte" in the book edited by him,

Kirche im Prozess der Aufklärung (Munich: Kaiser, 1970), especially pp. 73-90. However, as James Hitchcock has pointed out, there is a great tendency on the part of intellectuals to substitute their own personal expert authority for other more traditional forms of authority. Thus one does not end up with a purely democratic authority-less society, but with a society dominated by other authorities. See his "The State of Authority in the Church," *Cross Currents*, 20 (Fall, 1970), pp. 369-381.

2 Boston: Beacon, 1973.

3 Margaret O'Brien Steinfels concludes her excellent review in *Commonweal*, XCIX (February 1, 1974), pp. 442, 443: "and if the choice between religious leaders becomes a choice between a feminist theology professor from Boston College and a carpenter's son from Galilee, I say stick with the working class." In this connection a comment about the problem of "intellectuals" might be in order. Intellectual is a term that refers not precisely to professional scholars or students. In fact, the term is somewhat loose and vague. Perhaps it can best be explained as referring to people who try to exercise power through the use of ideas or through their status as educated people. Able to manipulate ideas, they tend to use this ability to manipulate people, both as individuals and as society. For the "intellectual" in this sense the source and base of power is not heredity or tradition, social or political rank, physical strength, charismatic personality. It is his expertise, precisely in regard to ideas. In his contribution, "La part du Diable dans la littérature contemporaine," in the French symposium on the devil, *Satan*, Etudes Carmelitaines (Paris: Desclée, 1948), Claude-Edmonde Magny quotes Paul Valéry, "In truth, the existence of others is always unsettling for the splendid egotism of a thinker" (read "intellectual"). He then comments, "Valéry discovers everywhere outside himself the monster he bears within himself. Devoured by the secret and envious desire to be God, he cannot suffer any other creature to exist apart from himself. And he attributes to others, even to God himself, the same jealousy" (p. 575). I think this must be kept in mind when reading any intellectual. It can certainly help us to understand the at least rhetorical excesses of some of the very vocal advocates within the women's lib movement. That they would like to create the universe in their image and likeness is certainly clear in the writings of authors like Millett, Daly, Ruether and others. To prevent such a tragedy is one more, and a very powerful, motive for others to advocate women's liberation and to participate in the accomplishment thereof.

4 J. Jeremias, *The Prayers of Jesus* (Naperville: Allenson, 1967),

p. 111.

[5] "The First Feminist Theology," *National Catholic Reporter*, January 18, 1974, p. 10.

[6] I do not wish to insist too strongly on either the Psalm or Johannine texts as if they demanded that God be spoken of in feminine terms. In fact, according to the authoritative translation of Mitchell Dahood, *Psalms* III (Garden City: Doubleday, 1970), pp. 112-120, verse 3 has nothing to do with womb. My purpose is, rather, to show that the Christian tradition, however reluctantly and sparingly, has nevertheless found it acceptable to speak of God in a feminine context and in feminine terms.

[7] On all this see Conrad Pepler, *The English Religious Heritage* (St. Louis: Herder, 1958), pp. 360-336. All the direct quotations have been taken from *The Revelations of Divine Love of Julian of Norwich*, trans. by James Walsh (St. Meinrad: Abbey Press, 1974), pp. 156-165.

[8] *Woman.*

[9] Philip Nobile, "What Is the New Impotence, and Who's Got It?" in *Esquire*, October, 1972, p. 95. See also the remarks of Judd Marmor, *Newsweek*, March 29, 1971, p. 28.

[10] Betty Friedan, *The Feminine Mystique* (New York: Dell, 1966), p. 141.

[11] "Socialization and Persistence of Religion," *Concilium: The Persistence of Religion*, 81 (1973), p. 59.

[12] "Woman," *New Catholic Encyclopedia* (New York: McGraw-Hill, 1967), Vol. 14, p. 991.

[13] *Male Chauvinist Theology*, a *Cross Currents* reprint (West Nyack, N.Y.).

[14] Lionel Tiger, "Male Dominance? Yes, Alas. A Sexist Plot? No." *New York Times Magazine*, October 25, 1970, p. 35.

[15] "The Existence of Women and the Psychoanalytic Conception," *The Chicago Theological Seminary Register*, LX (March, 1970), pp. 36, 37.

[16] "Die Regulation des Sexualtriebs in psychometrischer Sicht," in A. Gross and S. Pfürtner (eds.), *Sexualität und Gewissen* (Mainz: Grünewald, 1973), p. 50. It is interesting to note that when medical and anthropological sciences are asserting (or re-asserting) a fundamental specificity of the two sexes, theologian S. Pfürtner is quoting the older anthropological studies which tend to pass over such specificity (pp. 50, 154, 155 of the same book). There is also an important summary of current thought on this topic by Jakob David "Auf der Suche nach der Rolle der Frau," *Orientierung*, 38 (June 15, 1974), pp. 128-130.

[17] *Rites and Symbols of Initiation* (New York: Harper Torchbooks, 1965), p. 25.

[18] They might have read about it in so non-specialized a publication as *Newsweek*, March 29, 1971, p. 58. The idea has been around since 1926. It is one more reason to suspect that the desire to be male, not equal, is very strong among certain women.

[19] *The Feminine Mystique*, p. 126.

In the preceding pages I have presented the background, especially philosophical and religious, of women's status and esteem in current Western society. Just as I finished the final draft of the manuscript two items closely connected with this topic came to my attention. One is a chapter aptly entitled "Women's Liberation" in Ben J. Wattenberg's *The Real America*, a book whose subtitle claims that it is "A Surprising Examination of the State of the Union."

On the basis of various polls and surveys he concludes that "American women are finding some grounds for agreement with the Liberationists." In response to his musing whether the "precepts of Women's Lib have taken the country by storm," he answers:

That would be a very great overstatement. It is accurate

Appendix /1
IS WOMEN'S LIBERATION
THE WAVE OF THE FUTURE?

to say some of its precepts have made great headway. Americans agree that women should speak up, that women's status should be strengthened, that women have to work harder than men to get ahead in the world, that a husband should help with housework, that equal pay for equal work is only fair, that birth control, divorce and sex education should be available. Other data show women becoming more relaxed about social fear and less compulsive about household chores.

That's a lot, but there it ends.[1]

Even on that issue which many of the most vocal and ardent proponents of Women's Lib have adopted as the symbolic and real issue (the crux and parting of the spirits), abortion, the general public has by no means been converted. In the 1972 referendums in Michigan and North Dakota 61% and 77% respectively voted against liberalized abortion legislation. In March of 1974 the Gallup poll found that 38% of men and 49% of women opposed the Supreme Court ruling allowing the termination of pregnancy by abortion during even the first three months of the pregnancy.

The impression obtained by Wattenberg is that "American women simply do not see life the way the Women's Movement sees it." His description of the reaction to the Women's Liberation Movement in general is well summed up in the following three paragraphs:

On some of the truly critical questions raised by Women's Lib—questions that go right to the root of a sexist America's failure and guilt, there is a massive rejection. American women have not accepted the notion that females are the oppressed sex, that they are mere sex objects, that domestic life is demeaning, and so on.[2]

In short, American women don't believe they are living in a rotten corrupt sexist society that has crushed them. They are, in fact, more satisfied than men. They do not believe that America has failed, or failed them. They see problems and they are prepared to actively seek some specific changes, but they like being women and they even like being women in this kind of society.[3]

Beyond such specifics is rejection of some major intellectual underpinnings of the Movement: women don't feel their education is wasted, they don't feel unfullfilled, they feel a husband and children are properly the focus of their lives—and in general they feel satisfied, more satisfied than men. They reject the notion of failure and guilt and crisis—at least they reject that notion as cast by the Feminists.[4]

Against this background it was most intriguing to watch NBC's three-hour television special "Of Women and Men," hosted by Barbara Walters and Tom Snyder on January 9, 1975. I watched the program with the members of a graduate seminar in humanities I was conducting at the University of Evansville. Their reaction was generally what can be described only as disbelief. In fact several suggested that the program must have been a put-on—that we were not really to take the program seriously. These viewers were not simple peasants or the brainwashed devotees of some sexist religious sect. The group includes a university professor, an actress, several high school teachers and business-persons, professional people both female and male.

Their reaction, it seems to me, clearly illustrates why the Woman's Lib ideology has not and will not "take the country by storm." It is also a striking confirmation of Wattenberg's thesis: first, that American women do not perceive that ideology as an accurate description of their experience in an admittedly sexist world; second, that they also find the proffered solution unsatisfactory and at least to some extent offensive, both morally and generally.

The NBC program illustrated the contention of many that the professional full-time advocates of Woman's Lib are themselves a sort of sexist oppression. Comprised of a numerically small selection from an equally limited social, economic and cultural section of society, they seek to impose their own analysis of and solution of society's ills on all of society. There is a different way than in the past, but still only one way to be a woman.

And that way often seems to be in the image and likeness, not of Yahweh, but of the upper middle class suburbanite executive. And up. One is tempted to wonder whether Freud wasn't correct in spite of himself. How often Women's Libbers seem to be living certifications of his "woman-as-penis-envy" theory. The reaction of my seminar was often that the women portrayed on the NBC special wanted neither liberation nor equality, that they did not want even shared roles. Rather they wanted reversal. One can hardly avoid the impression that for so many of the special's women fulfillment and happiness could come only when they did what men had traditionally done. Hence, although many people, wanting a more human culture, advocate the abolition of boxing, little girls are now introduced to participative pugilism so that they might be liberated and become more human.

Perhaps the most intense manifestation of this desire to be a man was the clothed woman photographer who was taking the pin-up pictures of the unclothed man. One could almost hear her saying (breathily?) to herself, "Oooh Boy (Girl?)! I've really made it. Now I'm just like a man!"

Then Joan Nicholson presented her theory of the pin-up—an objectification of women, symptom of male dislike of and hostility toward women, the expression of the male's fantasy, which is described as his desire to dominate women. The shibboleth of male dominance is omnipresent! The female pin-up is indeed and beyond all doubt a product of the male fantasy. That it is a manifestation of his fantasy-desire to dominate tells us much more about the mentality of the female theoretician than the male patient. The fantasy is clearly for a world of perfection and pleasure which can be hinted by the unblemished inhabitant of the centerfold, perhaps approximated by earthly encounters but only fully realized in that trans-earthly heaven of which the pin-up is most certainly the fantasy.

Women's Lib spokespersons often claim that they are really working for human liberation. And that is probably true. And certainly commendable. What a program like "Of Women and Men" clearly illustrates is that contemporary as well as earlier cultures do not necessarily have adequate concepts of Women, Men or Freedom. Any proposed new liberation could easily become a new oppression. We have seen this in our study on "The Humanity of Women." And Mr. Wattenberg's investigations indicate that the contemporary Women's Lib ideology has no fail-safe guarantee that it will necessarily *avoid* the same fate.

NOTES TO APPENDIX 1

[1] Ben J. Wattenberg, *The Real America.* (Garden City, New York: Doubleday, 1974), pp. 213-224.

[2] Ibid.

[2] Ibid., p. 219.

[3] Ibid., p. 221.

[4] Ibid., p. 223.

In chapter eleven I presented a lengthy discussion of the question and problem of women's ordination to the priesthood through the sacrament of Holy Orders. In this appendix I want to offer a theological theory which maintains that the question has already been answered and the problem solved. That is, in point of fact, women have already been admitted to the sacrament of Holy Orders, at least in the Roman Catholic Church. I include these remarks in a separate appendix because I concede that they are quite speculative. Consequently I do not want them to obscure in any way the data and conclusions I presented in chapter eleven, which I consider to be doctrinally beyond dispute. I readily admit that the argument of this appendix is not widely, at least not fully, understood and accepted. However, the absence of a comprehensive theory has not and need not prevent the Church from taking

Appendix/2

HAVE WOMEN ALREADY BEEN ORDAINED?

a practical pastoral position it deems necessary for the good of the faithful. This is one of the great advantages of belonging to the Roman Catholic Church. It does accept the existence of a theology of lived reality. The theory need not always precede the fact.

What is the fact done by the Church to prompt my contention that it has already admitted women to the sacrament of Holy Orders and a partial participation in the priesthood? It has admitted both men and women to the office technically called special (extraordinary) minister of Holy Communion. It has done this officially and publicly, by an act of the hierarchy. I emphasize this to eliminate from consideration the merely seeming or apparent minister who would owe his ministry to the private initiative of any individual minister or community, whatever the excuses or presumed theological justification offered therefor. I also want to disallow whatever might happen only once or even sporadically because of a peculiar and extraordinary crisis.

Now, to the argument. The legitimate special minister of Holy Communion is duly appointed, designated or authorized by the Bishop for service to the Church in a particuler place and time, known technically as a local Church. One will notice that the word "ordination" is assiduously and diligently avoided in the official literature dealing with this office of special minister. Admittedly the service thus authorized by the Bishop is quite limited. What is generally overlooked, however, is that every office, ministry or ordained service in the Church is always more or less limited. This applies most obviously to the deacon, but also to the priest and even to the bishop himself. The latter is severely limited, geographically, to his diocese, or functionally, to his non-territorial, non-diocesan office. Universal jurisdiction is attributed only to the papacy. However, this is clearly a singular office and power in the Church, and is itself not purely or simply unlimited, as if the Pope were either an omnipotent god or an anomic dictator. Even the very "papalist" era of Pope Pius IX and Vatican Council I was aware of this.

The decisive question can now be posed. Is the admittedly limited service of the special minister of Holy Communion such that it can qualify for inclusion within the ministry authorzed by the sacrament of Holy Orders. In other words, does what the special minister of Holy Communion actually performs have a special relationship to or participation in what ministers normally associated with the sacrament of Holy Orders do? An affirmative answer is indicated by the former's similarity to theology's "classical" description of what the traditional deacon did. According to standard theological textbooks, citing the Pontificale Romanum, the deacon's office is to serve at the altar, baptize, and preach. This office is then described in accordance with the prescriptions of canon law. The deacon assists the priest, who is the principal minister, in the liturgical celebration of the Eucharist. Although the deacon may also preach (canon 1342, 1), his preaching is not considered the same as that of the priest. More important for our question, the deacon is the extraordinary minister of solemn baptism; although he may not use this power without permission of the Ordinary or Pastor. This permission may, however, be legitimately presumed in case of urgency or necessity (canon 741). Likewise the deacon is an extraordinary minister for the distribution of Holy Communion to the faithful—again only with the permission of the Ordinary or Pastor as in the case of solemn baptism (845, 2). Finally, the deacon also enjoys a limited role in the Benediction of the Blessed Sacrament, in viaticum for the sick (canon 1274, 2) and the burial of the dead.[2]

The salient point for our considerations is that the special minister of Holy Communion is officially empowered by the Bishop to distribute Holy Communion publicly under certain circumstances in a local Church. The restrictions levied on these special ministers are no different than those on the traditional deacon. Furthermore, the special minister is empowered to do precisely what had been regarded as the most important actilvity of the deacon, namely the distribution of Holy Communion.

Are there no difficulties with this assertion? There are, but some are not very difficult. For example, it is frequently asserted that the special minister is intended only for special cases, namely the shortage of priests. However, this is precisely the theological explanation given for the origin and institution of deacons (and priests)—a reasoning theological manuals trace all the way back to the action of the Apostles appointing the Seven "Deacons" to assist them. This is described in chapter 6 of the Acts of the Apostles. Of course, these Seven "Deacons" were hardly deacons in the later customary meaning of this term. It is also asserted that the special minister of holy communion is limited spatially and temporally. Such a limitation would not be without its own considerable theological difficulties. Nevertheless, there is no compelling theological evidence that such limitations would necessarily preclude the special minister from sharing in the power of Holy Orders. As we noted above, all "power" in the Church, whether sacramental or jurisdictional, is always limited. Theologians dispute whether such limitation is of the power or "merely" of its exercise. But the basic principle has always been whatever the good order and efficient life of the Spirit in the Church requires. Hence the limitations on the sharing in and the exercise of the Church's power have varied greatly throughout the Church's history. In the words of the Bishops' study text, the power of the Church has been shared

---

314 APPENDIX

and exercised in more expansive or restrictive ways as "pastoral needs so demanded."

The arguments against the sacramentality of the special minister of Holy Communion rest on certain undifferentiated assumptions contained in the presentations of the theological manuals of the last two centuries. These assumptions are made in regard to the rite of ordination as well as the nature of office in the Church and the sacrament of Holy Orders. They generally overlook the great development and diversity of both the theory and practice of Sacramental office in the Church. In particular this approach tends to absolutize the tripartite division of the Sacrament of Holy Orders into Deacon, Priest, Bishop. It also tends to overlook the great difficulty theologians have in describing the nature or essence of each of the three offices, and most importantly, the justification for the restriction of the power assigned to any individual office. In our own days we have witnessed significant rearrangements of the power of Holy Orders and jurisdiction—in regard to the conferral of the sacrament of Confirmation and the more relaxed granting of jurisdiction to hear confessions.

Even a brief look at the history of the Church shows us that from the very beginning the Church has been aware that it possesses within itself a power of administration and leadership.[3] This power is one of the many gifts of the one Holy Spirit (Ephesians 4:11; 1 Corinthians 12:28). The Church also seems to have been aware that it could arrange this power in various ways to meet its needs in new and different conditions. Thus the Twelve (Apostles) did not hesitate to appoint the Seven Deacons to assist them. There is no indication however, that the Seven Deacons ever simply waited on tables or even did only those limited tasks later assigned to the office of Deacon.[4] Rather, they shared in what later came to be understood as the power of the sacrament of Holy Orders—

whether to the extent of Deacon, Priest or Bishop is not indicated. The great variety and diversity of ministries, of offices, of administration and government in the early Church are another indication of the Church's awareness of its ability to distribute its power of order (that is, its power of administration and leadership) as it saw fit. The later development into major and minor orders, into sacramental and non-sacramental ministries is further evidence that the Church has not always had an absolutely clear and distinct theology of office and Holy Orders in the Church.

It is quite possible, then, that we are currently witnessing a new development in both the practice and theory of Holy Orders. And, as has so often happened in the past, the practice has preceded and anticipated the theory. I do not think it fanciful to find at least the possibility of such an awareness in the commentary of the Bishop's Commission on the Liturgy, *Ministries in the Church* (Study Text 3).[5]

> The apostolic letter, Ministeria quaedam, reserves institution into the ministry of reader and acolyte to men. It should be clearly understood, however, that although the liturgical rite of institution is so limited, in terms of actual ministerial function women are not necessarily excluded.
> By special indult from the Congregation for the Discipline of the Sacraments, granted in 1970 at the request of the American episcopal conference, women have fulfilled the role of reader in liturgical celebrations. They have also undertaken the acolyte's function as special minister of holy communion when pastoral needs so demanded it.
> The original edition of the general instruction of the Roman Missal stated that "When a qualified man is not available, the conference of bishops may permit a woman to proclaim the readings prior to the gospel, while standing outside the sanctuary." On December 23, 1972 the Congregation for Divine Worship promulgated a list of changes in the Roman Missal. The above quotation was one. The revised text reads: "Those who exercise the ministry of readers, even though they have not been instituted, should be qualified and carefully prepared

so that the reading will develop in the faithful an appreciation of scripture. The conference of bishops may permit a qualified woman to proclaim the readings prior to the gospel and announce the intentions of the general intercessions" (no. 66).

Nevertheless, the exclusion of women from the liturgical institution in the ministries of reader and acolyte seems unnecessary and has been judged by many women to be offensive and discriminatory. In particular, the injunction of Gaudium et spes (no. 29) against such distinctions has been cited, especially since liturgical institution in the two ministries does not involve the sacrament of holy orders.

This position does not touch in any direct way the discussed and controverted disciplinary or doctrinal issue of the reception of orders by women. The Apostolic See has clearly and explicitly removed the two ministries in question away from the close relationship to the sacrament of orders which they had enjoyed as minor orders.

The concluding sentence in each of the last two paragraphs need not be taken as the final solution to the problem. They are, rather, a recognition of the problem. The entire quotation indicates an awareness that the new practices entail certain consequences for the theory of Holy Orders, consequences which have not yet been fully explored.

Furthermore, as we have pointed out above, the special minister of Holy Communion has a much more decisive similarity to the deacon than any of the traditional minor (and non-sacramental) orders had. The special minister of Holy Communion is involved in what was formerly reserved precisely to someone in Holy Orders—the regular, public, orderly distribution of Holy Communion in the public liturgy of the Church.

In any case, the authorization of women as special ministers of Holy Communion certainly indicates that the two most important and long-lived disabilities of women have been overcome. If women are allowed and enabled to distribute Holy Communion, they can no longer be considered liable in any way to the strictures of ritual uncleanness. Therefore they can no longer be excluded from the sanctuary, and, indeed, are not. Furthermore, if they are able to distribute Holy Communion to men (male), they can hardly be considered to be any longer in a "state of subjection" to them. As we saw above, these two "disabilities" or "incapacities" were the chief grounds for the general restriction of women in the Church and specifically for their exclusion from the priesthood. Hence it is possible that such a simple response to the "pastoral needs" of the Church as allowing women to be special ministers of Holy Communion can be seen as the decisive undoing of the famous curse of Genesis 3:16. Those who might still wish to restrict women in the Church can clearly no longer invoke this famous (or infamous) verse in favor of the subjection of women. The decision to admit women to this special ministry is also significant for two other reasons. First, it is an official and hierarchial action, not merely the efforts of an individual or small private group. The decision therefore enjoys a certain permanence and firmness in the life and history of the Church. Second, and finally, it is also significant because, in contrast to the ascetical and virginal emphases which have been dominant for so long, this decision restores the Christian liberation to its rightful and original sacramental context.

Notes to Appendix 2

[1] This is clearly stated in the "Collective Declaration of the Bishops of Germany," in which false interpretations of Vatican I's doctrine of papal primacy and infallibility were rejected and the orthodox interpretation presented. Both the original German text and a Latin translation, along with Pope Pius IX's acceptance and approval, are contained in H. Denzinger and A. Schonmetzer, *Enchiridion Symbolorum*, ed. 34. (Freiburg: Herder, 1965), pp. 603-607, nn. 3112-3116. This document was signed by the German Bishops in early 1875. In March of that same year Pope Pius IX ratified and

confirmed the document as legitimate Catholic doctrine. This document is very important because it protects the idea of limited office in the Church against the erroneous theories which want to allow for only unlimited or "full" office. What these erroneous opinions omit, of course, is what we shall emphasize throughout this appendix, namely that all office, even papal, is not absolute, but limited. Possible degrees of limitation are not, of course, determined in this document.

² On all this, see F. Sola, *De Sacramentis Vitae Socialis Christianae*, in J. de Aldama et al., *Sacrae Theologiae Summa*, IV. (Madrid: B.A.C., 1953), pp. 640-653.

³ Recent studies have again shown that the early Church did indeed have structure, institution, office. They have also shown that the early Church experienced a great variety and development in the arrangement of its structures and office. The real history of the Church, both in doctrine and practice, undoubtedly provides for a division of its leadership and governing office into the offices of deacon, priest and bishop. But it also allows for other arrangements and dispositions in regard to both ordination and the tripartite division of the Sacrament of Holy Orders. See especially R. Brown, *Priest and Bishop*. (New York: Paulist, 1970). A. Deissler, H. Schlier, J-P. Audet, *Der Priesterliche Dienst*, I and K. Becker, *Der Priesterliche Dienst*, II. (Freiburg: Herder, 1970). K. Rahner, *Vorfrage zu einem oekumenischen Amtsverstandnis*. (Freiburg: Herder, 1974). R. Dillon, "Ministry as Stewardship of the Tradition in the New Testament," in *Proceedings of Catholic Theological Society of America*, Vol. 24 (1969).

⁴ See P. Gaechter, "Die Sieben (Apg 6, 1-6)," *Zeitschrift für Katholische Theologie*, 74 (1952), pp. 129-166.

⁵ Washington, D.C., United States Catholic Conference, 1974, pp. 33f.

This bibliography neither intends nor pretends to be complete and exhaustive. Given the flood of publications in women's studies, such an enterprise would, in any case, be doomed to failure. The considerable flotsam in this flood also renders such an enterprise unnecessary.

Furthermore, I have not included articles available in standard reference works which as encyclopedias and various, special dictionaries. Nor have I included listings which are primarily scriptural commentaries. I have attempted, with a few notable exceptions, to include titles which are both generally available and intelligible.

What this bibliography does provide, then, is a reasonably adequate cross section of writings about the nature and role of woman in the history and culture commonly called Western. Some of the entries are heavier, some lighter; some are ob-

Bibliography

jective, to the point, others more cathartic, as Ms. **Pat Rotter** explicitly remarks in the preface to the anthology of fiction she edits under the title, *Bitches and Sad Ladies*: "We may not really want to lock our husbands in cellars of keep men as sex objects, but our acceptance of the anger in these stories (our own personal anger free of consequences) acts as a catharsis. The enjoyment of these power fantasies releases our own anger-energies to more positive purposes." We certainly hope so. Since such "anger" is present in the literature of the women's liberation movement in no small quantities, I have deemed the inclusion of representative literature to be not only desirable but necessary.

I should also point out that certain entries in this list include extensive bibliographies, for example, Kerns on patristics, Swidler and Meer on the ordination of women, Mayr on the feminine in God, and O'Faolain and Martines on historical documentation. Consequently I think that this bibliography's variety, both in kind and quality, will enable the reader to savor both the issues and moods which pervade the current discussion of the humanity of woman.

Alberione, James. *Woman: Her Influence and Zeal As an Aid to the Priesthood.* Boston: St. Paul Editions, 1964.

Anderson, Margaret, ed. *Mother Was Not a Person.* Montreal: Content, 1972.

Arnold, F. X. *Woman and Man: Their Nature and Mission.* New York: Herder and Herder, 1963.

Atkinson, Ti-Grace. *Amazon Odyssey.* New York: Links, 1974.

de Beauvoir, Simone. *The Second Sex.* New York: Bantam, 1952.

Bernard, Jessie. *The Future of Motherhood.* New York: Dial, 1974.

Bertinetti, Ilse. *Frauen im Geistlichen Amt.* Berlin: Evangelische Verlagsanstalt, 1965.

Bier, W. C., ed. *Woman in Modern Life.* New York: Fordham University Press, 1971.

Bird, Caroline. *Born Female.* New York: Pocket Books, 1968.

Borresen, Kari Elisabeth. *Subordination et equivalence. Nature et role de la femme d'apres Augustin et Thomas d'Aquin.* Oslo:

Universitetsforlaget, 1968.

Boston Women's Health Book Collective. *Our Bodies, Ourselves.* New York: Simon and Schuster, 1972.

Bouyer, Louis. *Man and Woman with God.* London: Burns and Oates, 1960.

Brothers, Dr. Joyce. *Woman.* Garden City: Doubleday, 1961.

Bullough, Vern with Bullough, B. *The Subordinate Sex: A History of Attitudes Toward Women.* Champaign: University of Illinois Press, 1973.

Buytendijk, F. J. J. *Woman.* New York: Newman, 1968.

Clapp, Marie Welles. *The Old Testament As It Concerns Women.* New York: Methodist Book Concern, 1934.

Culver, Elsie Thomas. *Women in the World of Religion.* Garden City: Doubleday, 1967.

Cuneen, Sally. *Sex, Female: Religion, Catholic.* New York: Holt, Rinehart and Winston, 1968.

Daly, Mary. *Beyond God the Father: Toward a Philosophy of Women's Liberation.* Boston: Beacon, 1973.

———. *The Church and the Second Sex.* New York: Harper and Row. 1968.

Danielou, Jean. *The Ministry of Women in the Early Church.* London: Faith Press, 1961.

Danniel, Francoise and Olivier, B. *Woman is the Glory of Man.* Westminster: Newman, 1966.

Dector, Midge. *The New Chastity and Other Arguments Against Women's Liberation.* Boston: Coward, McCann and Geoghegan, 1972.

Doley, Sarah, ed. *Women's Liberation and the Church.* New York: Association Press, 1970.

Donaldson, James. *Woman: Her Position and Influence in Ancient Greece and Rome, and among the Early Christians.* London: Gordon, 1907.

Dreifus, Claudia. *Woman's Fate.* New York: Bantam, 1973.

von Eiff, A. W. "Die Regulation des Sexualtriebs in psychometrischer Sicht," in A. Gross and S. Pfurtner, eds. *Sexualitat und Gewissen.* Mainz: Grunewald, 1973.

Eliade, Mircea. *Patterns in Comparative Religion.* Cleveland: World Meridian Books, 1963.

———. *Rites and Symbols of Initiation.* New York: Harper Torchbooks, 1965.

———. *The Sacred and the Profane.* New York: Harcourt, Brace and World, 1959.

Emmanuel, Sister Vincent. *The Question of Woman and the Priest-*

hood. London: Sheed and Ward, 1969.

Emswiler, Sharon Neufer and Emswiler Thomas Neufer. *Women and Worship: A Guide to Non-sexist Hymns, Prayers and Liturgies.* New York: Harper and Row, 1974.

Ermarth, Margaret. *Adam's Fractured Rib.* Philadelphia: Fortress, 1970.

Figes, Eva. *Patriarchal Attitudes.* New York: Stein and Day, 1970.

Firestone, Shulamith. *The Dialectic of Sex: The Case for Feminist Revolution.* New York: Morrow, 1971.

Ford, J. Massynberde. "Biblical Material Relevant to the Ordination of Women," *Journal of Ecumenical Studies,* Fall 1973.

Galot, J. *L'Eglise et la femme.* Gembloux: Duculot, 1965.

Gibson. Elsie. *When the Minister is a Woman.* New York: Holt, Rinehart and Winston, 1970.

Gilman, Richard. "The Fem Lib Case Against Sigmund Freud," *New York Times Magazine,* 31 January 1971.

Glazer-Malbin, N. ed. *Woman in a Man-made World.* Chicago: Rand McNally, 1972.

Gornick, V. and Moran, B. *Woman in Sexist Society.* New York: Signet, 1971.

Gorres, Ida Friederike. "Women as Priests?" *Herder Correspondence,* July 1966.

Grassi, Joseph. "Is the New Testament Anti-Feminist?" *St. Anthony Messenger,* September 1973.

Greer, Germaine. *The Female Eunuch.* New York: McGraw-Hill, 1971.

Hageman, Alice, ed. *Sexist Religion and Women in the Church: No More Silence.* New York: Association, 1974.

Harkness, Georgia. *Women in Church and Society.* New York: Abingdon, 1972.

Helman, Patricia. *Free To Be A Woman.* Garden City: Doubleday, 1971.

Hellwig, Monika, ed. "Hope and Liberation," *Liturgy,* October 1970.

Henning, Clara Maria. "Women in the Priesthood," *Commonweal,* 11 January 1974.

Henry, A. M. "Pour une theologie de la femininité," *Lumiere et vie,* July-August 1959.

Heyer, Robert J., ed. *Women and Orders.* Paramus: Paulist, 1974.

Hole, Judith and Levine, Ellen. *Rebirth of Feminism.* New York: Quadrangle, 1973.

Horney, Karen. *Feminine Psychology.* New York: Norton, 1967.

Howe, Irving. "The Middle-Class Mind of Kate Millet," *Harper's,*

December 1970.

Huizinga, J. *The Waning of the Middle Ages.* Garden City: Doubleday Anchor, 1954.

Jakob, David. "Auf der Suche nach der Rolle der Frau," *Orientierung,* 15 June 1974.

Janeway, Elizabeth. *Man's World, Women's Place: A Study in Social Mythology.* New York, Morrow, 1971.

Jennings, Sister Vivien, O.P. *The Valiant Woman.* Staten Island: Alba House, 1974.

Kennedy, S. Ethne, ed. *Women in Ministry.* Chicago: NAWR Publications, 1972.

Kerns, Joseph E., S.J. *The Theology of Marriage.* New York: Sheed and Ward, 1964.

Koedt, Anne, Levine, Ellen, and Rapone, Anita, eds. *Radical Feminism.* New York: Quadrangle, 1973.

Korda, Michael. *Male Chauvinism: How It Works.* New York: Random House, 1973.

Kress, Robert. "God Our Mother," *St. Anthony Messenger,* May 1975.

de Kruijf, T. C. *The Bible on Sexuality.* De Pere, Wisconsin: St. Norbert Abbey Press, 1966.

von LeFort, Gertrude. *The Eternal Woman.* Milwaukee: Bruce, 1954.

Leipoldt, Johannes. *Die Frau in der antiken Welt und im Urchristentum.* Leipzig: Koehler and Amelang, 1955.

Los Angeles Times, Sunday, December 29, 1974 (a special supplement on feminist issues in the Christian Churches).

Luskey, Margaret Langhans, "A Portrait of the Woman as a Girl Catholic," *Commonweal,* 11 January 1974.

Marty, M. and Peerman, D., eds. *New Theology* 9. New York: MacMillan, 1972.

Mayr, Franz. "Der Ausschluss der weiblich-mutterlichen Analogie fur Gott bei Thomas von Aquin," *Theologie und Glaube,* vol. 63, no. 2 (1973).

McGrath, Sister Albertus Magnus, O.P. *What a Modern Catholic Believes About Women.* Chicago: Thomas More Press, 1972.

McKenna, Mary Lawrence. *Women of the Church.* Baltimore: Kenedy, 1967.

Mead, Margaret. *Male and Female.* New York: Mentor, 1962.

Mailer, Norman. *Prisoner of Sex.* New York: Signet, 1971.

Van Der Meer, Haye. *Priestertum der Frau?* Freiburg: Herder, 1969.

Millet, Kate. *Sexual Politics.* Garden City: Doubleday, 1970.

——. *Flying.* New York: Knopf, 1974.

Ministry in the Church. A Statement by the Theology Section of the Roman Catholic/Presbyterian-Reformed Consultation. Washington, D.C.: 1971.

Moll, Willi. *The Christian Image of Woman.* Notre Dame: University of Notre Dame Press, 1967.

Morgan, Elaine. *The Descent of Woman.* New York: Bantam, 1973.

Morgan, Robin, ed. *Sisterhood Is Powerful.* New York: Random House, 1971.

Morris, Joan. *The Lady Was a Bishop.* New York: MacMillan, 1973.

Oakley, Ann. *Woman's Work.* New York: Pantheon, 1974.

O'Faolain, Julia and Martines, Lauro, eds. *Not in God's Image.* New York: Harper Torchbooks, 1973.

Raming, Ida. *Zum Ausschluss der Frau vom Amt in der Kirche.* Munster: University of Munster, 1969.

Richardson, Herbert W. *Nun, Witch, Playmate.* New York: Harper and Row, 1971.

Rivers, Caryl. *Aphrodite at Mid-Century.* Garden City: Doubleday, 1973.

Romero, Joan Arnold, ed. *Women and Religion.* Tallahassee: Florida State University, 1973.

Rotter, Pat, ed. *Bitches and Sad Ladies.* New York: Harper's Magazine Press, 1974.

de Rougemont, Denis. *Love in the Western World.* Garden City: Doubleday Anchor, 1957.

Rowbothan, Sheila. *Hidden from History.* New York: Pantheon, 1974.

Ruether, Rosemary Radford. *Male Chauvinist Theology,* a Cross Currents reprint. West Nyack, New York.

Ruether, Rosemary Radford, ed. *Religion and Sexism: Images of Women in the Jewish and Christian Traditions.* New York: Simon and Schuster, 1974.

St. Anthony Messenger, March, 1971 (an entire issue dedicated to the problem of women in the Church).

Savramis, Demosthenes. *The Satanizing of Woman.* Garden City: Doubleday, 1974.

Schall, Richard. *Human Dignity and Human Numbers.* Staten Island: Alba House, 1971.

Schillebeeckx, E., O.P. *Marriage.* New York: Sheed and Ward, 1965.

Smythe, P. R. *The Ordination of Women.* London: Skeffington, 1939.

Sochen, June. *Herstory.* New York: Alfred, 1974.

Stassinopoulos, Arianna. *The Female Woman.* New York: Random House, 1973.

Stendahl, Krister. *The Bible and the Role of Women.* Philadelphia: Fortress, 1966.

Stuhlmueller, Carroll, "Women Priests: Today's Theology and Yesterday's Sociology," *America,* 14 December 1974.

Swidler, Arlene. *Woman in a Man's Church.* New York: Paulist, 1972.

Swidler, Leonard. "Jesus Was a Feminist," *Catholic World,* January 1971.

Tavard, George H. *Woman in Christian Tradition.* Notre Dame: University of Notre Dame Press, 1973.

Thompson, Mary Lou, ed. *Voices of the New Feminism.* Boston: Beacon, 1971.

Thrall, M. *The Ordination of Women to the Priesthood: A Study of Biblical Evidence.* London: SCM Press, 1958.

Tiger, Lionel. "Male Dominance? Yes. Alas. A Sexist Plot? No." *New York Times Magazine,* 25 October 1970.

Tomalin, Claire. *The Life and Death of Mary Wollstonecraft.* New York: Harcourt, Brace. Jovanovich, 1974.

Trible, Phyllis, "Depatriachalizing in Biblical Interpretation," *Journal of the American Academy of Religion,* March 1973.

Trevett, R. F. *The Church and Sex.* New York: Hawthorn, 1960.

Ulanov, Ann Belford. *The Feminine in Jungian Psychology and Christian Theology.* Evanston: Northwestern University Press, 1971.

de Vaux, Roland. *Ancient Israel.* New York: McGraw-Hill, 1961.

Vos, Clarence. *Woman in Old Testament Worship.* Delft: Judels and Brinkman, 1968.

Women in the Church. A Statement by the Worship and Mission Section of the Roman Catholic/Presbyterian-Reformed Consultation. Washington, D.C.: NCCB, 1971.

Index

B

Bacon, F., 173
Balzac, H., 190
Baptism, 169, 232
Barak, 30
Barre, Poulain de la, 1
Basel, Council of, 160
Beauvais, Vincent de., 169
Beauvoir, Simone de., 189, 193, 199, 210, 277
Becker, K., 319
Benedict, R., 284
Beowulf, 127
Bernard, St., 272
Betrothal, 163
Biology, 32, 95, 157, 174, 203, 240, 245, 272
Bisexual, 141, 202, 211, 219, 269, 278, 282
Bishop, 226, 240, 248, 253, 261, 313
Blood, 35, 62, 174
Bonaventure, St., 233, 239
Boredom, 211
Breath, 21, 46
Bride, 112, 261
Bridegroom, 240
Brown, A., 224, 319
Brown, R., 66
Buckley, W., 296
Bunker, A., 9
Bunny, 190, 213, 278
Buytendijk, F.J.J., 277, 284

C

Cai, R., 294
Cain, 269
Calvin, J., 175-179
Canon Law, 163, 224-226, 254, 298, 313
Celibacy, 46, 71, 83, 88, 103, 136, 151-153, 179, 295
Cerebral, 286
Cervantes, L., 279

Chalcedon, 231
Childbirth, 26, 103, 118
Christ, C., 268
Chrysostom, St. John, 132
Church, 78, 96, 109-111, 117, 145, 179, 239, 258, 299
Circumcision, 34
Clean-Unclean, 34, 62, 150, 254, 318
Cleaver, E., 276
I Clement (Epistle), 90, 115
II Clement (Epistle), 116, 151
Clement of Alexandria, 119
Clothing, 93, 101
College Theology Society, 64
Commonweal, The, 300
Concilium, 253
Congregationalist Church, 224
Corinth, 84, 299
I Corinthians (7), 87
I Corinthians (11), 86, 94, 243, 246
I Corinthians (14), 86, 89, 226, 244
Cross Currents, 302
Cupid, 159
Curse, 27, 74, 104, 110, 115, 119, 133, 137, 176, 190, 246, 287, 292, 318
Cyprian, St., 137, 151

D

Dahood, M., 302
Daly, M., 266, 275, 300
Damaris, 78
Dance, 30-32, 280, 289
David, 31
David, J., 302
Deacon, 80, 226, 231, 312
Deaconess, 80, 146, 226, 231, 250
Death, 198
Deborah, 30, 244
Dector, M., 214, 297
Defectives, 57, 157, 191, 201, 245,